Teachers Investigate their Work

Action research is a method used by teachers and other professionals to improve their practice and their understanding of their practice situations, and as a way to generate knowledge about practice. It provides a practical way for professionals to uncover some of the complexities of their practice and thereby to improve the quality of their pupils' learning, or the care of their patients or clients.

Teachers Investigate their Work introduces the methods and concepts of action research through examples drawn from studies carried out by teachers and other professionals. Arranged as a handbook, it contains numerous sub-headings for easy reference and over 50 practical methods and strategies to put into action, some flagged as suitable "starters". Throughout the book, the authors draw on their international practical experience of action research, working in close collaboration with teachers and other professionals. This fully revised second edition has been rewritten with added contemporary cases from teachers and other professionals, and a North American perspective. A new chapter provides examples of published action research studies, whilst the final chapter, which focuses on the theoretical foundations of action research, reflects the changes in the field since the publication, over ten years ago, of the first edition.

Teachers Investigate their Work is an essential guide for teachers, nurses, social workers and other professionals, as well as those who coordinate their professional development. It provides methods and examples of how to identify starting points for research, how to collect and analyze data, how to develop action strategies and implement them, and ways to make action research public.

Herbert Altrichter is Professor of Education and Educational Psychology at Johannes Kepler University, Linz, Austria.

Allan Feldman is Professor of Education at the University of Massachusetts, Amherst, USA.

Peter Posch is retired Professor of Education at the University of Klagenfurt, Austria.

Bridget Somekh is Professor of Educational Research at Manchester Metropolitan University, UK.

Teachers Investigate their Work

An introduction to action research across the professions

Second edition

Herbert Altrichter, Allan Feldman,
Peter Posch and Bridget Somekh

Routledge
Taylor & Francis Group

LONDON AND NEW YORK

First published 1993
by Routledge
This edition published 2008
by Routledge
2 Park Square, Milton Park, Abingdon, Oxon OX14 4RN

Simultaneously published in the USA and Canada
by Routledge
270 Madison Ave, New York, NY 10016, USA

Routledge is an imprint of the Taylor & Francis Group, an informa business

© First edition 1993 Herbert Altrichter, Peter Posch and Bridget Somekh
© This edition 2008 Herbert Altrichter, Allan Feldman, Peter Posch and Bridget Somekh

Typeset in Palatino by RefineCatch Limited, Bungay, Suffolk
Printed and bound in Great Britain by
TJ International Ltd, Padstow, Cornwall

British Library Cataloguing in Publication Data
A catalogue record for this book is available from the British Library

Library of Congress Cataloging-in-Publication Data
A catalog record for this book has been requested

ISBN10: 0–415–37795–1 (hbk)
ISBN10: 0–415–37794–3 (pbk)
ISBN10: 0–203–97897–8 (ebk)

ISBN13: 978–0–415–37795–9 (hbk)
ISBN13: 978–0–415–37794–2 (pbk)
ISBN13: 978–0–203–97897–9 (ebk)

Contents

Methods and strategies

Figures

Acknowledgements

As with the first edition, this book draws considerably on the book by Herbert Altrichter and Peter Posch (1990) *Lehrer erforschen ihren Unterricht*, Bad Heilbrunn/OBB: Klinkhardt, and its subsequent editions. The authors thank Jinny Hay and Jackie Bridges for their insights into action research and for their contributions of examples of action research from other professions. We would also like to thank the many students at the University of Massachusetts, Amherst, who tried out the new methods and strategies in this edition, and especially those students enrolled during Fall 2006 who trialled this edition.

Chapter 1

Introduction:
What will you find in this book?

You have just opened this book, are slowly reading the first lines and starting to build up an impression of what may be contained in the following pages. How can we give you, the reader, an idea of the book's importance for us, what drove us to devote much energy and time to writing the first edition and why we have spent many months working as a team of four authors, rather than three, to revise it for this second edition? Wistful thoughts like these invade the consciousness of many authors sitting in front of a manuscript that has achieved a certain status – or at least size – through being written, rewritten and finally polished. It is now to be given the last finishing touch: the introduction, which will introduce some key ideas and whet the reader's appetite to read on.

We have decided to tackle the introduction in a particular way. We want to recount some personal experiences that convinced us of the importance of this approach to research – specifically, research conducted by professionals in order to develop their own practice. It also provides us with the opportunity to introduce the fourth member of our team, Allan Feldman. Allan brings to this edition of the book his experience of working with teachers and other practitioners in the United States.

In the early 1980s three of us were strongly influenced by the work of the Teacher-Pupil Interaction and the Quality of Learning Project (TIQL) in which teacher-researchers investigated what it means to understand a subject or a topic and how students' understanding can best be developed through classroom work (see Elliott 1991: 40–2).

Allan was similarly influenced by the work of the Physics Teachers Action Research Group Project (PTARG) during his doctoral studies at Stanford University (Feldman 1996). He also had the opportunity to become our critical friend when the first edition was at the draft stage, by trying out our strategies and approaches with the PTARG teachers. These projects were exciting because teachers investigated the development of students' understanding in their own classrooms, shared their experiences, tried to identify and explain common, and contradictory findings, developed and experimented with new teaching strategies, and wrote case studies of their work. Although we had different connections with these projects – as a TIQL Project teacher (Bridget), interested observers of TIQL (Herbert and Peter) and facilitator of the PTARG Project (Allan) – for each of us the experience was an important landmark in our professional development. The teachers' research provided us with new insights into the process of teaching and learning: it paid much closer attention to details and practicalities than other kinds of research; and it probed the differences between stated aims and actual practice in a way that integrated teaching with research. To show you what we mean here are some examples (all action research passages have been set in italics throughout the book):

In the TIQL Project, Carol Jones (1986), teaching a mixed-age class of 7 to 9 year-olds, investigated their understanding of their schoolwork. She kept notes of what the children did each day, the tasks she set and anything special about the way in which they carried them out. She soon realized that the children understood the tasks in terms of their previous expectations, and had developed an idea of the sort of work she, as their teacher, would be expecting. Her research then focused on, "the extent to which children operate according to criteria of their own, rather than according to the intention of the teacher". She enlisted the help of an outsider who visited her classroom and interviewed the children. By transcribing and analyzing these interviews she found that the children's criteria for judging the value and importance of their work were, indeed, different from hers. For example, when they were asked to observe Puss Moth caterpillars, and make drawings and notes of what they saw, they made a clear distinction between writing and drawing, "holding writing to be a more 'worthwhile', or higher status task, than drawing". In addition, because they were used to being given cards to help with spelling, one child had not understood that the work card gave instructions about how to observe the caterpillars, and instead said, "it just tells you the spellings". These data suggested that the children were not engaging in the kind of observation and interpretation that Carol had intended, but instead had turned the work into "a routine writing task". She also found that the children did not value working in collaboration as she did, but instead used the criterion of "liking to have your own ideas" and rejected sharing ideas, calling this "copying".

In addition to developing their own teaching, some of the TIQL teachers worked in schools where a number of other colleagues were also engaging in research. Thus, it was possible to discuss what they were doing and begin to develop new shared understandings. This kind of work can be a valuable professional development experience for many individual teachers, but in some schools, with the support of a member of senior management, teachers undertaking research can also make a significant impact on the development of the curriculum as a whole. For example, in a large secondary school, Brian Wakeman, one of the Deputy Heads, coordinated a group of teachers who all carried out research into aspects of their pupils' understanding and in this way built up a

Would a Team or colleagues add Value to AR

picture of the kind of changes which it might be helpful for the staff as a whole to implement (after Wakeman *et al.*, 1985).

A few years later, Allan worked with the teachers of the Physics Teachers Action Research Group (Feldman 1996). The Physics Teachers Action Research Group was an example of a group of teachers who taught in different schools who came together to engage in collaborative action research on their practice as physics teachers. PTARG was formed in 1990 and met on a regular basis for three years. The teachers continued to meet occasionally through the year 2000.

Although the teachers helped each other with their research, each had his or her own focus. One of the teachers, Sean Fortrell, had as his starting point for research[1] the dissonance that he noted between the students in two different levels of introductory physics. He found that those in the "Conceptual Physics" class put their effort into attempts to arrive at conceptual understandings of physics. Students in his other course, who he thought to be more able, were principally concerned with getting the correct answers to quantitative physics problems. When he talked about this dissonance at a PTARG meeting, one of the other teachers, Andria Erzberger, told of how she required her students to write down the "approach" that they used to arrive at a numerical solution. This idea, which she had got from a physics text, has the students writing down in words the way that they will go about solving a numerical problem. Sean began to have his students do the same on their homework so that they would begin by describing how they solve problems rather than by writing down equations.

At the end of the school year, Sean reported to the PTARG group what he had learned from the data that he had collected about using this method to encourage his students to think about a problem before attempting to solve it: "What I found was that some students were comfortable with this idea of writing down an approach and others were not. Those who were not, generally did not do it very much. Those who were, I found, latched onto it and used it pretty much the year through, especially in test situations. Most of them used it when the problems were difficult and they were searching around for 'How do I do this?' They would really sit down and write out their steps. I'm not sure how well it necessarily helped them. . . . For those students who were really reaching and trying to figure out in writing their approach, it would make very clear [to me] that they had no idea of what they were doing. They would write out an approach and you could see, 'This is what they're trying to do and it doesn't make sense. That's not the way it should be done.' Very rarely would you find a problem where somebody wrote down an approach in full and then went through and did it all, and did it all right. . . . And so their approach didn't describe how they would solve the rest of the problem. So sometimes it really helped them, other times it just showed that they didn't understand what they were doing."

While Sean's adoption of Andria's technique did not necessarily give him his hoped-for results, as the year went on the other teachers became aware through their discussion of Sean's project of a similar dissonance between their goals to teach conceptual understanding of physics and the students' concern with getting the right answer. Ultimately a concern for students' conceptual understanding led the group to the agreement that their goal for the next year would be to develop teaching methods and assessment techniques that would encourage conceptual as well as quantitative learning in all students.

(After Feldman 1993)

Looking back after a number of years it is easy to explain the deep impression these projects made on us from our different points of view.

- For Herbert and Peter, as visitors from Austria with experience in educational research and teacher education, it was important and unusual that the TIQL teachers not only saw themselves as 'users of knowledge produced by professional researchers' but also did research themselves – producing knowledge about their professional problems and substantially improving their practice. In their developmental work the teachers sometimes made use of external support (for example, in-service training courses and external consultancy from the project team) but, on the whole, retained the initiative in the work themselves. It was impressive that the TIQL teachers were reflecting on their experiences and self-confidently discussing them in public, thus successfully overcoming the notorious disregard for teacher's knowledge and the tradition of teacher 'privatism'.
- For Bridget, as a TIQL participant, it was an opportunity to stand back after 12 years' experience as a teacher and analyze the complexities of teacher-pupil interactions and their impact on children's learning. For the first time she described, and theorized about, her professional practice and found that others were interested. She realized that as a teacher she had insights into classroom processes that were of value in developing educational knowledge.
- For Allan, as facilitator of the PTARG Project who had himself just recently been a high school physics teacher, it was both an opportunity to see how many ways in which teachers similar to him could work together to generate new knowledge about their practice, and to learn about the practice of action research. As we noted above, Allan was at that time a doctoral student at Stanford University and was a student in a course on action research taught by Peter. In fact, Peter met with the PTARG teachers and helped them with the analytic discourse (M9), and provided the teachers with new ways to think about their learning. This can be seen in Sean's comments about action research:

It reminds me of what Peter Posch was talking about last time, he impressed on me the idea that it's often more useful, especially in this sort of stuff [action research], to not give the conclusions but to tell the whole story because you

*can glean so much more from somebody else's experience hearing the whole
tale than you can if you hear 'I've found that this kind of student conversation
is good and this is how you should implement.' It's kind of empty, it loses
something.*

(Feldman 1993: 112)

In both these projects, practitioners understood themselves as "teacher-researchers" and they are not alone. Through the Classroom Action Research Network (CARN),[2] and contacts with a large number of schools and universities, we have met enough individuals and teams working in a comparable way to understand why some people talk about an action research "movement".

In the 15 years since we wrote the first edition of this book, action research has become much more widely accepted among many professional groups as a methodology for supporting development and change. The examples throughout the book are drawn from specific social contexts, in many cases school and higher education settings such as classrooms, and in some others hospitals, clinics and schools of nursing. Our own experience has been that drawing on cases from different professional groups is enormously helpful in allowing us to better understand our own practice as action researchers. Differences destabilize our assumptions and make it possible to ask new kinds of questions about our own cultural norms. Although we did not want to change the title of the book, we decided to include Chapter 9, in which we look specifically at the different ways in which action research is practiced within different professional groups. We invite you to explore whether this is also the case for you, by making conscious comparisons between your own professional workplace and those described in our examples.

In this book we attempt to collect and present in concise form the various ideas, methods and strategies for research that have been developed by European and American action researchers in recent years – in particular, in the fields of in-service education of teachers (Feldman 1995, Capobianco 2000), initial teacher education (Somekh and Davis 1997, Altrichter 1988, Hewson *et al.* 1999), staff development in higher education (Weiss 2003), curriculum innovation (Somekh 2006) and environmental education (Hart *et al.* 2006)

THE PURPOSES OF ACTION RESEARCH

A well-known definition of action research is given by John Elliott whose work has been influential in this "movement." He writes:

Action research might be defined as *"the study of a social situation with
a view to improving the quality of the action within it"* (original italics). It
aims to feed practical judgment in concrete situations, and the validity

of the "theories" or hypotheses it generates depends not so much on 'scientific' tests of truth, as on their usefulness in helping people to act more intelligently and skillfully. In action-research "theories" are not validated independently and then applied in practice. They are validated through practice.

(Elliott 1991: 69)

This definition directs attention to one of the most essential motives for doing action research. It lies in the will to improve the quality of professional practice as well as the conditions under which people work in organizations.

Action research is intended to support practitioner researchers in coping with the challenges and problems of practice and carrying through innovations in a reflective way. Experience with action research over more than 30 years has shown that teachers are able to do this successfully and can achieve remarkable results when given opportunities and support; more recently the same effects have been achieved by other professional groups, such as nurses, social workers, and community support workers. Teachers, for example, have not only carried out development work for their schools but have also broadened their knowledge and their professional competency. They have passed on this knowledge to colleagues, pupils, and parents, and, in written form, to the wider public. They have shown that teachers can make an important contribution to the knowledge base of their profession. And they have demonstrated that they can engage successfully with professional problems without recourse to external direction. They did not restrict their work to adopting a set of practical routines, but acted as professionals precisely in developing new theories about their practice, including a critique of its educational and social contexts.

These teachers are 'normal' teachers, who reflect on their practice to strengthen and develop its positive features. They are not prepared to blindly accept the problems they face from day to day, but instead reflect upon them and search for solutions and improvements. They are committed to building on their strengths and overcoming their weaknesses. They wish to experiment with new ideas and strategies, rather than letting their practice petrify.

Allan offers another definition, with reference to Laurence Stenhouse (1981, 1983):

Action research happens when people are involved in researching their own practice in order to improve it and to come to a better understanding of their practice situations. It is action because they act within the systems that they are trying to improve and understand. It is research because it is systematic, critical inquiry made public.

(Feldman 2007a)

Through our book we aim to encourage all professionals to investigate those aspects of their practice that they want to improve and develop in their daily work and their relationships with colleagues, clients of all ages and managers/administrators. We want to provide a range of methods that can help them to gain a more comprehensive view of their situation, develop action strategies to bring about improvement and evaluate the outcomes of their efforts.

We want to encourage professionals to share their experiences and, by this means, to give a degree of publicity to the professional knowledge that informs their practice. The book contains some suggestions to make this possible. We believe that sharing ideas with colleagues, and keeping the public well-informed about professional concerns and endeavors, may contribute to raising the self-confidence of professionals and, thereby, improving both performance and job satisfaction.

Finally, the book is intended to stimulate the various professional groups to recognize the value of their work to society as a whole, in particular by taking control of the development of their organizations, and of the identification and resolution of crucial professional problems. The current period of rapid social change (while challenging stability) offers exciting possibilities to build a more dynamic culture across the social services. This implies a need, however, for professionals and their leaders, individually and collaboratively, to reflect upon their practice, analyze the functioning of their organization and its strengths and weaknesses, develop perspectives for the future, translate them into actions and structures, and monitor their impact on real situations.

GETTING STARTED: LEARNING TO BE A RESEARCHER BY DOING RESEARCH

Familiarity with action research can develop in various ways: one way is to read about practical methods and theories – another is to study what other practitioners actually did in order to reflect on and improve their practice. The wealth of examples in this book as well as collections of action research case studies; for example, Cochran-Smith and Lytle (1993), Mohr (2003) and Hart et al. (2006), among others, and journals such as *Educational Action Research, Action Research, Journal of Research in Nursing* and *International Journal of Nursing Studies* may enable you to do this. However, the royal road to action research is to explore it by doing it yourself. Thus, the most meaningful way of reading this book would certainly be to exploit it as a reservoir of tools and ideas, and test its usefulness while reflecting on and developing some issue from your own practice.

Doing research involves acquiring some new skills, which is not easy until you have a sense of the whole process. So, we want to start by giving you an overview of what is involved in being a researcher, so that you can quickly plan how to begin and what to do next. Carrying out research is a project and like any other project it requires good organization and a combination of prior planning and on-the-job adjustments to the plan, moving from the initial starting point to some kind of conclusion. As a professional teacher – or another professional such as a health worker or manager – you already have skills in planning a complex project and carrying it through; and this book is designed to help you experiment with more specific research skills in data collection and methods of analysis, so that you will learn to develop tentative explanatory theories about your working practices as the basis for developing action strategies. Researching one's own practice is immensely interesting and rewarding and, rather than thinking of research skills as something to be acquired in advance, we recommend you engage in small-scale research activities immediately and learn through experience.

The key to being a good researcher is not, however, just a matter of acquiring skills; it is important to understand the research process as an art to be continuously perfected rather than a set of procedures that can be applied unproblematically. There is never one clear, right answer to matters relating to human behavior, and research into social situations always involves uncovering the unexpected. To be a good action researcher you need to learn to reflect on what you do, speculate on the possible implications of every situation, and generate theories to be tested in action. The diagram below, which is reproduced in the final chapter of this book, presents action research as an iterative process that integrates theory with practice, through reflection and action planning.

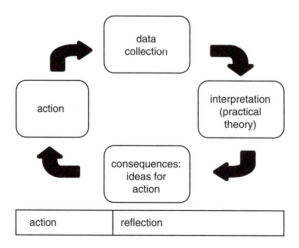

Figure 1.1 The circle of action and reflection

What would an example be?

QUICK START GUIDE IN NINE STEPS

As a starter, think of your research as being made up of nine steps that you need to take. These are all interrelated and not necessarily sequential, but it helps to list them separately as a mental checklist:

1   *Identify a research support group*
    If possible you need to establish yourself as part of a group that can share experiences and provide mutual support. Often a research support group is made up of people who are not all from the same workplace. The important thing is for all members of the group to be involved in their own research, and to agree to meet regularly and be good listeners for one another. There are various strategies described in the book, such as analytic discourse (M9), which help groups to provide each other with high-quality support.

2   *Identify your collaborating research partners*
    These are usually people directly involved in the situation you will be researching. They might be colleagues or clients (children if you are a teacher). When you are choosing them, remember that the more closely involved these partners are in your research the more powerful it is likely to be in terms of bringing about change, but the less control you will have over the direction of the change.

3   *Begin keeping a record of your research activities*
    This is often called keeping a 'research journal' and Chapter 2 provides a lot of ideas about different kinds of research diaries, their purposes and how to make them most useful to you. The key idea is to build up a record of all the impressions and ideas that come to you in the course of your professional activities so that you can think back on these over the weeks and months to come. On the day itself and the one or two days following these are vivid and powerful but they are only held in short term memory and will soon be lost if they are not written down. As you are more and more involved in researching your practice, the focus of your research journal will shift to more explicit recording of research activities.

4   *Decide on the starting point for your research and begin investigating it*
    This is discussed fully in Chapter 3. Starting points can be of many different kinds. There may be some aspect of your professional practice that you find problematic and would like to investigate in order to understand it better. You may want to develop a new approach to some aspect of your practice in order to improve it. You may have a very specific question you want to investigate, but more likely you will just have a general area of interest. All of these approaches are fine, because in any case your area of interest is bound to be changed or refined once you start researching.

5 *Clarify your starting point*

This is the process of progressively refining your area of research through beginning to collect data and analyze it. It is discussed in Chapter 4. You may find that your original focus is considerably changed during the early stage of your research. Sometimes this stage can be frustrating because data analysis is an important skill that you need to develop over time, so you may not immediately see anything very significant in your data. However, this stage can sometimes be very exciting as you begin to see things from new points of view. There are several methods and strategies (Ms) in Chapter 4, some to be carried out alone, and others involving your support group in giving mutual help with this process.

6 *Collect data systematically*

Data collection has already been an important part of your research in steps 3, 4 and 5 above, but Chapter 5 gives a lot of ideas for different methods of collecting data more systematically. It is important to experiment with different approaches and learn how best to collect rich data. For example, interviewing is a complex process and different approaches to interviewing will result in very different accounts from the same interviewees. Some data is in this sense "richer" than other data. But what counts as "rich" will vary and is very much a decision for you to make. Comparing different kinds of data and discussing how they were collected and what makes them more or less "rich" is always a very useful focus for the research support group.

7 *Analyze data*

The most fascinating, but also initially the most difficult, part of the research process is data analysis. Typically, new researchers find it difficult to "see" what is significant in their data, but there are a number of techniques that are very helpful and the methods and strategies (Ms), as well as the more detailed theoretical discussion of the process of analysis, in Chapter 6 should make this stage of becoming a researcher particularly interesting and rewarding. Once again, involvement of your support group and/or research partners will make an enormous difference to how quickly you can acquire the necessary sensitivity to data to become good at analysis.

8 *Developing action strategies and putting them into practice*

In practice, as soon as you begin recording your impressions and reflections in your research diary you will feel the urge to start taking action. This very immediate feedback from research into practice is one of the great benefits of professionals getting involved in action research. When you are beginning to develop greater competence as a researcher, you will be able to plan action strategies more systematically on the basis of explanatory theories you have developed. This process is fully described in Chapter 7. When action strategies result in the improvements you predicted this takes your research one further step forward by demonstrating the power (validity) of your explanatory theóries. Social situations are very complex, however, and there are always a large number of variables influencing what happens, so you should never expect to find clear and unambiguous proofs.

9 *Make your knowledge public*

Research was defined by Stenhouse (1983) as "systematic inquiry made public", and however powerful your research is for your own professional development, it cannot claim to be effective as research until it is shared with others. In Chapter 8 we discuss the many different ways that professionals can make their research knowledge public, and the reasons why this is important for both the status of the professions and the benefit of clients (students, patients, etc.). In practice, action research is never a "finished" process because each set of "findings" gives rise to new ideas for action strategies, and another cycle begins. However, it is important to decide on a cut-off point and write up the research and/or present it formally to an interested group (peers, parents ...). Often written accounts of action research will be in the form of case studies and, when several such accounts are brought together for cross-case analysis, the findings become increasingly stable and capable of informing the action strategies of other professionals working in comparable settings (Somekh 2006).

An important cautionary note is that much of what is written about action research, including this book, may give the impression that it is a step-by-step method that follows a set pattern called the "action research cycle". For example, the nine steps in our Quick Start Guide above proceed from data collection to data analysis to the development of action strategies, and finally to the implementation of those strategies. However, while this pattern is a useful way to talk, write and learn about action research, the practice of action research is often more complex because it is research on ongoing practice. That is, even as we collect data, we are immersed in the practice we are studying. The collection of data affects our practice directly and also indirectly because as we collect data we become more knowledgeable about our practice, which changes the way we talk about it and the way we choose to act in our practice situations. The converse also occurs – as we engage in our practice we become aware of new aspects and contingencies that affect our choices of starting points and data collection methods.

What this suggests is that as we go through an action research cycle, we are actually going through many "mini" action research cycles as our doing of research and our practice interact with one another. As you read on through Chapters 2–8, keep in mind this notion of mini-action research cycles and how they constitute the larger action research cycle.

DIFFERENT KINDS OF ACTION RESEARCH

In the *Hitchhiker's Guide to the Galaxy* (Adams 1979), Ford Prefect and his friends want to find out the meaning of "life, the universe and everything". Their crazy adventures challenge our understanding of human existence: how we can tell what is "real" (a matter of ontology) and how we can say that we "know" something (a matter of epistemology). These are the central questions for researchers and different methodological approaches to research assume different kinds of answers – but nothing as clear as the joke 'answer' in *Hitchhiker's Guide*, which is "42".

Different ways of categorizing action research build on epistemological and ontological assumptions. For example, Carr and Kemmis (1986) assume that access to knowledge is constrained by the operation of power and privilege in societies, so they categorize action research according to its function of enlightening and empowering the researcher. "Technical" action research, which focuses on seeking solutions to relatively simple problems, is therefore of less value than "practical"[3] action research, which focuses on improving practice (but without engaging with the ideological constraints that shape it); and "critical" or "emancipatory" action research is seen as having a higher value than either of the others because it problematizes assumptions about knowledge and reality and seeks to challenge oppressive social structures and create conditions for a socially just society.

Elliott, on the other hand, gives a high priority to engagement with practice and practical problem solving, and rejects the idea that professionals such as teachers are unable to engage in critical reflection and be effective agents for change without first being empowered. He argues that teachers do not need to be liberated from oppression, but are able to generate knowledge and understanding of their practices through engaging in systematic research and reflection: "Practical traditions are dynamic and changing in response to internal critique" (Elliott 2005a).

Noffke's (1997) three "dimensions" of action research – "political," "personal" and "professional" – provide yet another typology of action research, and are useful because they do not imply any hierarchy of status. They provide a useful tool for characterizing the differences between the kinds of action research carried out by groups within different cultures and contexts. For example, action research carried out in situations where there are serious disparities between the rich and the poor, or where some sections of the population are systematically discriminated against by a colonial power, is more likely to have a strong political motivation;

and action research carried out under the auspices of university programs leading to academic accreditation is more likely to have a personal development or professional orientation.

FEATURES THAT DISTINGUISH ACTION RESEARCH AS PRESENTED IN THIS BOOK

In writing this book we draw most closely on the traditions of action research deriving from the work of Elliott and Stenhouse, which in turn draws heavily on the work of Dewey and Bruner. In summary, this book suggests that:

1 Action research is carried out by people directly concerned with the social situation that is being researched. In the case of the social situation of a classroom this means in the first place teachers who take professional responsibility for what goes on in the classroom. While action research will usually be initiated by individual practitioners (teachers, nurses, social workers, etc.), sustainable improvements will rarely be possible if other concerned persons do not become won over to its purposes. According to the problem being investigated, these might include in the case of teachers: students, parents, LEA[4] advisers, governors or representatives of the local community. In the case of nurses they might include patients, their families, physicians and health insurance administrators. Thus, the long-term aspiration of action research is always a collaborative one. In cases where action research begins as a more private and isolated concern external consultants are often involved, for example from higher education institutions. However, in these cases the role of the outsider is to provide support and not to take over responsibility and control over the direction and duration of the project.

2 Action research starts from practical questions arising from everyday professional practice (and not from those that might be "in fashion" in some learned discipline). It aims to develop both the practical situation and the knowledge about the practice of the participants.

3 Action research must be compatible with the educational values of the workplace and with its working conditions (see Chapter 5 for a more extensive discussion of this point). However, it also contributes to the further development of these values and to the improvement of working conditions.

4 Action research offers a repertoire of methods and strategies for researching and developing practice that are characterized by a sensible ratio of costs to results. Methods are tailored to what is achievable without overly disrupting practice.

5 Action research is characterized by a continuing effort to closely inter-

link, relate and confront action and reflection, to reflect upon one's conscious and unconscious doings in order to develop one's actions, and to act reflectively in order to develop one's knowledge. Both sides will gain thereby: reflection opens up new options for action and is examined by being realized in action.

THE CONTENTS OF THE BOOK AND HOW IT MIGHT BE USED

The intention of writing this book was to introduce readers to action research. It is primarily for professionals who want to engage in innovation and development in their workplace. The most rewarding use of this book will be for those who are prepared to engage in an action research process alongside their reading. They can make immediate use of the suggestions and proposed strategies while, at the same time, critically examining and further developing them. In this way the book is intended as a source of practical support for those engaging in research, without in any sense being prescriptive.

We present this research approach on two levels:

- On the one hand, we have collected a variety of practical suggestions that have been developed by action researchers for investigating and introducing innovation into their practice and practice situations. To do this we use many examples drawn from studies by practitioners. The book does not contain any complete case studies written by practitioners, but if you are interested in reading this kind of outcome of action research you can find them in the sources that we cited above and throughout the book.
- On the other hand, we also want to explain the theoretical background of action research that underpins the methodological suggestions and gives them meaning. We do this from time to time as part of the process of clarifying the various research strategies, as well as in Chapter 10, which offers a theoretical grounding, what we think of as the 'support structures from behind the scenes'. However, for a more systematic and detailed analysis of the various theoretical approaches to action research, readers who are interested might turn to Elliott (2007), Carr and Kemmis (1986), Somekh and Noffke (forthcoming), Zeichner and Noffke (2001) or Cochran-Smith and Lytle (1993).

It may be best to gain a quick overview of the book by skimming its contents and finding out how the chapters fit together and interrelate, and then to regard the chapters as a series of resources to be given a second deeper reading, in the order best suited to need rather than reading them sequentially.

Chapter 2

The research journal
Companion to the research process

The research journal is one of the most important research methods and is very commonly used by practitioners doing research on their practice. It also makes a good way into research. We want to suggest that you regard it as a companion to the whole research process, rather than simply as a means of collecting data or recording analysis. Our suggestions for writing and using research journals are based on personal experience as well as experience of working with others keeping similar journals. At the end of the chapter we provide some exercises that should make it easier to start a research journal.

WHY JOURNALS ARE USEFUL FOR RESEARCH

We believe that these are the characteristics that make research journals so useful.

1 Writing a research journal *builds on an everyday skill* of many practitioners. In this sense writing a research journal is simpler and more familiar than other research methods, such as, for example, interviewing. In addition, journal keeping is easier to organize than most other research methods. It is always possible to make a journal entry if paper and time are available, whereas to carry out an interview you need a partner who is willing to answer some questions, which may or may not have been prepared in advance.

2 A research journal *can also contain data collected by other research methods*. For example, it is a good place to record notes from unstructured observations or the description of the context and conditions of an interview just carried out. In this way the research journal becomes similar to the laboratory notebook kept by scientists. Scientists' lab notebooks contain their hypotheses and research questions, their research design, the data that they collect and their data analysis. They also make records of their discussions with colleagues and any ideas that come to them during the course of the research. In short, the

laboratory notebook is as much as possible a complete record of the research endeavor. Although you may not want to use your research journal in this way, the point that we are making is that it can be used for much more than purposes of reflection.

3 Short memos or ideas about the research issues can be recorded frequently in a research journal. Because of this *continuity* a research journal can develop a quality that makes it more valuable than other research methods: it becomes a companion of your own personal development through research; it links investigative and innovative activities; it documents the development of perceptions and insights across the different stages of the research process. In this way it makes visible both the successful and (apparently) unsuccessful routes of learning and discovery so that they can be revisited and subjected to analysis.

4 Research journals *draw on a tradition*. "From the very beginning of European culture texts have been written with the aim of increasing self-understanding, becoming aware of self-delusions, and articulating and reducing pain" (Werder 1986).[1] Journals in which the self and its surrounding conditions were investigated have ranged from Saint Augustine's *Confessions* to Handke's *Weight of the World*. Such texts published with philosophical or literary intentions are rare islands in a sea of anonymous journals by writers whose reflections on themselves and on their everyday lives remained unpublished. At first sight such journals appear to us as self-reflective or introspective texts or as "literature" but only rarely as research. This does not mean, however, that introspective journals cannot lead to important insights or that they are necessarily self-indulgent: Elias Canetti (1981) regards conversation with oneself in a diary as a dialog with a "cruel partner". One of the main points of this chapter is to show how action research can learn from these literary and self-reflective diaries. Mary Lou Holly (1989: xi) presents a similar point of view in describing, "how keeping a journal can facilitate observation, documentation, and reflection on current and past experiences, including one's life history and the social, historical, and educational conditions that usher in the present".

5 Journals in which researchers recall the fruits of their daily observation in the research field hold a *central position in many disciplines*: for example in zoological field research, DeVore's (1970) journal containing his observations on the behavior of apes; or in ethnographical research, Malinowski's (1982) use of a journal to record his detailed observations. Qualitative sociological research makes intensive use of research journals in building up thorough insights into the functioning of institutions through participant observation and through conversations with key informants; for example, the famous studies of the Chicago School; such as, Whyte (1955) and Cressey (1932). Whether

they are called journals, logbooks, field notes or lab books, these records are important companions to the research process.

6 There is also a tradition of using research journals in *qualitative educational research* as a result of the influence of ethnography and sociological field research. Examples include the highly readable ethnographies by Alan Peshkin (1986). An early example of this qualitative school research is Philip Jackson's (1968) *Life in Classrooms*. In this book the author tried to "move up close to the phenomena of the teacher's world" (p. 159). As a participant observer he had to use a mixture of methods and perspectives since "classroom life . . . is too complex an affair to be viewed or talked about from any single perspective" (p. vii). More recently, Jackson has turned to autobiographical methods to reflect upon his experiences both as a pupil and teacher to delve into the complexities of teaching and learning (Jackson 1992).

Action research has drawn upon this tradition of journal keeping in educational research. Research journals containing observations, ideas, plans etc. have been increasingly used during the past years by those interested in action research (e.g. Strieb 1985, Glover 1992). For example, Fuller (1990) and Williams (1990) made a journal the basis of their data collection to investigate ways of enabling children to become more autonomous learners. It is important to note that its legitimacy as a research method has increased dramatically in the past ten years as narrative forms of inquiry including autobiography, memoirs and autoethnography have become accepted forms of educational research (Ellis and Bochner 2000, Elbaz-Luwisch 2004, Attard and Armour 2005). In fact, for some, journal writing has become synonymous with practitioner research. In North America this has been due largely to the influence of the Writing Projects (Lieberman and Wood 2002, Jago 2003). These local collaboratives of teachers of writing and of literacy practices have made teacher research a central part of their work, with the process of journal keeping and reflecting in and on it being the prime research method (Holly 1989).

To sum up, on the one hand research journals can contain *data* that are obtained by participatory observation and by conversations and interviews in the field, sometimes enriched by explanatory comments and photographs; on the other hand, they can contain written *reflections* on research methods and on your own role as researcher (perhaps similar to the conversation of the ethnographer with him/herself in a foreign culture). In addition, ideas and insights can be noted that lead to the development of the theoretical constructs that, in turn, can be used to interpret the data and guide action. Keeping such a research journal ensures that data collection is not artificially separated from reflection and analysis, nor from your actions as a practitioner. Strauss and Corbin (1990) have emphasized that analysis accompanying such data collection should be actively used for the further development of research: preliminary results of an analysis show that data are still necessary to fill in the gaps in a theoretical framework and to evaluate intermediate results through further investigation. In addition, the regular keeping of a research journal in which you record data and reflections and other interpretations results in an almost continuous stream of the mini-action research cycles that we discussed above.

SOME SUGGESTIONS FOR WRITING RESEARCH JOURNALS

In this section we present some ideas and suggestions for writing research journals. These are based on our own experiences, some of which have been positive and others frustrating, but all of which have deepened our understanding of journal keeping as an instrument for action research.

Writing a research journal is an individual matter. In due time, every journal writer develops a style and idiosyncrasies that are an important part of making journal writing valuable as a research method. For this reason, our recommendations are offered only as suggestions that you should adopt or reject after due consideration.

Getting started with your journal

1 Journals should be *written regularly*, at times that fit in with the kind of research question being investigated, for example, after each lesson in which a particular teaching strategy has been implemented, or after each meeting with a "difficult class". Some people find it is useful to reserve specific periods of time for this activity by writing them into their timetable, to prevent journal keeping being drowned in the whirlpool of daily necessities. These "journal times" can then be complemented and expanded by irregular recording of relevant scenes, experiences and ideas.

2 People who are not used to journal keeping often experience some barriers to establishing the habit. Sometimes it is necessary to go through a difficult period before journal keeping becomes personally satisfying. When deciding whether the exercise is worth the time and effort, it is worth considering its side effects. For example, regular journal keeping generally increases the quality and speed of one's own written articulation. We found journal keeping easier if we collaborated with a research partner to whom we could read extracts from our text and talk about them. This, in turn, had spin-offs in terms of increased understanding that enriched the whole research process.

3 The above suggestion, however, does not take away from the *confidential nature of a journal*. The decision to make parts of it available to other people should always remain with the author. It is particularly important to stress this again and again in projects, courses and workshops, in order to prevent the recurring subtle, social pressure to go public, on the principle: "I have said something, now it's your turn."

4 Feel free to disregard *considerations of style* or punctuation while writing it. Self-censorship often disturbs the free flow of thoughts; this can come later if the results of your research activities are to be published. Remember that because is it *your* journal, you need not share it with anyone.

How to keep a research journal

5 For our journal entries we use thick notebooks (of more than 40 pages). We have found that these become more and more "elegant" the more we enjoy journal writing. Journals are highly personal artefacts. For us, the use of notebooks facilitates reflection on our own process of learning. Other researchers write their notes on loose leaves that they can file later under different categories. An elementary school teacher, who focused on introducing innovative methods of teaching reading, wrote her journal notes on colored sheets that she put between the white sheets of her lesson notes. In this way she obtained a good record of the relationship between plans and the experience of putting them into action. Some people use a computer to keep their journal. While this makes it easier to do subsequent data analysis and to include non-textual material such as photographs, videos, and audio files, computers are not as portable or accessible as a notebook. Find a form to suit yourself.

6 Leave a wide *margin* on each page (or buy a booklet with a ruled margin). This can be used to record changes, additions, or references to other parts of the research journal or to other data, at a later date. Such a margin is especially helpful for the analysis of journal data (which we will return to in Chapter 6). Notes (from single words to sentences) can be entered here indicating the meaning or interpretation of a journal sequence within the framework of your research aim. This process is illustrated in the journal extract that follows in the next section. For example, as preliminary analysis (and in preparation for a written report), the margin can be used for coding and for identifying examples to illustrate particular concepts (see M33). Generally, we use different color ink to record provisional codes or analytical commentaries on journal entries, because it contrasts with the ink of the normal text and catches the eye more easily.

7 Each entry should be accompanied by the following information:

- the date of the event (and date of the written record if it took place on a different day)
- contextual information, such as time, location, participants, focus of study, and anything else (such as unusual weather or a fire drill) that seems important for the research.

If this is ordered in the same manner for all entries, it is likely to be easier to "read oneself back in" to the data at a later date.

8 It is easier to orientate yourself quickly and analyze the data if paragraphs, headings, subheadings, and underlining are used to *structure the text*. Some people like to number paragraphs and headings to make cross-referencing easier.

9 It is helpful to make a running *list of contents* on the first or last pages of the journal to make it easy to go back to particular pieces of data.

Using a research journal for data collection and analysis

10 Everything that you put in your journal is data. Some of the data are more factual or descriptive, while other data are more interpretive or inferential. The important thing to remember is that all information that helps you to develop a more profound understanding of your practice situation and can help you to reconstruct it later can and should be included in your research journal. Therefore, make sure to include "feelings, reactions, interpretations, reflections, ideals and explanations" (Kemmis and McTaggart 1982).

11 Research journals can also contain a great number of vivid descriptions of situations, sometimes called "thick descriptions" (Geertz 1973). These provide a quarry of examples for in-depth discussion. They also provide vicarious experiences that are particularly useful as a means of helping other teachers to reflect on practice. We find that materials of this kind are very useful for in-service courses, enabling practitioners to learn more independently and still remain close to experience.

12 You can also include items in your journal that seem relevant to the research process: ideas jotted down on a piece of paper, photographs or copies of documents such as pupils' work. If research activities and the data obtained by them (for example, a transcript of a lesson or an interview) cannot be written directly into the journal because of lack of space or for other reasons, it is a good idea to make a cross-reference to them in the journal.

13 In this way a research journal contains various kinds of records. This wide-ranging approach corresponds to our everyday form of tackling problems, but it is open to some pitfalls. For example, in general

we expect research to go back and forth between description and interpretation. Because of their practical forward-looking interests, teachers, nurses, social workers or other practitioners doing research are often inclined to neglect detailed description. It is useful, therefore, with each journal entry to make clear whether it refers to description or to interpretation. One way of coping with the fuzzy borderline between description and interpretation is to use the "ladder of inference" described in M18.

14 As we noted above, it is often very helpful in extending the research process to read sequences from your journal to a colleague or a research partner. The conversation about experiences can provide deeper insights into the fine texture of practice situations. Such conversations are especially fruitful if the researcher is rigorous in relating speculations to interpretations and descriptions recorded in the journal or other data – in other words, relating ideas to specific events and reflections rather than allowing the conversation to become diffuse and generalized.

15 From time to time it is helpful to do a *provisional analysis* of the journal entries (see Chapter 6). This shows whether descriptions and interpretations are in a useful balance, which of the initial research questions can be answered from existing data and which data are still necessary. Through this provisional analysis it is often possible to reformulate the initial questions more clearly, to modify them or to pose them in a new way. It also helps you to plan the next steps in research and action in a more rational way. Last but not least, it reduces the danger of being flooded by "data overload" towards the end of an investigation.

Ethical issues relating to keeping a research journal

Our first step in discussing ethical issues related to keeping a research journal is to compare it to both the personal diary and the laboratory notebook. In some cultures the personal diary is thought of as a private record, and that for someone other than the writer to read it without prior permission would be an extreme breach of propriety. In fact, the traditional diary has a lock and key to help ensure its private nature. The laboratory notebook, on the other hand, is very much a public document. In addition to helping to ensure the validity of the research, it is considered a legal document for the purpose of acknowledging the primacy of discoveries and the granting of patents.[2]

As we see it, the action research journal lies somewhere between the personal diary and the laboratory notebook in terms of its private or public nature, and can be considered a semi-public document. While these journals are usually private to the researcher and may contain intimate accounts and reflections, there is the possibility that for the purposes of the research some of its contents will be made public. Because action research is research on practice and includes other human participants, the contents of the research journal should not be made public without consideration of the participants. That is, permission to do so should either be obtained before the collection of data begins (e.g. through the use of a consent form, if required by the institution, ethics committee or institutional review board (IRB), which we discuss below, or it should be obtained before any data involving them are made public. This should be the case even if anonymity of the participants is maintained (see Chapter 8 for more details).

When journals contain interview data or observation notes made by someone else (as in the extract from the English teacher's journal below), it is usually best to clear the data immediately with the person concerned. This can be done by photocopying the relevant passage, or even by handing over the research journal open at the relevant passage (though this has the disadvantage that the person is not able to reflect on it except in your presence – since the journal as a whole is confidential). If the data is in digital form you can share it electronically, but remember that email or other electronic files can be readily copied and distributed, and may be considered public documents. It is not usually necessary to clear your interpretations with participants.

An important ethical rule is never to allow research to become covert. Journal notes of conversations in the staffroom or in casual situations such as on the way to the swimming pool are often the most useful of all, and providing colleagues and children know that the research is being undertaken they do not all need to be cleared. To ensure research is not covert: (i) tell colleagues and pupils that you are undertaking it; and (ii) clear any data before you refer to it or quote it publicly.

The ethical issue that we are dealing with here is *informed consent*. We like to break this concept into two parts. One is the need to inform participants and stakeholders that you are engaged in a research study. The other is the need to seek consent of those involved in your research. This is especially important for those whom you have power over, such as pupils, patients and clients. You should provide them with a way to decline to participate in your research without negative consequences. For pupils, patients, and clients who are under age, you should seek permission of their parents or guardians.

The issues that we have discussed here are sometimes under the purview of an ethical committee or an IRB. Universities and other research institutions usually have a board or committee that reviews research projects to make sure that they comply with the rules and norms of ethical treatment of human subjects. You should find out whether your institution has an IRB or its equivalent and comply with its rules for review.

[handwritten margin note: Ask about this in class]

Similarly, local educational agencies such as school boards have enacted regulations that govern the doing of research in schools, and hospitals and social agencies also have rules governing research done in their institutions. It is imperative that all practitioners find out what those regulations are and comply with them.

MEMOS AND IN-DEPTH REFLECTION

In the remainder of this chapter we look closely at two different types of journal entries: memos and in-depth reflections. We provide examples of each type of entry after we describe them. You may find it useful to refer to those examples as you read about the types of entries. As with all the action research methods that we describe in this book, do not feel you must know how to keep a journal before you begin. Learning how to keep a research journal is best done by doing it.

Memos

Memos are the most frequent kind of entries in research journals. Memos are produced when trying to recall and write down experiences that occurred in a specific period of time (for example, during a lesson or session with a patient or client). The memo often provides the only possibility of collecting data on your own practical activities without too much investment of time and energy. Sometimes, action researchers fear that after a delay of an hour or more they will not be able to remember in enough detail, or with sufficient accuracy, to write useful memos. In our experience this is not too much of a problem, particularly if you follow procedures that help to improve the quality of your recall. For example, Bogdan and Biklen (2006) suggest:

- The earlier a memo is written after an event the better.
- Before writing down from memory you should not talk about the events with anybody as this may modify your recollection in an uncontrolled way.
- The chronology of events is generally the best way to arrange written records. However, as it is important to make entries as "complete" as possible, anything you remember later can be added at the end.
- Sometimes it is possible to jot down catchwords and phrases during the course of the activity you want to record: for example, when pupils are working independently, with partners or in groups; when you are listening to pupils reporting back to the class; or when you are not teaching but observing a colleague or a student teacher. Later on, when writing the journal, these catchwords and phrases jotted down during the lesson prove very useful as *aides-mémoire*.

- Memory improves if you can find time and leisure for recall. If activities are to be documented in a memo, it is useful to reserve some time afterwards that can be kept free of interruptions. The time necessary is often underestimated. In general it is easy to spend a full hour writing down observations and reflections. You should plan to spend at least half an hour, particularly as you may find you get delayed in starting!
- Memos are written primarily to describe and document events after they have taken place. At the same time these descriptions are usually frequently interspersed with interpretations. Within memos it is important to make a clear distinction between *descriptive sequences* and *interpretive sequences*.

Descriptive journal entries

Descriptive entries contain accounts of activities, descriptions of events, reconstructions of dialogs, gestures, intonation, and facial expressions; portraits of individuals – their appearance, their style of talking and acting; and the description of a place or facilities. Your own behavior as the action researcher is, of course, an important part of these descriptions.

In any descriptive passage the detail is more important than the summary, the particular is more important than the general and the account of an activity is more important than its evaluation. Whenever possible speakers should be quoted exactly (indicated by quotation marks) or in a paraphrase (some people indicate this in a journal by single quotes). Words and phrases that are typical of a person, group or institution should be written as exactly as possible.

Interpretive journal entries

Memos should contain not only descriptive entries but also interpretive entries: interpretations, feelings, speculations, ideas, hunches, explanations of events, reflections on your own assumptions and prejudices, development of theories etc. Interpretations will occur not only when writing down experiences but also at a later date, when journal entries such as observation notes etc. are reflected upon.

AN EXAMPLE TAKEN FROM A RESEARCH JOURNAL

It seems important at this stage to give an example from the kind of research journal we have been describing. You may find it useful to cross-check the example with the suggestions outlined in the previous section – which ones have been adopted and which not, and why might that be? The excerpt is not intended as a model of "the right kind of research journal", rather it demonstrates the personal and highly focused nature of journal keeping.

The excerpt is taken from a research journal kept by an English teacher in a secondary school who was introducing computer use in the teaching of writing. It was kept over a 6-month period. In this excerpt a visitor (who is hoping soon to become a teacher) was asked to make observation notes (some of which are quoted and commented upon in the journal). The teacher saw this as a good opportunity as none of her colleagues had been able to observe her classes. There were eight groups of children writing stories collaboratively: four groups had access to writing on one computer at the same time (using four replacement keyboards and software that divided the screen into four separate writing areas) and four groups were doing their writing on paper. As well as this story writing the groups were engaged in drawing maps, making lists of necessary equipment, and other related activities. In practice, two pupils from each group were usually at the computer at the same time – one sitting at the keyboard and the other standing behind and sharing in the process of composition. The other two group members were working on the maps, equipment lists etc.

On the left-hand side of the journal the teacher left a margin. After a first review (a provisional analysis) of the journal she entered several catchwords and references that are explained in more detail later in this chapter, for example: MNs (methodological notes) and TNs (theoretical notes). While this example is of a planned observation, entries in research journals can and should include observations, reflections and comments that come about spontaneously.

Ask (handwritten margin note)

? (handwritten margin note)

Extract from a secondary English teacher's research journal

Nov. 14: Notes and reflections after talking to Susan, a visitor who observed my lesson.

MN1 *method* (handwritten)
observation
notes

Susan focused more than I expected on the high level of noise. Her expectations seemed a bit unrealistic – told myself that she must have gone to a very formal school, but I felt quite vulnerable although probably didn't show it. Is it worthwhile getting observation notes in this way from anyone who happens to come along? It would be nice to have a regular critical friend/partner, but as I don't this seems the best compromise.

Susan said:

So talking in class is a method (handwritten)

What is box for? (handwritten)

1 Group 1 seemed to be very reliant on Amnon – that at the beginning Billy was "crawling all over the table . . . very disruptive".

TN1 individual differences ☐?

Comment: Is this because Amnon is known as the computer expert? Billy misses some classes for help with reading. Can I give him extra time to make up?

Theoretical notes (handwritten)

2 Group 2 was working well – Robert and Tim mainly at the table and Quentin and Keith at the computer – periods of lapses, but on the whole working OK. Quentin and Keith were the motivating powers. Quentin wanted to ask Keith's advice. Keith felt he was in control. They had Carlo on their left and his keeper, Edward. Carlo seemed OK for about half an hour and then got very aggressive.

3 Group 5, Carlo and Edward were talking about their work. Edward was making suggestions and Carlo writing them down – later having an argument about a sentence at the end. Carlo very reluctant to change it. Edward, in rather a nice way, pointing out they could improve it. Edward feeding spellings – sometimes Carlo getting it right himself. The time span was too great for him.

I don't get these. Go + notes are numbered. (handwritten)

Who said this? (handwritten)

TN2 Collaboration – benefits and drawbacks

Comment: really worried about Carlo. This didn't sound too bad, but he's a disruptive force. Edward's role seems very helpful, but what does he gain from it? Looking forward to Carlo and Edward working on the computer – maybe a pity I have left them out of the first four groups.

4 Group 6, girls at the front, in their stride – wrote a lot, didn't put down their pens – a marked difference from the beginning of the lesson when Susan felt they weren't very interested.

MN2 reliability of data?
TN3 effects of computer on my role

Comment: sounds good, but what were they writing? I neglected this group – problem when the computer is in the room is that I am concentrating my attention mainly on the children working on it. How can I guard against this? Maybe I can't until I am more used to it.

5 Didn't watch Group 3 because every time she had a look they were doing very nicely – they didn't move much – whereas other children moving round the room quite a bit. I suggested that movement was to do with groups using the computer – no need for Group 3 to move as they were all sitting near the computer, anyway. Susan agreed – they could communicate with whoever was at the keyboard – yes.

TN4 *movement*
related to com-
puter use

Comment: *using a computer for collaborative writing necessitates movement between those writing on the computer and other members of the group back at the table. Movement, discussion and noise are therefore consequences of collaboration. To reduce movement and noise it may be best to place the computer in the middle of the room and seat the groups at surrounding tables – would need an extension cable for the computer.*

December 10 ☑   – *I think I'll try this.*

6 *Group 4 were working well, too – though there was a difference of opinion. Fiona got really uncooperative. She stormed back from the computer and said, "That Caroline, she's been there for such a long time – she's messing about with commas that we can deal with when we get the printout. She should be getting the story into the computer." She was very irritated – she lost her stride after that – near the end of the lesson so it didn't matter too much, but she was extremely put out.*

TN5
collaboration –
raising tensions

Comment: *Really worrying that there seem to be these arguments. Billy's behavior is part of the same pattern, I think (there's actually been some racial taunting between him and the others in his group, who are from India, China and Israel). Working with the computer seems to be raising greater tensions. Why? Is it the way I've set up the work . . . or is it because they are all so highly motivated? If it's the latter then maybe they are all trying much harder than usual to keep some ownership of the task – so they are really trying to collaborate instead of portioning out bits of the task with differential levels of ownership and responsibility. Cooperating in collaborative group work requires specific social skills – should these be taught? Heavens, I find collaborative writing difficult myself. Maybe tensions within groups are inevitable, but deliberate teaching might make them more aware of the need to work together and of tendencies of group members to dominate or to withdraw. How can I do that? Perhaps it would be good to hold*

November 21 ☑   *a class discussion about the way they are managing their group work.*

I need to understand better the way the groups are organizing themselves – I'll try to fix up 5-minute interviews with every child in Groups 1–4 at the end of this first two weeks of writing on the computer.

[handwritten annotations in margin: why is this after date Dec 10 ?]

[handwritten at bottom: idea → Conferencing w/ students.]

REREADING THE RESEARCH JOURNAL

In daily life, any writing will usually be reread afterwards, which results in the discovery of mistakes (and, of course, treasures), and many things become clearer. While rereading it is much easier for you to judge which things are important and which are not so important than it is at the time of writing. You can discover new relationships between ideas and often some new insights that should be followed up. Questions emerge and it is easy to see what still needs to be done. Often it is possible to see how the thoughts expressed in the text could be usefully restructured.

Similar things happen if a memo is reread or analyzed. Analysis in research is a kind of rereading of existing data with the intention of reorganizing, interpreting and evaluating them with respect to your research interest (see Chapter 6). Although it might be tempting to see this as a reason to write the research journal using a computer, an important part of analysis is seeing the original text with emendations. Therefore, if you do use a computer, make sure that you keep both the original text and your revisions, and distinguish between them with different fonts, colors or brackets.

The English teacher whose journal we excerpted above reread her journal and put in analytical comments that we refer to as theoretical notes, methodological notes, and planning notes.

- *Theoretical notes* are used to put forward explanations relevant to the research question or issue being investigated. They identify relationships between events and note them for further research.
- *Methodological notes* are used to record your reflections on the research methods that you used. Ideas for alternative methods and procedures are noted to help develop your own competence as a researcher.
- *Planning notes* are used to record new ideas for the improvement of practical action that emerge as you write or reread your journal. For example, you may remember things that you wanted to try out some time ago, or flashes of thoughts from the last lesson that you may have forgotten.

We now look at each of these types of notes in more detail.

SUGGESTIONS FOR WRITING THEORETICAL NOTES (TNs)

Research is more than collecting data. It is also about making connections between data and understanding them. When you reflect on data various ideas come to mind. Theoretical notes in a research journal try to capture these ideas and save them from oblivion. Sometimes they are an integral part of memos as in our example from the English teacher's journal: she marked the theoretical notes with the symbol TN and with a key term or label, which indicates the main theoretical idea for subsequent analysis. Ideas for theoretical notes also emerge while analyzing data, while thinking or talking about your research plans or as sudden flashes of understanding on the way to work etc.

There are a number of purposes for which writing theoretical notes is useful. These include:

- clarifying a concept or an idea (see TN2 in the English teacher's journal);
- making connections between various accounts and other bits of information (TN5);
- identifying surprising or puzzling situations worth following up later (TN5);
- connecting your own experience to the concepts of an existing theory (TN1);
- formulating a new hypothesis (TN4);
- realizing hitherto unconscious assumptions and formulating their theoretical implications (TN3).

For practical purposes in making theoretical notes we suggest you might:

- Date each theoretical note and give it a label or key term indicating its content (see the examples in the English teacher's journal extract).
- Clarify the relationship between a theoretical note and the data it relates to. If necessary, the relationship may be qualified (for example, by writing 'uncertain', 'examine'); and cross-references to other theoretical notes and data may be added.
- Priority should be given to writing theoretical notes over other research activities (such as observation, documentation, formal analysis etc.). Whenever you have an idea for a theoretical note, other activities should be interrupted to record it in as uncensored a form as possible – even if it sounds rather fantastic or daring. These ideas may turn out to be keys to understanding the issue being researched.

SUGGESTIONS FOR WRITING METHODOLOGICAL NOTES (MNs)

Methodological notes record the researcher's self-observation when doing research. As with theoretical notes, sometimes they can be an integral part of the journal entry and sometimes added later as part of preliminary analysis. For example they might address these questions:

- What were the circumstances in which I used particular research methods (see MN1 in the example from the English teacher's journal)?
- What role did I play in the situation under investigation?

- What comments arise from my experience of specific research methods and strategies (MN2)?
- What decisions did I take about the future course of my research, and why?
- What conflicts and ethical dilemmas did I encounter and how did I deal with them?

While research on the research process itself might seem too complicated and self-indulgent, in moderation there are good reasons for making methodological notes. First, action research does not claim to produce unambiguous results regardless of the context. Therefore, it is important to reflect on research methods while doing research, and to build up a stock of methodological knowledge that action researchers can draw upon in future investigations. Second, documenting and reflecting on methodology while carrying out action research may be of particular importance for other people working in your field. Such records provide them with knowledge and practical examples, which are useful when working with other teachers, nurses or social workers who want to reflect on and improve their practice. Third, by paying attention to how you do research, you improve your research skills as you proceed through mini-action research cycles (see MN1 in the English teacher's journal).

SUGGESTIONS FOR WRITING PLANNING NOTES

When writing memos and reflecting on data we often "automatically" generate ideas about, for example:

- alternative courses of practical action;
- how to do it next time;
- what was forgotten this time and must definitely be made up for in the next lesson;
- what has to be thought through more carefully;
- what additional information seems essential and needs to be gathered.

Jotting down planning notes in your research journal makes more systematic use of the stream of ideas that, as we all know, go as quickly as they come. It provides us with a way to remember the plans that we want to put into practice at some later date. At the same time, it facilitates the shaping of a plan by recording the context of the original aspirations thus helping us to keep its purposes clear in the course of development. Some practical suggestions for writing planning notes are:

- As in everyday life, you should not make too many plans. Plans that are not put into practice often induce feelings of frustration and failure. On the other hand, you should not suppress evolving ideas too early just because they seem 'unrealistic' (see also Chapter 7).

- We mark plans by the symbol □ in the margin (see the English teacher's journal). A date may be added to the □ if planned activities have to take place at a specific time. You can check it when you have carried out a plan (☑ see the example in the English teacher's journal). In this way you can quickly see which plans you have completed and which still need to be put into practice.

In-depth reflections

Much of your journal will consist of the memos that we have discussed previously in this chapter. We also encourage you to include entries that are the result of in-depth reflections that draw on a range of experiences over an extended period of time, rather than focusing on a specific situation.

In-depth reflection and other creative-introspective methods are important ways for action researchers to gain access to, and reach, an understanding of their tacit knowledge, which is the result of their experience but, normally, not directly and consciously at their disposal (see further discussion of this in Chapter 10). Writing in journals and the use of other methods and strategies (Ms) described in this book can help to make explicit your tacit knowledge. These methods may also be particularly helpful for exploring recurring situations that are problematic in any way, for example:

- situations that occur frequently but that you do not fully understand;
- situations that end up in problems and conflict again and again;
- situations that you repeatedly feel uneasy about although no obvious conflicts surface, for example: dilemmas, ethical uncertainties, difficult decisions, and 'vicious circles' in which you feel trapped into behaving in a particular way (see further discussion of this in Chapter 6);
- problems with pupils, patients or clients that do not seem to have any logical reason.

In-depth reflections in journal entries can contain descriptive and interpretive sections, just like memos. Since these reflections usually refer to longer time-spans the descriptive element is sometimes neglected, but you should be aware of the danger of losing touch with reality if you allow your thoughts to range too widely. Therefore, it is important to link passages of in-depth reflection with their roots in events and actions.

Research notebook extract illustrating in-depth reflection

To illustrate in-depth reflection we include here an extract from a particularly ingenious example. A teacher of a special class, for pupils with learning difficulties, used this method to explore her experiences during breaks between lessons. Once again, while reading it we suggest that you keep a check on how this example relates to the points we have made above.

In particular, my twelve students' ways of modifying closeness and distance – both among themselves and towards me – during the breaks inspired me with some ideas of how to do them (and myself) more justice in the classroom. Using (one child) as an example to illustrate what I mean, I will not describe persons and situations but what was impressed on me through my observations: perceptions and subjective images influenced as much by my will to see and learn as by what was really taking place.

I have used the following procedures to reproduce these images as authentically as possible:

1 *When thinking of one particular child I display my associations in the form of "clusters". These serve as a starting point for the next steps (although not every idea is followed up).*
2 *I sketch some impressions of a typical situation during breaks in which this particular child was involved.*
3 *In doing so I reconstruct my part in these situations as far as I am conscious of it.*
4 *Comparisons with the situation during lessons then indicate starting points for improvement that emerge from the observations during breaks.*
5 *Finally, I roughly describe the development in the course of the school year and, in particular, my reflections on the observations in order to learn from them.*

Winfried: a distorted mirror image of myself
(an example of my method)

1 *Associations*

2 *Behavior in breaks*
   Winfried occupies the center and smiles, beamingly. Smaller children cling to him, drag him around. He laughs: "You will tear me to pieces!" Like a mother whose children are tugging at her. His peers struggle for his attention. He distributes it equally in the circle around him, provides judgments and laughs at somebody fooling about in front of him. What he says, counts. He is a source of tranquility – amid all the ado around him. Apparently, he has nothing to do with it. And yet, it arises from the competition for his attention.

3 *My part*
   In addition to that, I put him on a throne. It is so comfortable. If I want to re-establish discipline I merely need to express my displeasure by standing close to Winfried. He will immediately reprimand his classmates in an appropriate manner. The wrongdoer is embarrassed, the case is settled. "I'm glad that he is here!" comes to my mind again and again. But it is also a strain on him. He is tugged to and fro, not only physically. Sometimes his smiles go in all directions

Figure 2.1 Bergk's cluster

and seem to be a mask. This is linked with a certain aloofness from the others. He is there for everybody, but would he also be able to cling to anybody who is there for him?

I notice the similarity with my own role. Do the right thing and be available for everybody! That is what I always have to do – and it is a strain.

4 *Comparison with the situation during the lesson*
 Winfried rarely starts any disruption. But many children want to talk to him or show something to him during the lesson. This interferes with my plans when I want to talk or show the class something. It is a repetition of the situation during break – only this time I don't like it. Again, Winfried is under strain as a result. He cannot concentrate on his own writing, picture, or math problem. Therefore he is slow. His neighbors, competing for his favor during the breaks, surpass him during the lessons and even prevent him from catching up when he falls behind. Winfried really grieves about his learning difficulties. On two occasions I found him shedding silent tears.

5 *Development in the course of the school year*
 Winfried clearly demonstrated a typical teacher's problem to me by adopting

[handwritten marginalia: "That would interest me really...", "interactions of social status in classroom"]

parts of my role: being the authority who judges and evaluates is exhausting and produces unrest all around. His peers sucked assurance out of Winfried that – had their self-confidence been greater – they could have gained more efficiently from their own work, self-reflection and self-appraisal. I could support Winfried best by helping all the students to develop more independence in their learning. . . . If I stepped down from my judge's or master's throne and furnished all the children with spacious masters' seats, Winfried could also leave his throne and take a position among the others.

At first it was difficult. The children's minds were set on hierarchical structures and teacher-oriented instruction. Winfried sat in the center of the first row, appropriate to his "task" as "co-teacher" and "mother". At first, my attempts at pair and group work failed because the younger ones, in particular, did not accept each other as 'partners' but sought feedback from Winfried. Only as the groups became more independent and I removed him physically from the center stage, did Winfried calm down slowly . . . and so did I (Bergk 1987: 2).

GETTING STARTED

Familiarity with action research can develop in various ways: you can read about practical methods and theories – or you can study what other practitioners actually did in order to reflect on and improve their practice. The wealth of examples in this book, as well as collections of action research case studies, may enable you to do this. However, the royal road to action research is to explore it by doing it yourself. Thus, the most meaningful way of reading this book would certainly be to exploit it as a reservoir of tools and ideas, and test its usefulness while reflecting on and developing some issue from your own practice.

Among the descriptions of Methods and strategies some act as Starters (M1, M2, M3, M4 and M12). These are particularly useful as ways of getting started on research. They arose from our experience in in-service courses, university workshop-conferences, and innovative projects. We realized that teachers and other practitioners, overwhelmed by the complex aim of researching, developing and documenting an aspect of their own practice, often did not easily find a worthwhile starting point for their work. Often they needed specific suggestions of ways to get started. Because of their preoccupation with their grand aim, they were unable to begin their research and find small-scale progress rewarding. However, our experience also tells us that action research does not lend itself to precise pre-planning. On the contrary, every action researcher must find his/her path according to the specific research question and the particular working situation. There are specific methods and approaches from which to choose, but these need to be selected and tailored by the individual. Too many tasks, too precisely defined, hamper the development of an individual research path and press action researchers onto a generalized course of research that often does not fit the particularities of the situation. Our suggestions try to balance these extremes.

The Starters are intended as "suggestions": they attempt to formulate some ideas and recommendations about how to approach the complex task of researching your own practice. You should use these recommendations to get you started. As soon as you have found your own way, which will be bound to deviate from the suggestions, you may confidently abandon those ideas that are no longer helpful. Just as Lawrence Stenhouse (1975) claimed for all curricula, recommendations are, at best, intelligent proposals that have to be tested and developed by reflective practice.

We assume that different and original methodological patterns will develop as your research progresses and you engage in mini-action research cycles. Thus, you will find some Starters proposing small research activities at the beginning of the book.

M1 RESEARCH JOURNAL (STARTER)

Use a research journal during the whole course of your research. We recommend a notebook, with large margins, at least 40 pages in length. You can record here all your observations and experiences during your research. Every idea or reflection that comes to mind in connection with research activities – be it positive, ambivalent, negative, or simply yet unclear – could be important for your subsequent work and provide a starting point for development and improvement. Jotting down all experiences, striking events, and ideas in your journal means preventing valuable information from being lost in the further course of project work.

A journal develops into a valuable research method only if it is used regularly. If you notice that there has been no single entry in your journal for a full working week check:

- whether you can reserve a period of time during the week that is relatively free of disruption;
- whether journals really fit your research plans.

However, remember that difficulties are bound to occur with something new (and, according to our experience, they are particularly frequent for novices in journal writing). Don't be discouraged too quickly. Don't forget to make use of the suggestions for journal entries contained in the whole of this chapter.

Our second starter results from our experience that it is often frustrating to wait too long to see the first research activity materialize. We recommend embarking on a small research activity even before you have begun to formulate a starting point for your research – to warm up your research muscles, as it were. This helps you start the journal and gives you the feeling that something has been achieved. You have begun your research even though it is not yet focused on a specific issue for reflection and improvement. As a bonus, such small exercises – even if they seem to be selected at random – sometimes point the way to an issue that becomes the starting point for further research. These exercises shouldn't be thought of as being distinct from your action research but as examples of what we are calling mini-action research cycles.

M2 THE SLICE OF LIFE (STARTER)

Another way to "jump start" your research is by writing a "slice of life" (Tremmel 1993). A slice of life is an informal, two-part piece of writing.

- The first part is a *detailed narrative of an event* that occurred in your practice. The event should be of relatively short duration. For a teacher that might mean something that happened during one class on a particular day. It should be as detailed as you can make it but keep your story to no more than two pages. This should help to keep the narrative portion of the "slice of life" as low on the "ladder of inference" (see M18) as possible.
- The second part of the slice of life is a *reflection* on the first part. While your reflection can be analytical, you should also record your feelings that arose during the event as well as any new understanding or feelings that arise from writing the narrative and then reading it.

If at all possible you might share your slice of life with others, either members of your collaborative action research group or a critical friend (see M10).

M3 EXERCISE TO WARM UP YOUR RESEARCH MUSCLES (STARTER)

If you have not yet definitely decided on your research issue ("this is what I am going to study and nothing else!") we suggest that you carry out *one* of the following five exercises:

- Select one of next week's lessons. Write a memo about the course of events in your journal. Include all thoughts that come to your mind during reflecting and writing.
- Tape one of next week's lessons. Select 5 minutes of the tape for transcription (see M27 if you need help for this activity). Leave a margin for comments beside your transcription. Then, note in the margin all associations that come to your mind when reading specific sections of the transcript (it is not the "correct" interpretation of the event that is at stake – allow every association).
- Prepare a *cluster* of all associations that come to your mind when you think of the phrase "Being a teacher", "Being a nurse", "Being a social worker", etc. (for a description of the "clustering procedure" see M4).
- Every day next week cut out from a newspaper some words, phrases or pictures that you intuitively like or that you spontaneously feel concern your profession. At the end of the week prepare a *collage* from the cuttings. Feel free to complement the collage by hand-written words and your own drawings.
- Imagine an extraterrestrial visitor entering your classroom (or your personal workroom) from the top left corner without being noticed by anybody in the room. Describe in a short piece of writing what he/she would see and think.

To close this warm-up exercise we suggest:

- If you are working on your own, read what you produced again after a few days. Add a sentence that concisely expresses the impression you have when rereading your own writing.
- If you are collaborating in a group, what you produced might be read to the group. However, sharing should always be voluntary. Alternatively, you could report back on the exercise in a few sentences. Other group members might ask questions but should refrain from making comments and putting forward interpretations. (For further ideas on this, see also the analytic discourse method in M9.)

M4 IN-DEPTH REFLECTION (STARTER)

In-depth reflection is an opportunity to think through your own actions and make your "tacit knowledge" accessible to yourself (see Chapter 10, p. 271). The following procedure, known as "clustering" (Rico 2004), provides one way of starting this process.

1 The procedure of "clustering" begins with a *core word (or phrase)* that is written in the center of a blank sheet. For example, a possible core phrase might be "Being a teacher", "Being a nurse" or "Being a social worker". Other stimuli may be used in a similar way: a situation that has been of concern to you for some time, a picture, some writing, a dream, a piece of music etc.

2 Note down all associations to this core word as *word-chains*. These start from the central concept and display your associations in various (linear or branched) graphic arrangements. A core word plus word-chains is called a "cluster". The following example, taken from Bergk's example used earlier, indicates what clusters might look like:

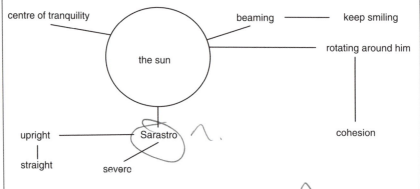

Figure 2.2 Example of a cluster

3 When you have noted down the most important associations, the next step is to switch over mentally from the flow of associative images to the recognition and systematization of patterns. Let the cluster inspire you and use its elements as the basis for some writing. This writing might either be rather prosaic or emphasize creative elements – just as you feel (see sections 2–5 in Bergk's example).

4 Later on, you might do some editing of the text. You might also read it to others (colleagues, family) and discuss it.

Chapter 3

Finding a starting point for your own research

The first step in a research process is to find and formulate a feasible starting point. What issue in my practical experience is worth studying over a period of time? Does it fit my capabilities and do I have the resources? Is there a fair chance I can get somewhere if I research this issue? These are questions one needs to ask when beginning action research. In this chapter we provide some suggestions and ideas to help you to answer them.

WHAT DO WE MEAN BY STARTING POINTS FOR RESEARCH?

What does a feasible starting point for action research look like? How do teachers reach such starting points? Let's have a look at how Susan Lincoln, a high school teacher, described her starting point to other students enrolled in a university course on action research taught by Allan (see M11 for more information).

One of the challenges that a teacher must face in the classroom is the presentation of subject material to students of mixed abilities. In any class, a teacher can expect to have students with disabilities, individual education plans, students with limited aptitude with the English language and extremely capable students. How can a lesson work for all of these students? What kinds of modifications need to be made to accommodate all the learning styles represented in a typical classroom? How does a teacher fairly assess each student's learning?

The solution that comes to mind is cooperative group work in which groups comprised of students with different strengths and needs work together to achieve a common goal. The common goal is usually a task or problem given to the group by the teacher, accompanied by some strategies for tackling the problem. The choice of tasks and learning strategies, as well as appropriate assessments, is the focus of my investigation.

According to Chapter 612a(5), the US Individuals with Disabilities Education Improvement Act 2004 all students should be educated in the least restrictive environment, that is,

> To the maximum extent appropriate, children with disabilities, including children in public or private institutions or other care facilities, are educated with children who are not disabled, and special classes, separate schooling, or other removal of children with disabilities from the regular educational environment occurs only when the nature or severity of the disability of a child is such that education in regular classes with the use of supplementary aids and services cannot be achieved satisfactorily . . .
>
> (Individuals with Disabilities Education Improvement Act, 2004)

My classrooms are not truly heterogeneously grouped. The science courses at the high school in which I teach are leveled primarily by the integration of math skills into the curriculum. However, within each level, English language learners, pupils with documented learning disabilities and pupils with other special needs are integrated. I find planning appropriate lessons for all of my students a challenge, feeling that I'm often "reinventing the wheel" with each activity, project or assessment.

Through my action research project, I would like to outline the objectives for my lessons and the special modifications that I must make to accommodate all of my pupils. This will give me a clearer idea of what I need to cover in a lesson and how the class can best achieve the goal. In order to gain a better sense of the effectiveness of my efforts, I would like to systematically analyze the outcome of my lessons by using formative assessments such as regular short answer questions, 2+2 questions[1] that follow a lesson, mid-unit essays for understanding and a brief end of unit survey of pupils' preferences of activities.

In order to accommodate the diverse group of learners in my classes, I will employ two basic strategies, differentiated tasks and differentiated outcomes (Churton et al. 1998). By analyzing my goals and the pupils learning styles and needs, I will develop activity options from which the pupils can choose to meet the goal set by me for the unit. In so doing, each pupil can choose an activity that best suits his/her learning style. By using formative assessment techniques, I'm hoping to see a pattern emerge that will help me predict what form of activity works best for a certain learning style.

For tasks that are not differentiated, I will employ rubrics[2] to help pupils achieve success through differentiated outcomes. Once again, I will refer to the outline of objectives and needs to define a rubric that can allow for success for all learners. By building options into the expectations, pupils will have a small degree of choice in the activity. Again I would try to obtain feedback from the class regarding the fairness and accuracy of the expectations built into the rubric. Customized rubrics can be developed for those pupils with specifically recommended modifications, such as a need for more time, use of specialized equipment, or use of verbal assessments.

Some references that I wish to use include:

- Tomlinson (2001), How to Differentiate Instruction in Mixed-ability Classrooms.

- Churton, Cranston-Gingras, Blair (1998), Teaching Children with Diverse Abilities.
- Gredler (1999), Classroom Assessment and Learning.
- Turner and DiMarco (1998), Learning to Teach Science in the Secondary School.

In addition to the research literature, I am planning on working with the various resource room staff and special education professionals in my school for feedback and resources that might help me in planning these many lessons.

As in much of action research, it will be difficult to establish a control for this study. Although I feel as though I've always given a good deal of consideration to diverse learning styles when planning lessons, I have never approached the problem in a systematic way. Perhaps one measurement that I can make with regard to the effectiveness of the study would be a comparison of quarterly grades. The first marking period came to an end just as I started to collect data for my study. Because the material that is covered changes with each marking period, I would only use this comparison as part of a larger set of observations, however.

FEATURES OF STARTING POINTS

What are the essential features of starting points for action research? First, they have a *developmental perspective*: for example, a teacher wants to improve a practical situation, such as, how to best teach a heterogeneous grouping of pupils, and to further develop his/her own competences. Second, they have a *research perspective*, an interest in understanding: practitioners want to understand the practical situation, its context, their own action within it and their effects in order to develop this situation in a productive direction. This "double goal" is one of the main characteristics of action research (see Chapter 1) and leaves its mark on the design of action research projects.

Typically, starting points for research begin with *experiences of discrepancies*. They can be:

- discrepancies between plans and expectations, on the one hand, and actual practice, on the other (for example, Susan wanted to address the problem of teaching to a population of diverse learners).
- discrepancies between the present situation and a general value orientation or an aim (for example, although the federal law requires heterogeneous groupings and Susan believes it is good for the pupils, she was challenged by the task of coming up with appropriate lessons to meet all students' needs).
- discrepancies between the ways in which different people view one and the same situation (for example, the whole class with a large

number of special needs students will be stigmatized as a low ability class).

Discrepancies like these give food for thought once they are consciously recognized. Action research begins with reflection upon such discrepancies and tries to save them from being forgotten in the maze of everyday work (see M8). They become the focus for further development of the teaching process and for the generation of knowledge about that process. Such discrepancies need not always be negative and problematic for the teacher, nurse, social worker or other practitioners. Action research can also focus on trying out good ideas for improvements or on the further development of one's own strengths.

SOURCES FOR STARTING POINTS

What are the main sources for finding starting points for research and development? In our experience, action researchers turn to the following sources (see Figure 3.1):

1   *Own experiences in their practice settings*
    Most often it is their own observations and experiences in their work settings that give practitioners ideas and reasons for their development work. Starting points may be derived from very different types of experience. Marion Dadds (1985) mentions three types of starting points that derive from experience:

    a   an *interest* – for example, trying out a promising idea, developing a strength or coping with a routine obligation in a more considerate and economic way;
    b   a *difficulty* – for example, wanting to improve a difficult situation, solve a problem or compensate for a deficiency;
    c   an *"unclear" situation* – action researchers often begin with bigger or smaller 'puzzles' – situations that are not clearly positive or negative, enjoyable or burdensome, but that raise an issue they want to understand more fully. Often their work begins with unexpected experiences that they are unable to interpret, but believe might serve as a useful starting point to further develop their practice.

It is very likely that every starting point contains characteristics of all three types in various combinations. In our example, Susan wanted to improve the opportunities for all the students in the class to learn regardless of individual differences (a); but faced the problems caused by the complexity of the problem and her lack of knowledge (b); and was unclear about the effectiveness of the learning tasks she was setting (c).

Figure 3.1 Possible sources for starting points

Source: Altrichter *et al.* (2006: 65)

> across Curve

2 *Mission statements, on-going programs and development programs of the institution*
   Topics that are important for the institution or unit, such as class-rooms, schools or clinics, provide a potential focus for research and development work by practitioners. So, what is promised in mission statements, programs, profiles, and management plans may involve necessary reflective development work for which action research may provide a feasible model. Similarly, complaints, diminishing numbers of students, clients or patients or developments in the community or the surrounding region may produce questions and chances to be tackled by systematic research and development (Calhoun 1994).

3 *Results from feedback and evaluations*
   Personal feedback provided to teachers, social workers or nurses by students, clients, patients, or other stakeholders may stimulate research and development work. Similarly, results from institutional self-evaluation, continuous quality management, external evaluations,

or comparisons with other institutions or units ('benchmarking') may make visible questions that are in need of more thorough study or new pathways for development (see Altrichter *et al.* 2006).

4) *Participation in development and in-service programs*

Participation in initiatives by central and regional institutions that seek to stimulate innovation through development programs, prizes, or specific funding (see Feldman 1995) may also provide ideas and impulses for further research and development by practitioners: if, for example, high quality learning in science classrooms (see Feldman and Capobianco 2000) or cooperative open learning in upper secondary schools (see Wittwer *et al.*, 2004) is to be supported, this obviously necessitates reflective development work by practitioners. Also, in-service programs may offer ideas for development of practice, and they may also be organized as support systems for reflective practical development work (see Altrichter and Posch 1998).

5 *Curiosity and "theoretical interests"*

Worthwhile ideas for development need not necessarily stem from one's own experiences (as in 1 and 2) or have been circulated by external agencies (as in 4). They may also derive from observing colleagues, from contacts with other fields of practice or from reading books or hints from the Internet. You may be curious whether or not what works well with colleague X or has been found out by researcher Y also makes sense in your circumstances. You may be interested in better understanding other people's ideas and in putting them into your practice (Feldman 1996). Such considerations, by the way, show that action research – even if concepts such as discrepancies, problems and difficulties are often used in the initial phase of projects – is not just appropriate for 'negative' and 'problematic' situations. Rather, good ideas may be tested or strengths may be developed. All in all, action research is oriented towards development and resources: it aims at detecting the strengths and potentials of the people involved and at the sustaining and development of their competences.

ISSUES FOR ACTION RESEARCH

What kind of issue is an appropriate focus for action research? Broadly, any professional situation about which practitioners want to gain a deeper understanding, and that they want to change, is a potential starting point. The issues could relate to the work or context of an individual action researcher, or it could relate to issues that confront the entire institution or unit. Here are some examples of the former:

Portfolios

- a teacher investigated parents' perceptions of the innovatory relationship she had established with them seemingly successfully over several years;
- a lecturer at the university researched her own teaching of a new course and developed modifications of teaching and learning strategies;
- nurses developed ways to better intervene in the care of patients recovering from strokes (see Chapter 9);
- social workers' supported community-based action research to improve the well-being of families (see Chapter 9);
- a teacher experimented with a new form of assessment of her students' work and carried out action research to improve and refine it;
- nurses developed new ways to work with their patients in a variety of settings and studied the implementation of the methods and how it affected their practice (Jenkins et al. 2005).

Conferencing

These examples are drawn from a wide range of practice situations. They also demonstrate that action research studies can go beyond the technical aspects of practice to focus on interpersonal relations or other social issues, or even issues beyond the confines of the institution or unit, such as the establishment of productive relationships with parents, other family members and the community.

As we noted above, action research can also tackle issues of institutional development:

- In Chapter 1 we referred to a school that developed as a result of collaboration between a number of teachers each focusing upon their own classroom, coordinated by a deputy head (Wakeman 1986).
- A secondary teacher researched the processes of decision-making and the operation of power in the school where she worked, drawing colleagues into collaboration in the process, first by eliciting their views in interviews and later by inviting them to contribute to redrafting the written report (Somekh 2006, Chapter 3).
- In a primary school, the team of teachers responsible for teaching the youngest children focused on the use of computers to support language development in their students, for the majority of whom English was a second language (Ourtilbour 1991). Their collaborative research resulted in changes in the school's policies and practice.
- A secondary teacher, responsible for coordinating colleagues' professional development in the use of computers as educational tools, carried out action research upon her own role in bringing about institutional development (Griffin 1990).
- A police educator researched the implementation of a new strategy for the education of police managers (Adlam 1999).
- A medical team did an action research study of an in-patient stroke service in a London teaching hospital (Kilbride et al. 2005).

In general, institutional issues are more difficult to tackle than issues of individual practice. The practical, theoretical and political problems of action research tend to increase greatly when the focus moves beyond the classroom to institutional development. These can really only be tackled if the action researcher is already experienced, or if the research is undertaken in the context of a project involving a number of practitioners from the same institution or school.

FINDING STARTING POINTS

Those who decide to engage in action research either have:

a   one very specific question in mind, often needing urgent attention;
b   many different questions in mind, none of which constitutes an obvious starting point;
c   no concrete ideas from which to begin an investigation;
d   a starting point that is defined by a larger project of which they are a part. This is often the case for projects funded by outside agencies (e.g., Ashton *et al.* 1990, Feldman 1995, Somekh 2006, Chapters 4 and 7).

The suggestions and ideas below are especially intended for cases (b) and (c). However, they can also be useful for case (a) and (d), especially if someone is beginning action research for the first time and wants to check the feasibility of tackling a question by comparing it with alternative possibilities. We have suggested the following approaches to practitioners we have worked with:

• Formulate more than one possible starting point.
• Consider all the potential starting points in relation to everyday practice, over a period of time.
• Invest sufficient time to make the exploration of possible starting points as wide-ranging as possible.

The ease and speed with which a meaningful question is likely to be found is frequently miscalculated. Some time may be necessary before any single issue relating to an individual's professional practice emerges as the one of greatest importance and one that can be clearly formulated (see Hull *et al.* 1985). The amount of time needed will differ from person to person and context to context. In action research courses run at universities that last for a semester, the first 2–4 weeks are reserved for finding starting points. In action research projects[3] that we have facilitated and that lasted for 2–3 years, it was not unusual for a teacher to take over a semester to select his/her focus. Even within tightly scheduled projects there should be opportunities for individual variations in the amount of time spent on this important stage.

Your personal search for a starting point could be facilitated by the following exercises:

M5 INDIVIDUAL BRAINSTORMING: FINDING STARTING POINTS

One step towards finding a starting point for your own research could be individual brainstorming:

1 Think of your own practical experience:

- Is there any question that you have wanted to investigate for a long time already?   *1:1 time w/ kids*
- Which of your strengths would you like to develop?
- Are there any aspects of your work that you find puzzling and which have already been a focus for your reflection?   *reach kids*
- Are there any situations that cause difficulties and that you would like to cope with more effectively?

Let your thoughts flow freely and write down your first spontaneous associations in the form of catchwords. You might like to use your research journal to record these. Don't spend more than 6–8 minutes!

2 Once you have recorded your initial ideas you may be able to stimulate further ideas for starting points by using these incomplete sentences (Kemmis and McTaggart 1982: 18):

- I would like to improve the . . .
- Some people (pupils/parents/patients/clients/family members/colleagues) are unhappy about . . . What can I do to change the situation?
- I am perplexed by . . .
- . . . is a source of irritation. What can I do about it?
- If I . . . I am completely worn out afterwards.
- Again and again I get angry about . . .
- I have an idea I would like to try out in my practice.
- How can the experience of . . . (recounted by a colleague, or found in my reading etc.) be applied to . . .?

3 If you have already started to keep your research journal, read through what you have written and see whether it generates additional ideas for starting points for research.

4 You can enrich the formulation of your potential starting points – and at the same time carry out a first, provisional analysis of

each situation – if you use these questions to identify the most important characteristics:

- What happens in this situation?
- Who does what?
- Which contextual factors are especially important in understanding this situation?

5 Try to condense the results of this brainstorming exercise by formulating a question for each possible starting point as precisely as possible.

M6 GIVING CONSIDERATION TO SEVERAL STARTING POINTS[4]

We recommend that you do not make an immediate decision on a starting point, but instead keep several starting points in mind to test their feasibility in the light of your everyday experience. You can do this in the following way: take the list of possible starting points that you generated from the brainstorming exercise (M5) and select 3–5 situations that seem the most interesting to you. Write down on a card the specific issue that interests you in each of these situations. For example:

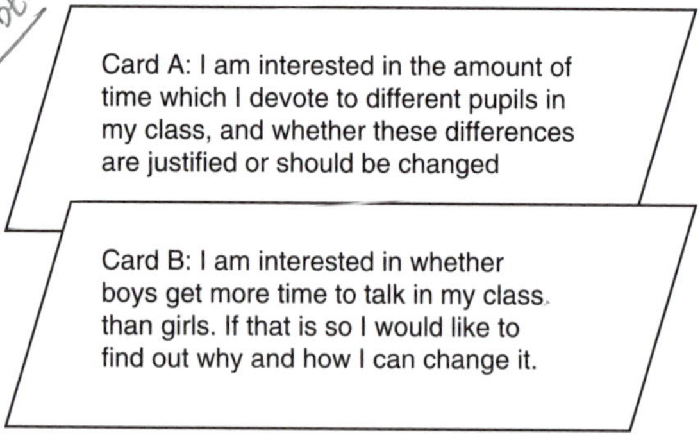

> Card A: I am interested in the amount of time which I devote to different pupils in my class, and whether these differences are justified or should be changed

> Card B: I am interested in whether boys get more time to talk in my class than girls. If that is so I would like to find out why and how I can change it.

Figure 3.2 Issue cards

Source: Developing Teaching (1984: 12)

At the end of each day over the next week take your cards and shuffle them. Then take the first card and for about 3 minutes reflect on the day and think about any events that seem relevant to the issue recorded on it. Write down your ideas in keywords either on the cards or in your research diary. Afterwards spend a minute on each of the remaining cards to think briefly about the other issues, possibly making brief notes in your journal.

APPROACHES TO CHOOSING A STARTING POINT

How can I choose a starting point from the many interests and questions that come to mind in relation to my own practical experience? Are some starting points more or less suitable than others? How can I identify the more suitable ones?

M7 CHOOSING A STARTING POINT

You can examine the available starting points in the following way:

1 Remember that action research has a *developmental perspective*. Check your starting point against these questions:

   - What is your focus for possible development?
   - What might you want to try out?
   - What might you want to change?

   Doing action research does not mean that you have to change everything. But nevertheless, it is important that when you embark on action research you have a genuine interest in development. Sometimes the main change is in your perception of the situation rather than in adopting specific new strategies.

2 Look at the starting points that you have formulated so far in the light of the following criteria, and write brief notes to record for each the pluses and minuses of adopting it as your main research focus.

   a *Scope for action* Does the situation come from my own field of experience? Can I really do something about this? Do I have any possibility of influencing this situation and/or taking action? Or am I too dependent on other people and institutional structures? Would an improvement in this situation depend primarily on changing the behavior of other people?

   b *Relevance* How important is this situation to me and to my professional concerns? Is this issue worth the effort in an educational, social or health-related sense? Is it concerned with important values? Is it likely that this situation will still interest me in a few weeks' time? Am I willing to invest a certain amount of energy in dealing with this situation? Am I interested in this situation in order to change and improve something?

c   *Manageability* Do I have the time to cope with this? Are there too many preparatory or related tasks to be coped with before I can start this project? Will it make too many demands of me? When you begin research don't choose a question that is 'too big'. When in doubt opt for the smaller or more limited project. In general it is better to build on successes even if they are small rather than having to reduce one's aims because they prove impossible to fulfill. There may be time later to extend your work.

d   *Compatibility* How compatible would this question be with the rest of my activities if I select it as my research focus? Would it involve things that I have to do anyway? How well does this intended research fit in with my forward planning? Would it be possible to build some research activities directly into my practice (for example, students interviewing each other, group discussions etc.)? If you are in doubt, decide on a starting point that fits thematically with those things you do anyway in your practice.

3 Now select the starting point that comes closest to these criteria. The result will not always be clear-cut, but sometimes may involve weighing up the advantages and disadvantages of two or three options. However, we believe that this process in itself can be an important help in identifying the question that best fits with your personal situation.

4 Next, try to document your starting point as vividly as possibly in your research journal. Formulating your starting point for research generally has four elements:

a   *A short description of the situation* What happens in this situation? Who does what? Which contextual factors are especially important in understanding this situation?

b   *Questions that indicate your research interests* What do I want to find out? What issues or relationships do I want to understand more thoroughly? What questions about my teaching do I want to answer more clearly?

c *Questions that indicate the developmental interests* What would I like to try out? What would I like to change/improve? In what direction do I want to develop the situation in order to make it better for myself, the students, patients or clients and other parties involved?

d *What is my next step?* What do I want to do in order to better understand the situation? What action could help to develop the situation into the direction I aim for?

Although this may all sound rather complicated, it is in reality relatively simple. Here are some examples of starting points (adapted from Kemmis and McTaggart 1982):

- When they are doing group work the students seem to waste a lot of time (a). What exactly are they doing? What productive and unproductive activities are frequently to be observed? Are different groups behaving differently (b)? How can I increase the amount of task-oriented time for students engaging in group work (c)? I want to talk to my colleague Cynthia who is said to run very stimulating and effective group work (d).
- My students are not satisfied with the methods I use to assess their work. What exactly do they complain about? What are the arguments? How can I improve assessment methods with their help? I want to ask my colleague Fred to interview some students in form 4.
- Most parents want to help their children and the school by supervising homework. What can we do to make their help more productive?
- My elderly mental ill patients often fall in nursing homes. What do I need to know to prevent this?

M8 The 'Gap': making discrepancies explicit

Previously in this chapter we discussed how starting points for action research can originate from discrepancies in one's practice. However, often these discrepancies are tacit and therefore you need some way to bring them to the surface. This method is done with at least one other person whom you see as your 'critical friend'. A critical friend is someone who has empathy for your research situation and can relate closely to your concerns, but at the same time is able to provide you with rich and honest feedback (M10). An even better way of doing this is with colleagues who are also engaged in action research with whom you take turns being the presenter.

1 Begin by doing a *freewrite* in which you explore the "gap" between how you would like to see yourself as a practitioner and the way you actually are. If you need to, look back in this chapter to the section on discrepancies to get some ideas of the type of gaps that there may be in your practice. The technique of free-writing was developed by Peter Elbow. He describes the process in this way:

> The idea is simply to write for ten minutes (later on, perhaps fifteen or twenty). Don't stop for anything. Go quickly without rushing. Never stop to look back, to cross something out, to wonder how to spell something, to wonder what word or thought to use, or to think about what you are doing. If you can't think of a word or a spelling, just use a squiggle or else write "I can't think what to say, I can't think what to say" as many times as you want; or repeat the last word you wrote over and over again; or anything else. The only requirement is that you never stop.
>
> (Elbow 1998: 1)

The gap activity is an example of what Elbow calls a 'directed freewrite'. What this means is that rather than being able to write about anything that comes to your mind, you are asked to restrict yourself to a particular topic or area, which, in this case, is your practice. As a result, you may find yourself in the position in which you "can't think what to say". If you find yourself running out of things to talk about, remember that you know much more about your practice than the people you are sharing your thoughts with (your critical friend or others in your collaborative action research group). Therefore, if you run out of things to write about in reference to your gap, you can always provide details about your practice situation.

2 *Tell your critical friend or collaborative action research group* about your "gap". Take no less than 5 minutes to tell your friend/the others what you wrote. You do not need to read out loud what you wrote; feel free to tell the story of your gap. If you find that you haven't used at least 5 minutes, fill the time by describing the details of your practice situation. You should not be interrupted when you are doing your telling. Once the 5 minutes are up, your critical friend or members of your collaborative action research group should question you about the gap in your practice. Use

the rules of "analytic discourse" (M9): only ask questions, do not make suggestions, and make sure that the questions are not suggestions in disguise.

3 Have someone else in the group or your critical friend (if he/she is also engaged in action research) take a turn *telling about the gap in their practice and answering questions* about it.

4 Be sure to *make a memo about* the gap activity in your research journal.

[handwritten margin note: Maybe we can do i Class 1-27]

The following example illustrates some of the difficulties that can occur if you choose a starting point without being clear of your reasons:

Case study – Anne McKenzie

Anne McKenzie was a new principal of a mid-sized comprehensive high school in the northeastern US when she enrolled in a graduate seminar in action research. She described her job in this way:

> When I started this project, my job as a high school principal overwhelmed me. I consistently felt as though "the tail wagged the dog" when I was at work. I spent the majority of my time at work in a reactive state, waiting for an unforeseen crisis to manage. Many of my day-to-day duties felt unimportant or uninteresting to me. I experienced my job as high in stress and low in intellectual stimulation.

> (McKenzie 2005: 6)

Clearly this is not what she envisioned the job to be. She wanted to be an educator who prepares young people "to be engaged, free thinking, and socially responsible citizens in a democratic society" (ibid.: 7). Anne identified this gap in her practice (see M8) and developed the following hypothesis:

> If I were to better balance the managerial aspects of my job (mundane, tedious, supervisory work) with the leadership aspects of my job (creative, intellectually stimulating, development work focused on teaching and learning) I would be a more effective and happier principal.

> (ibid.: 6)

Her initial response was to seek a technical solution – to find ways to better prioritize her daily tasks by reviewing her job description. As it turned out, there was no formal job description on record in the school board's (LEA) offices, and when she attempted to write one, she was only able to "generate a list of unrelated tasks" with no "cohesive underlying framework that connected them" (ibid.: 7).

Her reading of the educational leadership literature also was not fruitful – she found that the more she read, the more overwhelmed and ineffective she felt (ibid.: 9).

The action research seminar that Anne was enrolled in did several of the Ms, which helped clarify her starting point. She found that:

> *the problem had more to do with my perception of my work. I realized that the job of the high school principal is not the problem but perhaps how I perceive the job and thus experience the job represented the problem. At one point in the development and clarification of my research focus, I attempted to write a job description. As I wrote the description, I realized that I did not have a clear vision of what my job entails ... It became clear to me that perhaps my work felt purposeless because I had not defined the purpose of my work.*
>
> *(ibid.: 7)*

This led her to replace her original hypothesis with, "If I intellectualize my work, more of it will be meaningful." She also changed her research question from, "How do I balance my managerial and leadership duties?" to "How do I connect my actions at work to my vision of what it means to be an educator?" (ibid.: 8) To understand how to do this, Anne interviewed four teachers on her staff. She asked them to describe what it means to be an educator; to discuss their personal missions; and to talk about the ways in which their daily behaviors reflect their understanding of what their work should entail. She also asked them to depict what it means to be an effective high school principal (ibid.: 11). As a result of doing these interviews and analyzing them (see Chapters 5 and 6), she found that she was thinking differently about her job. She wrote the following in her research notebook:

> *I have often described my job as putting on my armor day after day, walking into the arena, and hoping some of the lions are sick or just too tired to eat me. After talking to colleagues, I realize that there are others in the arena with me. We can fight the lions together. Better yet, we can join hands and walk out of the arena.*

It also gave her ideas about how she could better structure the time between teachers and students, such as to use pupils' detentions as a time and place for meaningful conversations among students and teachers. She also began to look forward to discussion with other principals, especially women administrators, about vision, mission, roles and responsibilities, and "how gender plays into perceptions, attitudes, and practices of female administrators" (ibid.: 17). She concluded her action research report in this way:

> *Engaging in this research project has changed my thinking. Changes in thinking have profound implications. To paraphrase Ralph Waldo Emerson, the ancestor of every accomplishment is a thought. When we change our*

thinking we change our world. I would like to think that I am on the way to changing the world.

(ibid.: 18)

This example illustrates two further important characteristics of action research:

1 Whatever is formulated as the starting point can only be a first view of a situation that is very likely to change in the course of the research process. Action research tries to avoid the dogma of fixed hypotheses that, in more traditional research approaches, cannot be modified once the research has begun (see Cronbach 1975). Instead, the researcher remains open to new ideas that may influence the course of the research while it is taking place. In this way, any development of the initial starting point becomes an important indicator of the learning of the practitioner carrying out the research.
2 Whatever is formulated as a starting point often touches only the surface of a problem. A more detailed clarification of the problem situation and a further development of this 'first impression' help to develop a deeper understanding of all the related factors and open up new possibilities for action.

Chapter 4

Clarifying the starting point of research

A starting point for action research is best thought of as the *first impression*. In this chapter we give some suggestions for going beyond this first impression to a deeper understanding of the practical theories that govern our actions.

FROM THE "FIRST IMPRESSION"

Jonathan Haraty was a teacher at the SAGE School located in an urban area in the US. SAGE is a collaboration between the local school district (LEA), the Department of Youth Services and a local college. The school was founded to serve pupils charged with crimes or on probation. The primary objective of the school is to modify behaviors so that the pupils attend school and do not return to the court system. Jonathan chose to teach in this school because he wants to help the pupils to be successful in school and in life. To do so, he believes that he must treat each of his pupils as an individual.

Jonathan began his action research study by writing a "slice of life" (M2) about an incident that occurred in one of his classes:

> *Today one of my middle school students, Natalie, asked me why I was not making her work up to her potential. . . . She stated that her mother had looked over her schoolwork and felt that she had already done this in previous grades. She went on to state that she was beginning to get bored and that when this happened, she generally stopped coming to school.*

He elaborated on this in his action research report. He wrote that this exchange with Natalie led him to think about whether

> *I was reaching all my pupils who at their intellectual level or whether I was gearing my classes towards those pupils who need the remedial work and pace. I started looking at my pupils in this class, and the other three science classes that I teach, looking for pupils that I may not be allowing to reach their full potential by pacing them with the rest of the class. I noticed several pupils who have always completed the assigned work, and were getting very good*

grades, seemed to be looking out the windows a lot or were distracting other pupils.

He decided that he would use a simple, open-ended survey with all of his pupils to identify who felt they were not moving fast enough in the class. Using the responses to the survey and his observations, he would then select several pupils to do a personal interview. He also decided to interview a pupil from the preceding year who was currently enrolled in community college.

Start w/ survey

Jonathan learned from his data that rather than treating every pupil as an individual, he had assumed that all of his pupils needed remedial work and had directed his teaching at that level. He also saw that rather than helping his pupils succeed in school, his teaching methods may actually have caused some of them to drop out. He also found that there were pupils who would welcome extra work. One pupil said it would make him feel good because it would mean he was on top of the class. Another told Jonathan that he would feel important. A third said that she wouldn't mind the extra work "because that just means that I am improving".

Jonathan found his interview of a pupil who had already graduated the most insightful:

> *When asked in the interview if he would have done more work, or different work from the class, he stated, "Don't you remember? You gave me more work that allowed me to go at a faster pace than the rest of the class. Sometimes I resented it, but now that I'm in college, it helped."*

This interview triggered a new interpretation of his educational situation and made him look at what had changed in the last year. The major change was that in addition to enrolling pupils in the court system, SAGE had begun to admit pupils who had documented learning disabilities. In response to this new population, Jonathan was told to focus on "reading and writing across the curriculum". In the past years he was able to differentiate his instruction because he focused on what he knew how to do – teach science. The new task to teach reading and writing to pupils with learning disabilities, for which he lacked the skills, now appeared to be the main reason why he taught all the pupils the same way and targeted his instruction towards those who were most needy.

One of Jonathan's first impressions was that he had somehow for some reason abandoned the "better" pupil in his classes. It was not until he further investigated his situation that he began to take into account the changes in the make-up of the pupils and the change in curricular emphasis in his school. We believe that there are at least three points in Jonathan's action research that are of special interest. The first one is so obvious that it is easily overlooked: what we think about an issue and what we do or say may not be wholly consistent. For instance, in this example, Jonathan was not aware that he was treating all of his pupils as if they needed remediation, which conflicted with his belief that he should differentiate his instruction based on the needs and abilities of his pupils.

The second point is closely related to the first: what we intend by what we say and do can be interpreted quite differently by our pupils, patients or clients. The fact that our intentions and actions affect others only via their perceptions and interpretations can lead to problems when we change our practice. Jonathan implemented new methods that he hoped would help the learning disabled pupils to better their reading and writing skills. But his new way of teaching was interpreted by the "better pupils" to be below their abilities and uninteresting, which led to them being turned off to school. The introduction of new practices presupposes a change in the routine perceptions and actions of teachers and pupils, nurses and patients, and social workers and clients. This is often a long-term process in that all the participants have to become conscious of the new roles, explore them and test their reliability.

The third point arising from Jonathan's action research study is that our first interpretation of a situation does not always get to the heart of the matter, even if it sounds plausible and even if new strategies for action can be derived from it as illustrated in the example above. Our first impression often relies on familiar assumptions and long-standing prejudices. If we want to bring about improvements in practice situations it is important to test the quality of the first impression in order to establish a sound basis for development. Answering the following questions can achieve this:

1 *Does the first impression neglect any existing information?*
   The first impression often gives a plausible picture because we use data selectively and ignore information that contradicts or deviates from our view of the situation. Jonathan's first impression – that he had somehow for some reason abandoned the "better" pupils in his classes – ignored the fact that the nature of the pupil body had changed and that the school's administration had made a major change in the curriculum. By ignoring the larger context in his first impression, Jonathan saw the problem as his personal professional failure, rather than the result of being asked to do something for which he was ill prepared.

2 *Does the first impression contain any vague, ambiguous concepts?*
   Often the initial interpretation uses concepts whose ambiguity may have been a contributory factor to the problem. Jonathan changed his practice when the school administration told him that he must teach "reading and writing across the curriculum". The phrase was originally used to describe a particular way of infusing the teaching of literacy skills into all subject areas, not just language arts. However, by the time that Jonathan was told to do it, it had lost most of its meaning and had become an empty slogan. Because he had no knowledge of what it originally referred to, and because he knew little about how to teach

reading and writing, he acted upon the administration's request in a simplistic manner – he had the pupils take turns reading from their textbook. Clearly the vagueness of the meaning of "reading and writing across the curriculum" contributed to Jonathan's first impression of what was happening in his classes.

3 *Does the first impression deal only with the surface symptoms of the situation?* The first interpretation of a situation sometimes consists of a detailed description of diverse events and actions without uncovering or explaining their underlying implications. One could say that such a representation sets out the surface symptoms but does not progress to an in-depth interpretation. Surface symptoms comprise all observations and empirical generalizations that refer directly to the problem, for example: "I don't challenge my students to work hard." An in-depth interpretation puts forward a broad pattern of interpretation that appears to explain different phenomena and relate them to each other. For example, "The change in the student body and the change in the administration's expectations of teachers requires Jonathan to have skills and knowledge that he is missing for him to successfully differentiate instruction." Both levels are connected with each other: in order to grasp a problem fully an in-depth interpretation is essential because it reveals the interconnections between different factors in a situation – often it is not the event itself that creates a problem but the interpretations and tacit assumptions that individuals bring to the event. On the other hand the reliability of interpretations can only be tested by means of surface symptoms (see M16).

goes deep enough

4 *Has the first impression been accepted without testing it against other competing interpretations?* Jonathan's action research study illustrates this question quite clearly. The first impression, fed by tacit assumptions and previous experiences, provides a seemingly plausible interpretation – that his failure to make all his pupils work up to their potential was due to his failure to recognize their needs. This interpretation is neither doubted nor questioned in the light of possible alternatives. Prime among them is the effects on his teaching of the change in the make-up of the pupil body and the school administration's call for him to change his teaching in ways that were not clearly defined and for which he had little or no training.

Facing problems and dealing with discrepancies between plans and their implementation in practice is not pleasant. We tend to try to forget about them as soon as possible. By confronting first impressions with alternative interpretations, action research slows down the process of problem resolution. This in turn increases the chances of more reliable interpretations that can be used as a basis for improving practice.

ACTIVATING ADDITIONAL KNOWLEDGE EN ROUTE

It is easy to draw false conclusions from a first impression. To help you avoid this we suggest you spend some time clarifying the starting point. What happens when we clarify the starting point for research? Two processes generally characterize this phase:

- The researcher tries to get access to additional knowledge and to use it for reflection.
- The first impression or initial formulation of the starting point is questioned by this additional knowledge and refined, extended or changed.

As we do this, we are again going through what we call a mini-action research cycle. This can be seen in the example at the beginning of this chapter, in which Jonathan gained access to additional information on the starting point from his pupils. The information from these interviews served to question his interpretation of the situation and suggested an alternative meaning. Besides interviews there are a number of other ways of tapping additional knowledge, including activating tacit knowledge; collecting additional information; collecting views on similar situations from non-participants; and by experimenting by introducing changes in existing situations.

Activating tacit knowledge

A fundamental aspect of being human is that as we live our lives, we learn as we experience the world (Lave and Wenger 1991). However, we are not always aware of what we learn (see Chapter 10). Because in many ways, as action researchers, we are our own primary research instrument, it is important for us to make knowledge, such as the routine actions and assumptions that develop through our lived experience, accessible to self-reflection. There are a number of methods that we can use to activate this tacit knowledge (Polanyi 1962):

- *Activating tacit knowledge by journal writing and review of journal entries* The act of writing memos and other types of journal entries can in itself make tacit knowledge explicit (see Chapter 2). As Mary Lou Holly wrote,

    Writing about experience enables the author to view his/her experiences within broader contexts: social, political, economic and educational. . . . Writing taps tacit knowledge; it brings into awareness that which we sensed but could not explain.

    (Holly 1989: 75)

In addition, when we read what we have written, we have the opportunity to view it as an outsider and to see the text as describing what has happened to others. Patterns that we were not aware of become distinct in the text, and assumptions are made problematic. By writing and reading what we have written, we construct and reconstruct our experience (Holly 1989). In this way, journal writing can help to formulate new interpretations and cross-links that were missed in the first impression of the situation.

- *Activation of tacit knowledge by conversations and by being interviewed* Story-telling facilitates introspection because we have to order our experiences before we can tell someone about them. It helps to clarify the situation further if the listeners can contribute actively to generating the story, for example by posing questions, asking for additional information and reflecting back to the narrator their pro-visional understanding of the situation. Analytic discourse (M9) tries to create such a conversational situation by means of a few simple rules. A conversation with a critical friend (M10) is useful in a similar way for teachers who do not have access to a support group of colleagues. Another method is the combination of sharing stories and questioning called *enhanced normal practice* (Feldman 1996). When practitioners engage in enhanced normal practice they tell brief stories about their work. The others in the group hear and listen to the storyteller, and respond with their own stories or with questions. There are generally three types of responses: other stories; questions about the details of what was described or explained in the story; and more critical questions that ask "Why?" as well as "What, where, how, and when?" When practitioners share stories about their work with one another in this way, there is an oral exchange and generation of knowledge and understanding by the recounting and questioning of some event or explanation of one's understanding to others.

- *Activating tacit knowledge by ordering conscious knowledge* There are a variety of different ways that we can order our conscious knowledge to activate our tacit knowledge. For example, by generating graphic representations of our knowledge we can often formulate existing experience more completely and identify blank spots in our awareness (M12). We can also take observations and descriptions and organize them into a story (M13), or construct a story from photographs of our practice situations (M14). In M15 we suggest a method for making assumptions and categories explicit and using them to generate hypotheses about your practice.

- *Activating tacit knowledge by reading one's own actions* The following example from an action research study done by a teacher named Pavani illustrates what we mean by "reading one's own actions".

Pavani often organizes group work on a "division of labour" basis and is generally satisfied with the results. However, she is not satisfied with the sharing of information between groups: at the end of the day, either there is not enough time for groups to report back to each other, or the pupils are too tired to do it well. A colleague's proposal that reporting back on group work should be done the following morning, and her intuitive opposition to this proposal, provide her with a new perspective. The teaching strategy that she has been putting into practice seems to say, "The reporting back from groups is a tail end, a kind of time-buffer that can be dispensed with in case of time pressure." She found that it would be difficult to change this practice, despite the contradiction with her conscious aims.

Reading an action implies that there is a kind of knowledge embedded in action that has been previously ignored because it does not conform to familiar meanings and stated aims. We can gain access to this knowledge through a naive reading of our actions:

- rejecting the familiar meanings and stated aims that we normally associate with an action;
- revisiting an action as if it were something strange and exotic, pretending to know nothing in order to know better.

Another way to think about "reading one's own actions" is to imagine that your actions are the answer to some unvoiced question. This can be done by asking yourself, "What question am I answering through my actions?"

Sometimes teachers and other practitioners formulate starting points and state aims that are contrary to their deeply rooted practices. This contradiction remains undiscovered if the knowledge hidden in action does not become conscious. In such cases new action strategies to improve a situation (for example, a new plan for storing resources, or a new strategy for improving the way groups report back to each other) cannot easily be put into practice because of their tacit contradiction with established routines of action.

Collecting additional information that is available in the situation

One possible way of testing our knowledge of a situation we want to improve and develop is to obtain additional information – perhaps by carrying out an observation or by interviewing other people involved. The whole inventory of data collection methods can be used for this purpose (see Chapter 5).

Collecting views on similar situations from non-participants

To discover alternative interpretations of a research situation we suggest you:

- ask colleagues about similar situations;
- read relevant books and articles in magazines and journals.

Other people's views can provide starting points for our own reflection, helping to actuate our tacit knowledge, or stimulate us to collect additional information. It is important to remain clear that such explanations are hypothetical, providing stimuli for research and development rather than replacing them. It is also important to remember that we are rarely the first person to be in the situation that we are investigating. The research, professional and practitioner books and journals can be important sources of alternative interpretations. It is also important to remember that just because that information is published, it does not necessarily carry more weight for the interpretation of your situation than ones that you develop yourself or with your colleagues.

Experimenting by introducing changes in existing situations

The detective Sam Spade said, "My way of learning is to heave a wild and unpredictable monkey-wrench into the machinery. It's all right with me, if you're sure none of the flying pieces will hurt you" (Hammet 1989). Kurt Lewin, one of the originators of action research, suggested a somewhat less destructive way of understanding practice situations: "One of the best ways to understand the world is to try to change it" (quoted in Argyris *et al.* 1985). By introducing changes, trying out new actions and observing their results, our view of the situation in which we find ourselves is often deepened. We provide information and suggestions for trying out this strategy in Chapter 7.

SUGGESTED METHODS FOR CLARIFYING THE STARTING POINT

At this point we want to present some of our own experiences of this phase of research:

1 It is important to engage consciously in clarifying the starting point but at the same time its importance should not be exaggerated. After all, clarifying the situation is the task of the whole research process: if we aimed for absolute clarity about all aspects of a situation before beginning, we would never start at all. "The process of analysis is an endless one, but in action research it must be interrupted for the sake of action. And the point of interruption should be when one has sufficient

confidence in the hypotheses to allow them to guide action" (Elliott 1991: 174).

2 The time needed for clarifying the situation can vary considerably. It will depend on the complexity of the problem to be investigated, the researcher's prior experience and depth of reflection, the accessibility of crucial information, the relative ease with which explanatory patterns and theories emerge, etc. There is a comforting rule of thumb: the total time needed in research for clarifying the situation will always be nearly the same: if you take less time in the earlier stages, you will have to invest more time later on, and vice versa.

3 Even if a lot of effort is invested in clarifying the situation in consider-able depth in the early phases of research, understanding will change during the process of further research – not because the initial under-standing was "wrong" but because this is an outcome of the research. The researching practitioner is not merely interested in confirming insights once they are gained, but in further development in depth and analysis of understanding. All actions – those that are primarily to do with one's practice and those that relate to the research itself – can open new insights, no matter whether they happen at the beginning or the end of the process. To neglect and discount these insights – as some-times happens in academic research aimed at confirming or refuting initial hypotheses – is not sensible for the practitioner. Repressed problems will come back sooner or later and waste the time and energy of teacher and pupils, nurse and patients, and social worker and clients.

4 Sometimes clarifying the situation is the single most important result of the research. For example, for one teacher a taped interview with an apparently difficult pupil led to clearing up a misunderstanding and seeing the pupil in quite a new light. Because of seeing her in a new light the relationship between the teacher and the pupil became more relaxed, that in turn changed the way the teacher treated the pupil. In this case the situation changed at the time of clarifying the situation, because interview data enabled the teacher to see the pupil differently. There was no need for a systematic testing of new strategies of action.

Towards elaborating practical theories

Before introducing methods and exercises for clarifying the starting point we look at one of the ways in which this can be done – through the articulation of a practical theory of the situation to be studied. A practical theory is a conceptual structure or vision that helps provide practitioners with reasons and explanations for actions (Sanders and McCutcheon 1986). They can be thought of as rules-of-thumb based on experience and consisting of "a repertoire of practices, strategies, and ideas" (Sanders and

McCutcheon, 1986: 50) that help practitioners incorporate into their work
their best practices and those of others (Nussbaum 1986). To John Elliott,
practical theories are "developed within practice situations in which
judgment needs to be exercised ... [and arise] in the context of action,
where the practitioner is attempting to understand a practical situation
s(he) experiences to be unsatisfactory" (Elliott 2005b: 5) (see Chapter 10 for
more about practical theories).

Individual elements of practical theories and their interrelationships

The clarification of the starting point and the articulation of practical
theories happen together. For example, the clarification is attempted by
formulating individual elements of the practical theory and the connections between those elements.

1 Formulating individual elements of the practical theory

By finding a pattern in the complexities of the situation identified we can
identify the starting point for research. To do so, we first try to identify the
most important individual elements of the situation, to distinguish them
from less important elements and describe them as vividly as possible.
We can do this by asking:

- What is happening in this situation?
- Which events, actions and features of the situation are important?
- Which people are involved, in what kind of activities?

Let us try to illustrate the process of clarifying a situation by an example.
A possible starting point for the research could be:

> *Pupils seem to be very noisy during discussions in class. How can I organize
> the discussion so that it is less noisy?*

The starting point begins with a statement that describes the situation
(M7). We can now investigate this more carefully:

- *Which pupils are noisy?*
- *What are they doing when they are noisy?*
- *Does their noisiness result from taking part in the discussion or from some-
  thing else?*
- *Why does it matter if they are noisy?*
- *How can I define exactly what I mean by 'noisy'?*
- *Is there a particular time of day or environment when discussion is noisier
  than at other times or in other places?*
- *How do I respond when they are noisy in discussions? Do different responses
  from me have different effects on them?*

When we formulate important individual elements of the practical theory we should not restrict ourselves to what happened in the situation, but also take account of the context. Action research doesn't take place in a laboratory in which the researcher controls most of the context. For example, nurses work with real patients in hospitals, hospices, and elsewhere. Their own actions are embedded in a framework of other people's interests and actions. Their research and development activities in turn have consequences for others. Guiding questions for clarifying the context could be:

- *Which other people are affected by my research and development activities?*
- *Who do I need to consult to ensure that I have freedom to act with the greatest possibility of success?*
- *Which features of the institution in which I work are likely to have an influence on the question I want to investigate?*
- *What are the broad social and political determinants that I need to take into account in relation to my question?*

2 Formulating the connections between elements of the practical theory

The answers to the questions above lead step by step to the second area that needs to be addressed in clarifying the situation: we are not only interested in single features of the situation, but also in the connections between them. We need to engage in analysis (identifying the constituent parts), and also in synthesis (drawing threads together). The point is that we need to become aware of our tacit theories that make connections between individual elements, and of how they influence our interpretation of the situation:

- How does this situation come about?
- What important connections are there among events, contextual factors, the actions of individuals and other elements of this situation?
- What is my instinctive personal interpretation of this situation?

On the basis of these questions it is possible to formulate statements of this kind:

- If a nurse assesses patients solely through asking them questions from a standard form, he/she may miss other important cues from the patient (Meyer and Bridges 1998).
- If a teacher tends to follow up the answer to a question with a supplementary question, pupils will tend to refuse answering questions even if they are sure of the answer.
- The finite amount of staff available in an emergency department means that the busier the department becomes, the harder it is to give proper, individualized care to all patients (Meyer and Bridges 1998).

- The greater the expectation in a school that well-disciplined classrooms should be quiet places, the more difficult it will be to conduct classroom discussions without giving rise to discipline problems.

Sentences like these establish connections between individual elements of a situation (for example, between the teacher's comments and the level of the pupils' participation in a discussion); and they put forward a possible explanation for these connections.

In scientific literature such statements are usually called *hypotheses*, and this term is useful in action research as well. Hypotheses can be used to express aspects of someone's practical knowledge (see Chapter 10). It is important to be clear about their nature:

- A hypothesis is a statement that is based on a possible explanation that ties the elements together. The second example above ties together the asking of supplementary questions with pupils' reluctance to answer any question. In generating a hypothesis, it is important to have some reason for thinking that the elements are connected in this way. In this case, it may be that pupils usually volunteer to answer questions they know the answers to. If they are required to respond to an unexpected follow-up question for which they may not know the answer, they may feel "stupid" in front of their classmates.
- A hypothesis does not have to be correct. The term itself implies that the explanation is tentative and needs to be tested against experience.
- A hypothesis throws light on only one aspect of a complex situation, rather than the whole situation. As hypotheses are derived from specific situations, even when they have been verified they will still need to be re-examined in new situations (see Cronbach 1975).
- A hypothesis tells us about the relationship between specific features of the situation and actions or events that result from them. Therefore, they can be used as a basis for planning future action (see Chapter 7).

Commonly held views that influence our practical theories

In our experience there are some commonly held views that influence practical theories about what happens in our practice situations. These views are like glasses that we look through without being aware of them. Of course, it is not possible for any human being to do without these glasses: for example, we are all influenced by theories and explanations prevalent in our time. However, it is a good idea to try to identify some of these "glasses" and the unconscious influence they exert on the way we interpret situations. When clarifying the starting point we suggest that it is important to try to become more conscious of these hidden attitudes and preconceptions. Useful questions to ask yourself include:

- Could things have been different?
- Can I interpret this situation in another way?

We want to go on now to describe some of these commonly held views in order to illustrate our point.

Positive and negative influences

Most of us think of negative factors first when we try to explain and understand our practice situations. Every analysis tends to focus on negative experiences, often because the starting point has been chosen in response to a painful experience. But this is not enough to solve the problem.

First, it is important to take into account the positive aspects of the experience because they offer possibilities for positive action and improvement. One way of getting a better overview is to make a table placing these positive and negative influences side by side for comparison. Second, the distinction between positive and negative influences is useful for another reason: often on closer inspection it turns out that something that on the surface seems to cause problems is a hidden opportunity. Here is an example from a teacher's research:

> *After a serious conflict with his class in which the teacher became verbally aggressive, he asked his pupils to write about their perceptions of the event. Their writing gave a very negative view of what had happened and of the teacher's use of "insulting" words.*

> *(Schindler 1993)*

When you read this your attention may be drawn to the negative points of the situation. However, on closer inspection you may find some positive points: for example, only in a relationship in which there is a lot of trust would the pupils dare to express such open and emotional criticism.

Another example comes from the work of nurses:

> *In the reflective group, the nurses on the ward expressed difficulty in looking after older patients with impairments in cognition (e.g. dementia) and/or communication, and shared how hard this type of work was. In my observations, I too had noticed the tendency for these nurses to prioritize the delivery of physical over psychosocial care.*

> *(Bridges et al. 2001)*

While the nurses felt negatively about aspects of their work and this perhaps led to a tendency to avoid these aspects in practice, their willingness to discuss this in a reflective group and explore how they could improve the care they delivered is very positive.

There are many instances in our practices in which the glass could be seen as half-full or half-empty. As you use the methods for clarifying the starting point found at the end of this chapter, think about whether you are viewing the situation from a positive or negative perspective, and try to find an explanation that reverses your view.

The practitioner as originator or pawn

Richard DeCharms (1973) distinguishes between two opposing self-images that people can hold. There are the originators who see themselves as responsible for their own actions, and there are the pawns who see themselves moved by powerful hands. Action research encourages researching practitioners to develop strategies for action to improve their situations. In doing so, it encourages them to develop a self-image as originator. This needs to be balanced by an understanding that human situations are conditioned by multiple forces and cannot be fully controlled by anyone. To achieve this balance, it is useful to pose some critical questions:

- What possibilities for action are there in different situations?
- In what situations do I feel confident to effect change?
- In which situations am I mainly dependent in my actions on other people?

Many people see themselves as dependent on external forces and underestimate the contribution they can make to the situation. For these people action research tends to challenge their self-concept, inviting them to explore possibilities for action and encouraging them to show greater autonomy.

There are also others who act like pawns because they believe that their practice is so constrained that they cannot make any changes in their actions. While there are many real constraints, such as regulations, laws, and ethics, there are many that are myths (Tobin and McRobbie 1996). These mythical constraints are often in the form of expectations or obligations to behave in certain ways. One way to separate real from mythic constraints is to ask yourself what you would do if there were no barriers to your practice. In doing so you can isolate the constraints and test their veracity.

A causal or a systemic view

Another approach that elaborates on these ideas is helpful in determining the starting point more precisely. Positive and negative influences are not seen as separate, but stand in either a causal or systemic relationship to each other.

CAUSAL RELATIONSHIPS

The *causal relationship* needs little explanation. A is the cause of B. Pupil X disrupts the lesson because she knows that this gives her status with her classmates. Patient Y refuses to watch his diet because he is only concerned with the pleasures of the moment and not with long-term effects on his health.

The advantage of causal interpretations is that they suggest definite reasons and apparently simplify the complexity of a situation. They also help us to place a moral interpretation on events by assigning guilt (to the pupil, a colleague, the parents or ourselves). However, causal interpretations have their problems. One is that situations are usually caused by a number of contributing factors. For example, a pupil's bad behavior might be traced back to preceding events involving other pupils, parents and two or three teachers. Her behavior can therefore be regarded partly as a reaction to other, preceding events. This is not an argument against causal interpretations, but it does mean that we must be careful not to settle quickly for one that is too simple because each cause may itself have layers of further causes.

Let's take the case of a young teacher taking a new class for the first time. She will be a bit nervous and, either instinctively or consciously wants to win the pupils over and gain control. This purpose will be expressed in her behavior. Let's look at the pupils: they sit tensely, perhaps rather skeptical, keyed up and interested in holding their own against the teacher, individually and as a group. This purpose will be expressed in their behavior. At the same time they will watch every action of the teacher closely and their interpretations of her behavior will influence their own behavior.

The noisiness of some pupils is interpreted by the teacher as a threat to her control of the class. The pupils notice the irresolute appearance of the teacher and it makes them feel insecure. Is the pupils' noisiness caused by the wavering appearance of the teacher or vice versa? This question cannot be answered as there is some evidence for both possibilities. Looked at from the pupils' point of view the first answer will be more plausible, looked at from the teacher's the second will be more plausible. As it is impossible to know whether the noisiness or the wavering came first we cannot tell which should be regarded as the cause of the other. If we identify a cause, it will be arbitrary.

THE SYSTEMIC VIEW

What happens if we decide that there is no point in searching for causes and the people responsible? An alternative is the *systemic view* (see Selvini-Palazzoli *et al.* 1978). According to this view a practice situation is regarded as a system in that each participant (for example, the teacher, pupils, parents, and administrators or nurses, patients, family members, and doctors/has a relationship to one another. Each person influences the other members)and is influenced by them. A change in the behavior of one member leads to a change in the whole system.

Every kind of behavior can be regarded as both the result of feedback from the behavior of others and an influence on their further behavior. Even "non-behavior" (for example, the silence of classmates when one pupil disturbs the lesson) can in this sense be seen as information for the "troublemaker", the teacher and the pupils.

A system is a network of mutual relationships (expectations, kinds of behavior, perceptions) in which the practitioner is caught up. It is easier to understand if we imagine the network consisting of threads that are alive. A particular action of a social worker is dynamically connected to the network so that he/she is both affected by all its threads and influences them. But there is limited room for each thread to move if the network is not to be destroyed. There are longer and shorter threads and there are knots in the network. These are the points at which threads intersect. Therefore, an occurrence in one's practice originates from the whole network even if some parts of the network play a more important role than others. An extreme example of this happened in the health care system in the US. Nurses and other health care professionals joined with their patients to call for greater patient rights. The main thrust of this was to provide information to patients and their families so that they could make knowledgeable decisions about their care rather than leaving it entirely in the hands of doctors and, in more recent years, health maintenance organizations (HMOs). A totally unexpected side effect of the success of this movement was that pharmaceutical companies began to market directly to patients rather than doctors because the patients now had a say in their care. Residents of the US are now bombarded by advertisements from the pharmaceutical companies that provide them with the "information" that they need to make decisions about their health care.

What can we learn from the systemic view? It enables us to ask new questions. Not questions that search for causes of events and attribute blame, but questions like: Which threads (for example, other pupils' and the teacher's expectations) contribute to the event (for example, a pupil's disruptive action)? What is the function of a pupil's disruptive behavior for other pupils (and for the teacher)? Which are the sensitive spots (knots where many threads meet) in the event?

The systemic view also has another advantage: it can help us to arrive at a less emotional, more detached and, therefore, probably also fairer approach to situations in class, because it broadens our view beyond immediate, concrete causes. The interdependence of the elements in a system leads to a kind of balance (the tension of the net) to which the quiet pupils as well as the troublemakers contribute. The actions of a trouble-maker can cause the "normality" of the "good" pupils and vice versa (thus many teachers have noticed that when a disruptive pupil leaves the class another will often emerge to take his/her place).

If we pursue this perspective it can also offer suggestions for action. In any situation, the system is kept in balance by feedback from its inter-acting elements (participants in the practice situation). However, this feedback can also change the system. This means, for example, that it is important to know what feedback (from other pupils or the teacher) reinforces a "troublemaker" and what does not (it may be that any form of attention acts to reinforce the bad behavior). We can start to solve the problem by influencing the nature of the feedback (for example, by giving other pupils a chance to express their opinions or by the teacher voicing his/her own perceptions of a situation).

A focus for analysis is to find the *knots* where the threads interact and particularly influence events. For example, a pupil who disturbs the class may be looking for reactions from higher status pupils in the class. There are also occasions that result in interactions that cause a difficult situation, such as when a pupil comes to feel humiliated by a teacher's actions. We believe that the methods at the end of this chapter will provide you with the tools that you need to go beyond a causal perspective and to uncover the systemic aspects of your practice situation.

Holistic and analytic perspectives

In this chapter we have given a number of hints for clarifying the starting point of research. This process of clarification is not value-free. By clarify-ing or analyzing situations and problems we are necessarily rather select-ive and reductionist (see also Chapter 6). When we reduce the complexity in our practice to a few central features it often results in a mechanistic view of reality. This tendency has to be counteracted from time to time during the research process. We must not equate a reductionist and mechanistic model with the reality in which we live and act, which is much more complex than our model. The following suggestions may help to prevent this:

- Once you have developed hypotheses don't view them in isolation from one another, but always look for possible links among them.
- Try to keep in mind the specific situation from which the hypothesis was derived initially, by asking from time to time: Under what con-ditions would the prediction of my hypothesis be likely to be valid? Under what conditions would it be likely to stop being valid?

ask team
Re: smBoard ↓16 group
Clarifying the starting point 73

METHODS FOR CLARIFYING THE STARTING POINT

my class

Conversations

Conversations with colleagues play an important part in action research. This holds not only for the stage of "clarifying the starting point" discussed in this chapter but for the whole research process. Conversation has long been seen as a method of research. In science new ideas are tested by engaging in grand, cooperative conversations that follow agreed-upon standards (Putnam 1995). Interviews can be held in a conversational manner (Seidman 1998) and an important part of ethnographic research is to engage in conversations with participants (Fetterman 1989). Conversation has also been recognized, from a feminist perspective, as a way to make meaning of data (Belenkey *et al.* 1986, Josselson *et al.* 1997).

We urge you to engage in conversation about your research. The partners in the conversation should be *critical friends*: they should have empathy for the action researcher's situation and relate closely to his/her concerns, but at the same time be able to provide rich and honest feedback.

one of our articles spoke about it as a team

A small team of action researchers will probably create better conditions for action research than a person working alone. Another good way of working is to form research tandems. The partners in each tandem have their own starting points for research but assist each other as critical friends, sharing experiences and helping with data collection (doing observations, interviews etc.).

M9 ANALYTIC DISCOURSE IN A GROUP

This procedure allows us to increase our awareness of the important characteristics of any situation and to enhance our understanding of their interdependencies. However, it presupposes that the analysis is carried out in a group rather than individually. In analytic discourse a problem or issue is analyzed in the following way:

1 It is the task of the action researcher who wants to analyze a problem to provide the group with basic information on the issue to be discussed (in about 5 minutes); and subsequently to answer questions put forward by the group as comprehensively as he/ she deems possible or feasible.

2 It is the task of the remaining participants to gain a comprehensive and consistent impression of the situation by means of asking questions. These rules have proved to be important in carrying out analytic discourse:

- There should be questions only: statements concerning similar experiences should be avoided. This rule aims at focusing attention on the situation of the reporter.
- Critical comments (including those in the form of questions) should not be permitted. This rule, of special importance at the beginning of a discourse, aims at preventing the reporter from becoming defensive rather than reflective.
- Suggestions for solutions should not be permitted. This rule is to ensure that the search for an increasingly profound understanding of the problem is not cut short by a compilation of recipes.

3 Adherence to these rules, discussed beforehand with all participants, should be monitored by a moderator (usually one of the participants, who is prepared to assume that role). He/She is allowed to ask questions and may use this as a means of opening up new perspectives.

4 For the analysis of a situation three types of questions are predominantly suitable:

- Questions concerning the concretization of remarks (for example, the request to give an example or provide more details).
- Questions concerning the underlying theories (for example, a request to give reasons for any action described, or any interpretations of events put forward).
- Questions concerning an expansion of the system (for example, the request to give more information about people or events who may be related to the problem but have not so far been mentioned).

An *analytic discourse* has proved to be an effective method of gaining an in-depth understanding of a problem. Through it the interrelationships of the elements of the problem including the "headache areas" become apparent. This can provide a basis for solutions or for a new line of inquiry. An analytic discourse can lead to a deeper understanding of the problem – particularly for the person reporting but also for the whole group.

It usually takes some time for an analytic discourse to open up a problem in depth and become an intellectually worthwhile and personally enriching experience. The personal enrichment has to do with the seriousness, the sympathy and also the personal concern that may develop in the group. The intellectual value derives from a growing understanding of the intricate relationship among observations, tacit assumptions and evaluations that are specific to one person's situation, but that have many implications for the other participants' self-understanding.

Usually the greatest benefit from an analytic discourse is gained by the action researcher for whom it is organized. Apart from the deepening relationship with colleagues that results, the reporter develops a clearer and more analytical view of the problem or issue. Sometimes this can be experienced quite dramatically, if the reporter's perception of the problem changes fundamentally or approaches to its solution emerge. At the same time a more analytical view of a problem is usually accompanied by an emotional relief.

The role of the moderator is not always simple because it involves seeing that rules are observed that are against the practice of everyday conversation and that, therefore, are "forgotten" easily. The moderator must see the rules are kept or run the risk of the discourse remaining at a superficial level.

It may sometimes be necessary to refuse to accept questions that go too deep and invite a level of personal and emotional commitment unwarranted by the mutual trust in the group. Too much emotional involvement can also interfere with analysis because it draws attention away from a systemic view of a situation to a one-sided, causal interpretation (possibly too personally focused).

In the course of an analytic discourse progress should be made in three areas:

- The situation in which the research problem occurs should be clarified (knowledge of surface symptoms).
- an understanding should develop of "positive" and "negative" factors and influences related to the problem (in-depth interpretation).
- an understanding should develop of the potential for change (in thinking and action). To this end coherence and holistic plausibility of analysis is often more important for a researching teacher than the "objective" quality of individual arguments.

It has proved to be helpful if there is still some time left at the end of an analytic discourse for discussion without the rules. Often there is strong interest in the group in talking about the experience. If this opportunity is announced at the beginning of the discourse, when the moderator explains and negotiates the rules, it takes pressure off the process because participants who urgently want to "tell their own story" know they will get their chance later.

M10 CONVERSATION WITH A CRITICAL FRIEND

If you have no group of fellow researchers willing to take part in an analytic discourse, you can do something similar with a single person whom you trust and feel you can confide in. Of course, one-to-one conversations will not follow the rules as strictly as we have suggested for an analytic discourse. Nonetheless it can still be very useful to adopt a similar discipline:

If you want to assist a colleague in clarifying a situation, it is useful to devote a period of time to gaining an understanding of the situation and:

- only ask questions that deepen this understanding;
- refrain from any anecdotes, adverse criticisms or suggested solutions that might distract or deflect the train of your colleague's reflective thinking.

M11 THE STARTING POINT SPEECH

One of the ways to organize your thoughts and ideas about your starting point is to write – and, if possible, present – an informative speech about it. The audience for the speech should be your research group, critical friend or possibly other interested colleagues. We suggest that it be a short speech (5–10 minutes) in which you explain why your starting point is important to your practice.

Here are some suggestions of what the speech could contain:

- a statement of your starting point;
- why it is important to your practice;
- the general idea:

  ○ "a state of affairs or situation one wishes to change or improve on" (Elliott 1991: 72);
  ○ the results of reconnaissance – a description of the facts of the situation, and an explanation of the facts of the situation (Elliott 1991: 73);

- a list of several places that you might look in the research literature to learn more about the problem;
- "a statement of the factors one is going to change or modify in

> order to improve the situation, and the actions one will undertake in this direction . . ." (Elliott 1991: 75);
> - your ethical concerns and what you might do about them.

USING DIAGRAMS

graphic design represent

Normally theories start with a verbal description (written or spoken) of a situation. After a period of reflection and discussion/writing, the salient points are then drawn out and expressed in succinct, verbal statements (i.e. the hypotheses). Of necessity these statements are reductionist, losing much of the complexity and detail of the situation they attempt to explain.

Miles and Huberman (1994) have suggested that narrative texts (and other ways of presenting theories linguistically) overstretch the human capability to digest information and therefore lead to oversimplified interpretations. They make a plea for more frequent use of diagrams and other graphical means of representing theories. Narrative texts organize information according to the sequential structure of language and pose a problem for the representation of non-sequential events. Diagrams, on the other hand, allow us to represent information and its interrelationships in a structured, rapidly accessible and compact form.

Miles and Huberman (1994) give some suggestions for constructing diagrams:

- Limit the diagram or chart, whenever possible, to one sheet of paper.
- Try out several alternative ways of representing the situation. Many changes and modifications may be necessary before you are satisfied. The graphical representation should not be thought of as a straitjacket to limit future work but more like a map of the area that has just been researched. A main purpose of research is to contribute to the development of maps.
- Avoid "the no-risk framework". If the elements of the situation are only defined in very general terms, and two-way arrows connect everything to everything else, it will be easy to confirm the theory but it is unlikely to have any explanatory value. It is better to express your ideas as concretely and definitely as possible. The more exactly a practical theory is formulated, the more helpful it will be for your further work (although it is likely to need considerable modification).
- Use the graphical representation for your own development. Outcomes of practical experience, existing theories and the results of important research studies can be "mapped on to" it at a later stage. This will help to identify parallels, overlaps, contradictions, and gaps, and in this way refine and deepen your understanding of the field of study.

relationship

It has also been suggested to us by Elliott Eisner that one of the purposes of a diagram is to make complex ideas accessible (Eisner 1994). While oversimplified diagrams may not sufficiently conceptualize the situation, ones that are too complex will befuddle you and your colleagues. If your research group or critical friend cannot understand your diagram without a lot of explanation from you, try to make it simpler.

In the following section we suggest a practical method for creating a diagram.

M12 GRAPHICAL RECONSTRUCTIONS (STARTER)

Graphical reconstructions help to clarify the situation but also with data analysis in general (see Chapter 6).

Procedure

1 Read all your data and your notes in your research notebook (for example, your short description of the situation and questions that indicate the developmental perspective – see M7).

2 Write the most important features, events and actions that you identify in your data separately on small index cards. Then write on further cards the *most important* contextual conditions of the situation. Try not to have too many cards (particularly at first) or it may be too difficult to keep them all in view: 8–16 cards are ideal as a rule. If you find there is a need to include further items as the activity progresses, new cards can easily be added.

3 Now try to express the kind of relationship between the cards. For that purpose you can use further cards with symbols for relationships. Probably you will need the following ones most frequently (see Figure 4.1). Other symbols can be written on blank cards as needed.

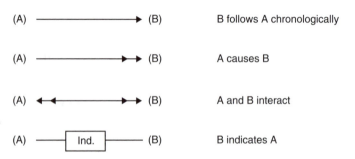

Figure 4.1 Symbols for relationships

like a 5card strategy

The point of *graphical reconstructions* is that in presenting the essential elements graphically (and not in a linguistic flow of ideas) you have to restrict yourself to essentials and be clear and concise. This helps to identify the most important features of a situation. Working with movable cards makes it easy to try out different configurations until you find one that satisfactorily reconstructs the situation you are considering. As you move the cards you go through a process of clarifying the relationships among all the elements of the situation.

4 When you have found a representation of the starting point that really satisfies you, copy the *graphic diagram* on to a single sheet of paper. Preserve this diagram. In the course of your research you will be able to see how your ideas change. You can also use the diagram to check how plans for actions fit your personal theory as represented in the diagram: From which elements of my theory do my plans for innovative actions originate? Why exactly do I think they originate there and not from other points on the diagram?

5 There is software that you can use to construct graphical representations. This type of software is used to visualize connections among concepts and ideas by providing users with the tools to construct diagrams like the one below. A popular one among teachers is called *Inspiration*®,[1] which includes features such as the ability to go from the diagram view to an outline view, and to incorporate text, images, video and audio into the diagram, and outline.

An example

The following is an example from the action research done by Karen St Cyr, a university supervisor of student teachers. Although its focus is teacher education, anyone who supervises novices should find this of interest.

> As a supervisor of preservice and novice teachers, my main goal is to assist teachers to teach well and be effective in their teaching. It is important for me to help to provide the framework for the teachers to analyze their performance and to reflect on ways to enhance their teaching skills, to develop competence, and to be able to exercise some autonomy in improving their performance. To facilitate this, I look carefully at their planning, observe their lessons, give immediate and objective feedback, assist them with diagnosing and solving instructional problems that they may be experiencing, and by employing various methods to enhance teaching and student performance.
>
> It is important for me as a supervisor to assist teachers to develop their teaching skills by developing reflective skills. Many novice teachers have

theoretical and practical insights of teaching that may not apply to specific situations with which they may be regularly confronted. Often the emphasis that is put on technical knowledge and skills in teacher preparation programs causes novice teachers not to be prepared to think deeply about how they are teaching and to make the necessary adjustments to make their practice more effective. The teacher's ability to reflect upon and analyze his/her own mistakes and to be proactive in correcting these mistakes is critical to develop proficiency as a teacher. If they do not develop these self-reflective skills, so often they feel like failures, lose confidence in their abilities, and may become an attrition statistic within 5 years of entering the teaching profession, even though they may be good teachers. This is why my role as a supervisor in assisting them to develop these essential skills is so important.

(St Cyr 2005: 30)

Based on Karen's preliminary data collection and analysis, the supervisor produces this diagram of the advisory framework that she describes (Figure 4.2):

M13 A STORY FROM CARDS

Try to observe practical situations that are important in relation to your starting point of research over a defined period of time (for example, between one and three weeks depending on the research question).

1 After each observation, describe the situation as precisely as possible on a large index card.
2 At the end of the time take all the cards and read through them.
3 Try to write a general explanatory statement that relates to all the situations you have observed.
4 Check this explanatory statement by answering the following questions for each card in turn.

   • Is it possible to present the situation described on this card using the concepts in my general explanatory statement?
   • How?
   • If the situation I observed is distorted or fragmented by this attempt, what changes or additions do I need to make to the explanatory statement?

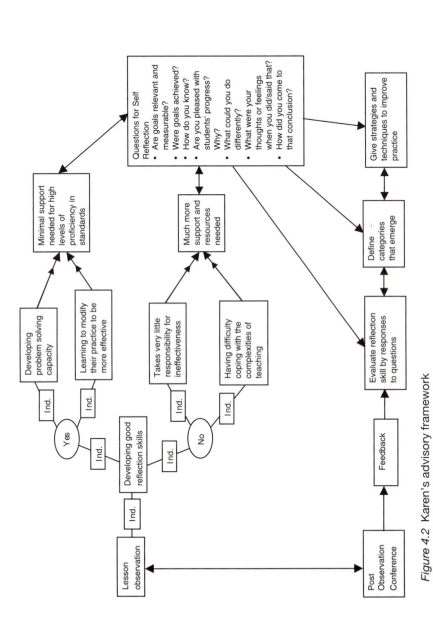

Figure 4.2 Karen's advisory framework

Source: St Cyr (2005: 15)

M14 PHOTOVOICE: A STORY FROM PHOTOS

Caroline Wang developed the Photovoice technique as part of her participatory action research work with women's health issues in rural China. Wang has three main goals for Photovoice:

> to enable people: (1) to record and reflect their community's strengths and concerns; (2) to promote critical dialog and knowledge about personal and community issues through large and small group discussions of photographs; and (3) to reach policymakers.

> (Wang 1999: 185)

Wang's website (www.photovoice.org) contains some examples of Photovoice projects. There are also several books available. Although it was not labeled as Photovoice, the use of photography by children in the documentary film *Born into Brothels* (Kauffman and Briski 2004) is an example of how photography can be used to gain new perspectives of your situation.

You can use the Photovoice technique to gather data about your situation, reflect upon it and construct a story through pictures that provides you with new ways to think about your starting point. We suggest the following steps:

- Take a series of still photographs of your practice situation. You may want to plan out your pictures ahead of time or just carry a camera with you for several days. If your photos contain pictures of your pupils, patients or clients, you will need their permission to share them with others, including your research group or critical friends. Even if you do not intend to share the photos, you should ask permission to take them.
- Select 15–20 of the photos, put them into some order and give them captions.
- Wait a few days and revisit your Photovoice project. It also helps to present your Photovoice project with commentary to your research group or critical friend. Then answer these questions:

  - What do the photos you selected and the captions you wrote tell you about your practice situation?
  - Were there any significant aspects of your practice that you did not include? Why didn't you include them?

M15 FROM CATEGORIES TO HYPOTHESES

Hypotheses are formulated in order to make the researcher aware of his/her tacit assumptions and provide an orderly framework for the research. The starting point is usually a loosely structured information base (experiences, knowledge taken from books or data). Working on this information the researcher tries to impose a pattern by identifying important characteristics or categories as distinct from unimportant ones and by making connections between these categories explicit. Unlike in graphical reconstruction (M12) the results of the analysis are not expressed diagrammatically, but linguistically. In what follows the procedure of formulating hypotheses is split up into steps each illustrated by an example (see also the practical hints for coding data in M33).

1 First try to identify your assumptions about the situation in question as they are documented in your research notebook, in other data you have already collected or in your memories from reading or experience.

   For example, a teacher made the following notes from memory after seeing a video-recording of one of his lessons (for reasons of space only brief sections are quoted).

The recorded lesson once again shows the problem I have identified: in this class there is no discussion that is kept alive by the pupils themselves for any length of time. Even if I ask questions or express provocative opinions there is normally little response and the topic is closed. . . . Watching the video I became aware of a pattern that occurred four times (the first time stimulated by a work-sheet that all the pupils had to read, the other times by a question from me). First a genuinely controversial topic is introduced for discussion. Then three or four pupils say something that is relevant to it. Then I put forward my opinion. Then only one or two more pupils say anything further (in one case nobody said anything further). Does the discussion die as a result of my statement?

2 Write down all the categories that emerge. To do this we need to know exactly what a category is. Unfortunately it is difficult to give one overall definition, but here is an attempt:

   • A category is a concept, usually represented by a noun (with some additional phrase). It can be used as a key to a text: it helps us to order the ideas in the text.
   • The order is created by using the category to stand for several

phenomena, which in the text are likely to be expressed in quite different forms.

- By putting them in a category, phenomena that are regarded as important are differentiated from unimportant phenomena (i.e. those that are not put in a category) within the framework of the research question.

It is easier to understand the concept of a category with the help of examples. As an exercise we suggest that you reread the description above and make a list of categories contained in the text that you think could be important in clarifying the situation.

My list of categories:..

....

....

We have also done this exercise ourselves and made the following list of categories:

- *class discussion* (developed from, "In this class there is no discussion . . .");
- *teacher's questions* (developed from, "Even if I ask questions or express provocative opinions . . .");
- *topic introduction* (developed from, "a genuinely controversial topic is introduced for discussion");
- *pupils' responses* (developed from, "there is normally little response . . .", "then three or four pupils say something . . ." and "only one or two more pupils say anything further");
- *discussion dying* (developed from, "Does the discussion die . . .?");
- *teacher stating views on controversial topics* (developed from, "Then I put forward my opinion").

We see some value in keeping categories close to the wording of the original text initially, and as the analysis progresses re-grouping some of these as more general categories. If your list is worded differently or contains different categories it need not be 'wrong'. Maybe you see a different pattern from us in this situation. In the end the "rightness" of a category is determined by its usefulness (i.e. its analytic power) for further research and action. In any case, comparing different lists of categories drawn up by different people (for example, yours and ours) helps us to understand the alternative perspectives expressed through the selection of categories. If you have the opportunity, discuss these differences with your research group or a critical friend.

3 When you have made your list of categories from your action research, check this interim result:

- Are there categories that actually describe the same phenomenon and can be summarized in one category?
- Are there any categories that represent different aspects of a more general concept (that is either already included in your list or should be added)? In our example, "discussion dying" is closely related to "pupils' responses". We keep the more general category "pupils' responses . . ." and cross out "discussion dying" on our list.

4 When reading the data and making the first list of categories, same patterns connecting categories usually emerge that need to be written down. Make a list of hypotheses that express presumed relationships between these categories. Usually hypotheses are formulated in an 'if . . . then' form. Try this out by taking two categories from your list and writing down a possible connection in the form of a hypothesis:

My hypothesis ....

....

....

For example, from our list of categories we set up this hypothesis:

If there is more "teacher stating views on controversial topics", then there will be less "pupils' responses".

Or in a stylistically more elegant form:

If the teacher expresses opinions on controversial topics more frequently, then the frequency of pupils' responses (to the controversial topic) will be reduced.

Remember that hypotheses need to do more than describe the relationship among categories – they should also provide an explanation as to why that connection exists.

5 Examine the list of hypotheses that you have drawn up, using the following criteria:

- Which categories do not appear at all in the hypotheses or only figure marginally? Why not?
  - Is it because you don't have a theoretical concept of these categories – in other words that you don't really know what they mean?

- ○ Is it only possible to identify trivial connections between them and other categories?
- ○ Is it only possible to identify connections that cannot really be investigated?

- To which hypotheses can you already bring a lot of experience (examples?) and which ones are very speculative?
- In order to test these hypotheses, what action could you take in your practice and what data would you need to collect?

DEVELOPMENT OR RESEARCH?

Through the clarification of questions the focus of your research should become clearer and clearer. It can have three key aspects: development, research and clarification of objectives.

1 *Development*

If your primary interest is in the development of specific actions (e.g. "How can I increase the extent of task orientation in group work?"), then you are focusing on a *developmental project*, moving from an evaluation of your situation (your practical theory) to practical action (see Figure 4.3). Your next step after clarifying your starting point is, in this case, the development of action strategies, which promise a further development of the situation (see Chapter 7 for details). If you evaluate your action strategies, research interests move to the center of attention: the action strategies are regarded as hypotheses, which are tested by using data.

2 *Research*

If your project is primarily guided by cognitive interests (e.g. "What kinds of productive and non-productive activities of pupils occur in my English lessons?"), then your focus is research. Information on practical situations is collected and interpreted depending on different theoretical and practical respects and (as you can see in Figure 4.3) you move from action via a collection of data to an interpretation of available information within a "practical theory". Your next step after clarifying your starting point is, in this case, to determine which additional data have to be collected and interpreted by which methods (see Chapter 5 for further details). On the basis of the situational understanding gained, new options for action can be developed in order to satisfy developmental interests.

There are two different kinds of approaches to research-type projects: *explorative projects* focus on a better understanding of practical situations; *evaluative projects* focus on the evaluation of a

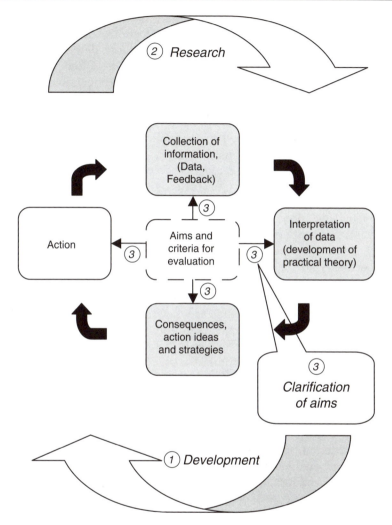

Figure 4.3 From practical theories to action

practical situation on the basis of developmental aims and success criteria. In this case the movement from action via data collection to interpretation of data, which is typical for research, is augmented by an evaluation of the relationship between aims and practice. The focus lies on the adequacy and effectiveness of an existing or innovative practice.

3 Clarification of aims

In both developmental as well as research projects the question eventually arises about which values and aims are represented in the phenomena investigated and how they can be justified in view of the values of the practitioner. Practical actions are representations of values in a concrete interactive form (Elliott 1991). So aims and values are ingredients of our everyday practice. Often we are only partially or not at all conscious of them. However, they can become obvious:

- if we or our partners are *dissatisfied* with present practice. The reason can be a discrepancy between our explicit aims and the implicit ones that are represented by our actions.
- if we want to engage in *cooperative development* with colleagues and other involved persons. Quite often it can be noticed that aims are agreed on the level of verbal formulations but that the views about their realization are different or that colleagues for whom different values are important resort to similar action strategies.
- if we or other persons *evaluate* our practice. For this purpose it is necessary to make explicit our aims and success criteria, and to determine which aims and corresponding indicators for success should be used for evaluation. Whenever an evaluation moves beyond self-evaluation, such as when it involves other persons or is conducted by an external institution, agreement about aims and indicators of success is not only a precondition of the technical quality of an evaluation but also one of social quality and justice, both of which demand fair negotiation processes.

In all of these cases a conscious *clarification of aims* is necessary, that is, the implicit aims of practice, and the hopes associated with innovations have to be made explicit. The people involved need to know which concrete actions, processes, features, results and so on, so that the aims can be observed and evaluated. If aims and values are formulated concretely enough to be used for observation and evaluation of practice we speak of *indicators* or – in the case of evaluation – *success indicators*. In the following section we present two methods that we have used in order to achieve an agreement about aims to be evaluated and corresponding success indicators.

Action research projects will always involve *activities relating to development, research and clarification of aims*. Practitioners want to better understand their practice to be able to develop it further; they want to implement ideas for improvement and to find out how successful they are in achieving their aspirations.

Where to begin when starting an action research process? There is no general rule. Whether the first step is research, development or clarification of aims depends on your specific situation and interests and different routes can be effective.

The *planning of an action research project* is an emerging, stepwise process. After initial research or development activities an interim check is made, in which current results are identified. On this basis the next step is determined, being research, development or clarification of aims. Planning a project starts with a question or developmental interest that may change during the research and development process. However such changes are not indiscriminate but typically occur when intermediate results suggest a modification.

Clarification of aims and development of success indicators

How can you proceed if aims are to be clarified and indicators of success are to be formulated? Below you will find two methods that we used with different groups of teachers involved in school development projects. In this context it is important to note that any kind of evaluative action research should focus on more than a clear and sound development of aims and success indicators but whatever is developed should also represent the claims and views of the different groups involved. Again, we want to make clear that although our examples come from our work with teachers, these methods can be used by anyone involved in professional practice, including nurses and social workers.

M16 CONCRETION OF AIMS AND FORMULATION OF SUCCESS INDICATORS

How are aims concretized and success indicators formulated? The following proposal suggests a few important steps. If a person, group, school or other institution wants to evaluate a situation it has to:

- elaborate aims and values (keyword "aims");
- clarify which characteristics of school life correspond to these aims (keyword "realizations");
- determine whereby one can recognize if and to what extent these characteristics exist (keyword "indicators");
- know instruments by which this can be substantiated (keyword "instruments").

The following section illustrates the way in which a school could deal with this process focusing on the issue "school and class climate".

Step 1: Aims
What are my/our aims?
Essential aims are formulated that should guide educational work.

Such aims are often implicit in action and can be elaborated by "reading one's own actions". Educational and other innovations are associated with different aims and expectations. For example, in a whole school they can often be found in its mission statement or quality programs.

With regard to the issue "school and class climate" such an aim could be as follows:

- We strive for a school climate in which teachers and pupils feel comfortable and are stimulated to high performance.

Step 2: Realizations
What is being done or has to be done in order to satisfy this aim?
This step refers to concrete measures that are expected to have special potential to achieve the aim, e.g. instructional arrangements and methods, curricular and extracurricular offerings, specific rules to orient behavior in relevant situations (e.g. in exams). In our example the following realizations could be elaborated:

1 Teachers and students demonstrate respect and esteem for each other.
2 The working rules are jointly developed and accounted for.
3 Mistakes are also seen as opportunities for learning.
4 The interior of classrooms is carefully planned and maintained in cooperation with pupils.

Step 3: Success indicators
How do you recognize if the aim is achieved?
Concrete and observable indicators are developed that allow you to find out if the anticipated aims are achieved. A few examples:

The climate of this school is higher than average if compared with schools of this type. Tests show higher than average achievements of the pupils.

1.1 *Teachers and pupils respect one another.*
1.2 *There are guidelines for the resolution of conflicts that are generally accepted and that respect the dignity of all parties involved.*
2.1 *The school rules have been negotiated democratically.*
2.2 *The rules are applied to all groups indiscriminately.*
3.1 *Pupils respond to teachers' comments on their tests.*
4.1 *Every classroom has an esthetically pleasing appearance.*

When aims are concretized, the most difficult part is the development of useful indicators. The more precise the indicators are, the easier the selection and employment of evaluation methods and the bigger is the chance to get utilizable evaluation results. However, the more precise – and thus more easily measurable – an indicator is, the less it is able to represent the original aim (i.e., in the language of evaluation, the lower is its validity with respect to the phenomenon to be measured). Because validity is an indispensable quality criterion of an indicator, and because indicators that do not represent important aspects of an aim are worthless, it is necessary to strike a balance between validity and precision.

Step 4: Instruments
Which instruments can gather the data to determine if the aim is achieved?
In this final step the instruments of data collection are determined by which relevant information with respect to the selected indicators can be obtained. In our example the following methods appear to be useful for the aims listed above:

1.1 *a standardized questionnaire measures school climate;*
1.2 *test items measure pupil achievement;*
2.1 *interviews with pupils and teachers and interviews with pupil representatives;*
2.2 *interviews with pupils and teachers and observations;*
3.1 *survey among pupils;*
4.1 *visit classrooms.*

This procedure should convey two important *messages*:

- The analysis underlying this process involves an intensive discussion of the aims of the persons involved and of the institution. It involves the *elaboration of a quality concept* in a dynamic process in which each of the four steps can influence each other step. The discussion of indicators (Step 3) can have repercussions on the understanding and on the formulation of realizations (Step 2) or on the aims (Step 1). The shaping of understandings emerging from such a discussion is no less important than its results, which can differ from institution to institution or practice to practice.
- The procedure also suggests that the process should *start with making aims concrete rather than deciding about methods of data collection.* The postponement of the selection of methods pays because it is greatly facilitated by well-defined indicators. On the other hand, if the indicators are not clear the choice of methods becomes a game of chance.

Aim: In pupil-centered instruction the pupils should be supported as much as possible according to their individual abilities, interests and needs. The team of teachers contributes by planning and implementing instruction accordingly in all subjects.

Realizations	Indicators
1 Curricular offers make allowance for different pupil prerequisites.	• Pupils can choose among tasks that range from simple to complex. • Pupils can use time slots of different length in order to achieve learning aims. (Analysis of instructional materials, interviews with pupils)

2 Methods of teaching, learning and social grouping are varied systematically.	• Pupils possess a number of competences and methods that they can use, e.g.
	  • Providing feedback to other pupils;
	  • Leading discussions; (Observation of instruction)

3 Teachers move beyond the transmission of information and act as organizers and aides for learning.	• Pupils are able to organize their work independently. • There is a positive and encouraging working climate. (Observation of instruction)

Figure 4.4 Realizations and indicators
Source: Modified from Hiebler *et al.* (2001)

Figure 4.4 provides an example of the results of such an internal deliberation process of a school. Realizations and indicators are assigned to an aim and methods of data collection are provided in parentheses.

M17 SUGGESTIONS FOR THE DEVELOPMENT OF SUCCESS INDICATORS

As already mentioned, the development of success indicators (or success criteria) is one of the most difficult tasks when concretizing aims. In Figure 4.5 we distinguish five kinds of indicators and typical measurement instruments that match them.

Here are some of our experiences with the development of success indicators:

• Teachers involved in the development of innovations, often intuitively use *"building blocks" of the development process* (generally input or process indicators) as success indicators and only rarely output or outcome indicators.

Typical kinds of success indicators		Typical instruments
Input indicators	• Are the requirements met for the realization of a plan? • Was the plan put into operation?	• Checklist • Checklist
Process indicators	• Does the quality of the process meet expectations?	• Observation • Interview • Questionnaire
Output indicators	• Does the quality of the result or product meet expectations?	• Test • Observation (of presentation, etc.) • Interview • (Questionnaire)
Outcome indicators	• Does the quality of long-term (sustainable) effects meet expectations?	• Post-test • Observation (of practice, etc.) • Interview • Questionnaire
Acceptance indicators	• How useful does the plan appear? • Are process or product accepted by the persons concerned?	• Single or group interview • Questionnaire

Figure 4.5 Indicators and instruments

- In a development project, for example, pupils should be trained in self-regulated learning. In such a project it can be important to know:
  - that the training is taking place as planned;
  - that there are negotiations between teachers and pupils regarding teaching and learning practices;
  - that teachers meet from time to time to reflect on the process and to decide on changes if necessary;
  - that diagnostic instruments are developed to assist pupils in providing feedback on learning styles, etc.

- All of these things are important building blocks of the innovation and are (probably) indispensable for the success of the project. On the other hand, in most cases the realization of these building blocks is not identical with the results or effects of the project. Although it can be important *to investigate if important building blocks of the innovation have actually been set in place* (Did the reflection meetings of the teachers take place as planned?) *and are of the intended quality* (Did they lead to substantial discussions and relevant consequences?), it is also important to go back to the ultimate aim of the innovation. If the aim was "pupils should become competent in self-regulated learning", then certain steps, such as training in self-regulated learning methods, achieving necessary agreements, design of diagnostic aids, *can be important intermediary results of the innovation,* but they are not the final result that promises *pupil competences.* Success indicators that refer to the intended final result (in most cases competences and attitudes of pupils) should not be forgotten.

- It is advisable to start the development of indicators with a brain-storming exercise that refrains from considering the usefulness of the ideas. In a second step those (few[2]) indicators should be selected that promise to provide good evidence for the aim to be evaluated. For the reduction of the number of indicators the following considerations are practical:

  - explanatory power with respect to the aim (validity is the most important criterion);
  - usefulness for the further development of the project;
  - plausibility for significant others (persons and groups who are affected by it);
  - practicability in view of the available resources (and the other tasks).

- Only after the determination of success indicators does it make sense to select those instruments for data collection that appear to be the best choice for ascertaining each indicator (the suggestions in Figure 4.5 can help in this respect).

Chapter 5

Data collection

How do action researchers get the material for their reflections, their *data?* The chapters on the research notebook and on finding a starting point have already presented some methods of data collection. This chapter deals with it more systematically. We begin by discussing what data are and the relationship between data and the situations we want to research. The main body of the chapter is taken up with presenting various data collection methods. We end with discussion of criteria for judging the quality of action research.

WHAT IS DATA?

We are able to take skilful and knowledgeable action in daily routines as a result of our experiences. Experiences are all the events and our interpretations of them that have taken place in the situations in which we are participants. We use them to plan, carry out and evaluate later actions. Some of them we soon forget, others are stored in our mind as knowledge (*practical theories* about specific situations) and can be retrieved to inform later actions. Others remain with us as tacit knowledge that we draw upon unconsciously but can be made explicit through some of the methods we described in the previous chapter. We can draw in this way not only on our own experiences, but also on other people's to which we have access through listening to or reading their accounts.

All the different kinds of *empirical* research, including action research, are based on experiences. Traditionally great importance is attached to profound *reflection* and *verification*. However, experiences can only be verified if they are not unique, but accessible to the researcher and others again and again. Experiences can be verified in different ways:

1 if the event the experiences refer to can be repeated;
2 if the event has left some traces, independent of the researcher, which can be investigated by the researcher and others;
3 if the researcher has used some means to represent the experiences (for

example in a research notebook or on audio or video-recording) and these representations are available to the researcher and others independent of the original context of time and place.

In action research, where we are dealing with human interactions in real situations rather than the laboratory it is complicated or impossible to repeat events (point 1), and in any case reflection takes more time than is generally available during an event, so researchers depend heavily on *data* that give *indirect* access to events (points 2 and 3). Data have two important features:

- They are material traces or representations of events and therefore are givens in a physical sense (from the Latin *datum* for 'the thing given'), which can be passed on, stored and made accessible to many people.
- They are regarded as relevant by a researcher, providing evidence with respect to the issue investigated.

What are or are not data depends on the research question. If the research concerns pupils' use of language, their written work or a recording of their verbal utterances will be important data; if the research is about interaction with patients or clients, clinical notes may be the most important data source.

Characteristics of data

Three characteristics of data are important:

1 Data can only represent events selectively: the audio-recording preserves verbal utterances from the area within range of the microphone for the period of time during which it is in operation; the questionnaire gets the opinions people give in answer to the questions asked. During the process of becoming data, either by being produced (for example, photos, transcriptions of interviews, memos) or by being selected (for example, pupils' writing, work sheets, school rules), some aspects of reality are stressed as important and others are neglected. To some extent this happens on purpose, as part of interpreting the research question or choosing a particular methodology; to some extent it happens accidentally, as a result of the researcher's unconscious prejudices, or some known or unknown bias of the methods chosen, or some restriction in the research situation (for example, the timetable making it impossible to interview a particular pupil, patient or client).

2 Whatever is produced or selected as data depends on interpretative processes by the researcher. The extent to which the researcher's interpretation contributes to the production of data can vary considerably. It is very slight if the researcher selects existing material as data because they seem important to the research question (for example a

letter to patients from the clinic selected as data for research into home-clinic links). But when the researcher transforms personal experiences into data, the degree of interpretation is much larger. For example, to produce a memo, an event is observed, interpreted (that is con-ceptualized) and finally recorded in written form. Data coming into being like this are events that have been interpreted by the researcher; that means the events are reconstructed, even if only by being described in terms of meanings already familiar to the researcher. In that respect experiences that have been recorded by the researcher are theory-laden.

3 Finally data are *static* because of their material character. Events lose their dynamic quality and cannot develop any more.

The following example will illustrate these three features. Let us assume that a social worker who is studying her own practice decides to audio-record a group therapy session. By choosing this method of data collection she has already expressed a certain view of the situation investigated: it is seen as a linguistic interaction, with less importance placed on non-verbal communication or the thoughts of the people involved in the situation. By placing the audio-recorder a certain section of reality is chosen and marked as meaningful in understanding the situation: the audio-recorder's position may pick up more of her talk, or of the clients'. The recorder itself embodies a specific observation theory in that, depending on the type of microphone, sound is picked up within a nearer or farther radius, with the consequence that the observed reality is selected differently. What has been recorded can be listened to again and again, but the relationship between social worker and client that has been made storable by the recording may have developed in the meantime: the results of the analysis based on this material may still be historically interesting, but may have become unimportant in under-standing the current situation.

We can summarize: data typically provide us, as researchers, with access to the world external to ourselves that we are investigating. We take data as information about that world, but we must bear in mind that they are not the world itself, but only its traces. They are always chosen or constructed from a certain perspective, and are therefore – to varying extents – theory-laden. This would not matter if we could make ourselves aware of all the theories, prejudices and biases involved in collecting and selecting data. However, we can only be aware of some of the theoretical perspectives contributing to the research process, while others remain unnoticed or *tacit*, although they still shape our research activities. In any case, it is important for us to acknowledge and be aware of the way these forces shape our research. The practical consequences of these con-siderations are small but, at the same time, wide-ranging. As our insights are built on data containing theoretical assumptions that, to some extent, are tacit:

- we must be modest in our claims and make clear the preliminary and hypothetical nature of our insights;
- we must re-examine and further develop the situational understanding we have gained (see the section on criteria for judging quality in action research in this chapter).

M18 THE LADDER OF INFERENCE

An aid to understanding the degree of reliability of data is the 'ladder of inference' (Argyris *et al.* 1985). This ladder consists of three rungs or steps to be climbed one after another – like a normal ladder. Each step of the ladder symbolizes data of a certain quality. Each step differs in the extent to which data are accessible to examination by people other than the researcher.

The first step of the ladder symbolizes data that can be regarded as relatively unambiguous representations of events, as they are accessible to observation. For example, with the help of an audio-recording we can check if the teacher has uttered the words quoted on the first step in Figure 5.1. The second step gives an interpretation of the teacher's words, which is shared by everyone in a defined cultural domain. We assume that the teacher's utterance "John, your work is poor" would be interpreted as criticism by everyone in our cultural context. The third step contains individual interpretations, which are probably not shared by everyone because they contain a number of additional assumptions.

From step-to-step the likelihood increases that different observers will interpret the same event differently. In order to avoid differences in the interpretation of events, we recommend the following:

- Start by examining the reliability of data on the lowest step of the ladder: identifying which data are factual observations, accessible to cross-checking by others.
- Move on to examining the reliability of interpretations on the second step, asking yourself if you are sure that they will bear scrutiny by others.
- The first two steps have provided relatively "hard data". Only now are you ready to proceed to the third step for further, more individual interpretations and conclusions.

You can approach it the other way around if you want to judge the

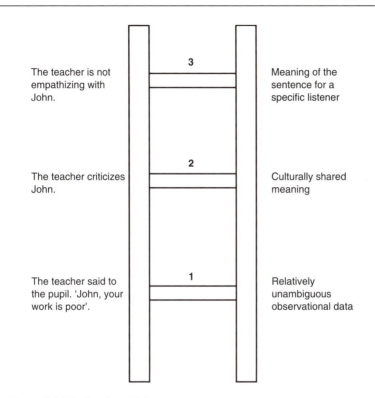

The teacher is not empathizing with John.

Meaning of the sentence for a specific listener

The teacher criticizes John.

Culturally shared meaning

The teacher said to the pupil. 'John, your work is poor'.

Relatively unambiguous observational data

Figure 5.1 The ladder of inference

reliability of an interpretation on step 3 ('the teacher is undermining John's confidence'),

- try to get information about step 1 (what was said or done?);
- find out if the interpretation of the data on step 2 will bear scrutiny by others;
- then it is useful to continue the analysis, possibly identifying more than one alternative interpretation at the third step.

The ladder of inference serves three functions (Argyris *et al.* 1985: 56):

1 It enables a careful scrutiny of interpretations based upon data drawn from a particular event.
2 It clarifies the relationship between interpretations and more factual data.
3 It facilitates reflection on action, by allowing us to trace interpretations of actions to the events to which they refer.

Can we say that the typical means of generating knowledge in research is through the collection of data, and that this distinguishes research from other activities? Unfortunately, we cannot draw such a clear line between research and everyday life, for the following reasons:

1 Data (as material traces and representations of events) do have a central position in the research process, but research results are not only and perhaps not even primarily dependent on the data. They spring also:

- from the researcher's consciously formulated theories;
- from the researcher's tacit theories based upon personal experiences (for which there may be no evidence in the data);
- from the collective tacit theories of the researcher's professional culture (for which there may also be no evidence in the data).

In a similar way all daily routines (for example a nurse's work in a hospital or clinic) are governed by a mixture of conscious and currently unconscious knowledge (see Chapter 10).

2 Data also have a central place in our daily routines. For example, tests and other measures are used to gather data about our pupils, clients and patients to assess their current status and their progress.

We want to emphasize that data collection does not (and cannot) replace what we learn from everyday experience, but is based on it and should support it where this is useful. For example, data collection is particularly useful when we want to understand and cope with difficult situations in which we are not satisfied with our routine actions, or when we want to re-examine our practical knowledge, develop it and make it accessible to our colleagues (see also Chapter 10).

DATA COLLECTION METHODS

Before we provide some examples of data collection methods, we want to give some suggestions on how to develop a data collection plan. Too often action researchers haphazardly begin the collection of data without giving much thought to why they need a particular type of data, what they expect to get from it or even what impact the data collection process itself has on others. Asking people's opinions, especially in interviews, heightens their awareness of the issues under discussion and this is a form of action in its own right. It is also important to look at what types of data are readily available because they are generated as the normal part of your practice (what Emily Calhoun (1994) calls existing archival data) and data that you generate through surveys, interviews, audio and video-recording, and so on. Therefore, we suggest that you develop a data collection plan. It is important to remember that because of the organic nature of action research, your data collection plan will most likely change as you collect and analyze your data.

One way to develop a data collection plan is to first write down a statement of your problem, question, or needs. Then answer the following questions in order:

- What do you need to know to better understand your situation and make decisions about your practice?
- What types of data will provide you with the information that you need?
- What types of data are already available to you (existing archival sources and other artefacts)?
- What types of data do you need to generate?
- What instruments will you need to generate and collect data?

EXISTING ARCHIVAL DATA

Action researchers have access to a variety of existing material that can be used as data. This material can provide evidence of past events relevant to a research question. *Written documents* are the most obvious: for example-pupils', teachers', nurses', and social workers' written work; pupil attendance records and patient and client schedules; and grade, performance and medical records.

There is also *unwritten evidence*: for example, the appearance of a classroom after the pupils have left, the cover designs and binding of books as well as their state of repair, signs of wear on the furniture, participants' demeanors, and so on. Here are two suggestions of ways to collect and use these existing data.

M19 MAKING A DOSSIER

A dossier is a "collection of documents relating to a particular person or topic" (Encarta 1999). For example:

- A teacher can collect the work of a particular pupil in order to study his/her development (all the work, a selection of the best or an arbitrary selection).
- A social worker can keep records of appointments, types of sessions, phone calls and so on to document a particular case.
- Each pupil can be asked to make a representative selection of his/her schoolwork.
- A whole class could put together a dossier of its work: first collecting all of the work and then selecting what is relevant for the dossier.

- A practitioner can document his/her activities over the course of a day, a week or longer.

Here are two examples of using a dossier for research:

A French teacher wanted to study the mistakes most commonly made by low-achieving pupils in order to identify possible causes and develop teaching strategies to help overcome them. She collected the exercise books of a selected group of pupils and listed the mistakes they had made over the past three weeks. She then analyzed the kinds of mistakes, their context and frequency. The list provided clues to possible causes. She then handed out the list to the pupils and discussed it with them in order to get a more complete picture of specific causes and possible teaching strategies.

Jackie Bridges gives this example from nursing:

> I was working in a practice development role with nurses on a rehabilitation ward for older people. Nurses had expressed difficulty in looking after older patients with cognitive impairment such as dementia. I was interested to see what proportion of patients had this kind of problem, and so took a 'snap-shot' look at prevalence by reading through the medical and nursing documentation for all the patients on the ward at that time. 17 out of the 22 patients had cognitive impairment documented on admission to the ward, ranging from mild to severe and from acute to chronic. The nurses felt that this proportion of 77% remained more or less constant despite a high turnover of patients. This finding made the lack of support for nurses providing this type of care even more surprising.
>
> (Bridges *et al.* 2001: 33–4)

Dossiers are useful in many ways:

- as reference material to be used in discussions with pupils, patients and clients' family members or colleagues;
- as a data base for discussions on ways to improve work patterns;
- as a stimulus for pupils, patients or clients to reflect on their work and behaviors to become more aware of their participation in their education or development. This often has the effect of involving all participants in the research process, by raising their awareness of their own practice situation and increasing the care with which they carry out their work;
- family members who have access to this kind of dossier are better able to judge achievements, progress and difficulties.

M20 RECORDING AND MAKING USE OF CLUES

It is often easy to neglect available data because they are embedded in everyday routines. They are so "normal" that it is difficult to notice them and they seem too banal to be taken seriously. We can learn from Sherlock Holmes. The secret of his method lay in his ability to detect clues in the most inconspicuous things. Dr Watson had just bought a new surgery, choosing from two located in adjoining houses. Without even entering the building Sherlock Holmes congratulated him on his choice. He had discovered that the steps leading up to Watson's surgery were much more worn than those of the surgery next door.

Here is an example of how clues can be recorded and used in action research:

A teacher who was annoyed by pupils' careless treatment of the school furniture decided to carry out an investigation. He began by asking how the problem manifested itself. Where did it happen? How did it show itself? He began in "his" class and inspected the desks, the floor, the "designs" on the walls; then he inspected the halls, looking for signs of wear on the windowsills, graffiti. He took photos of what he saw, and he also took photos of places where similar furniture etc. was in good condition.

He used this data to start a discussion with the pupils in his class, not in order to "preach" but to find out their point of view and get more information about the situations in which damage occurred. This led to further speculation about contributory factors, such as how careless behavior was sanctioned: for example, many offences of this kind went unnoticed when older pupils were responsible but were punished when younger pupils were involved. He followed up with interviews to try to find out more about the reasons for the pupils' behavior.

Clues can be used in other ways. Jinny Hay has provided us with an example of how social work professionals use clues within their daily practice that become part of their action research:

Social care professionals use "clues" within clients' homes to build rapport and to open up new lines of conversation that offer new insights. For example, photos will offer the opportunity to ask about relatives and the relationships with the client. Music/the garden will offer the opportunity to explore existing hobbies and interests. All will help to build a picture of the persons and of their preferred lifestyle and current barriers to achieving what they aspire to.

Using existing data has some advantages over data collected through a contrived process. In most cases it has higher credibility because it is independent of the action researcher's activities. A further advantage is that it can often be collected relatively quickly. Finally it provides evidence of events that may not be accessible by other methods, including those activities that occur away from the researcher.

On the other hand, using existing data has some disadvantages. Often it contains much more information than necessary, making its analysis very time consuming. Furthermore, even if the data have not been influenced by the research process, there will have been other influences that often can no longer be reconstructed in sufficient detail. This makes interpretation difficult. Documents also contain mistakes, omissions, and prejudices, and can even be deliberately misleading: it is difficult to discover these flaws and to take them into account if the circumstances in which they came into being are no longer known. For these reasons it is important to combine this method with other methods of data collection.

OBSERVING AND DOCUMENTING SITUATIONS

Observation is a normal process. Every type of practice in which we work with other human beings entails continuously looking for answers to practical questions: What is happening here? What does this situation "demand" from me? What happens if I act in a certain way? Will the situation develop the way I expect? These observations are normally intuitive and unfocused. Professional action requires an "eye for the whole situation" (a kind of intuitive "seeing" that is different from a carefully aimed "looking"). However, this kind of "seeing" has some drawbacks as a basis for developing professional competence. For example:

- It is diffuse: the focus is wide-ranging, details get lost.
- It is biased: observations are acted upon with a minimum of reflection. There is a danger of seeing "what one wants to see".
- It is ephemeral: observations are only held in the memory for a very short period of time so that it is difficult to subject them to detailed examination.

These weaknesses can be overcome by using systematic observation procedures. Diffuseness can be countered by observing something specific for a particular purpose. Bias can be controlled if observation is used to test assumptions against the "reality". Finally the ephemeral nature of "seeing" can be overcome by using techniques that "capture" events. There is the possibility that we lose our vision of the situation as a whole, so it is important that systematic observation procedures should not replace intuitive "seeing", but rather complement and correct it.

Here are suggestions for trying out four ways of observing and documenting a situation: direct observation, audio-recording, photography and video-recording.

Direct observation

Direct observation of a situation does not require any technical tools except perhaps pencil or pen and paper. It can be thought of as a form of *participant observation*, a well-known method used by anthropologists and ethnographers (Fetterman 1989). Normally participant observers are professional researchers who become part of social situations in order to investigate them. However, for action researchers, their prime task is their practice, not observing. When action researchers observe their practice systematically, they are taking on a second task that sometimes fits in with their practice but may sometimes conflict with it (Wong 1995).

When your practice requires your full attention or emotional involvement, it is difficult to achieve the 'distance' necessary for systematic observation. There is strong pressure either to abandon the attempt or to introduce technical aids (e.g. audio-recordings). On the other hand, there are times when some form of systematic observation is possible: for example, when pupils, patients or clients are the principal actors in the situation.

The most important skill in observing is sensitivity to what is observed. Observers have to cope with a dilemma that is normally insoluble. On the one hand, reality is what is reconstructed from the observer's current understandings. On the other hand, reality has its own "stubborn" character that resists interpretation and reconstruction. This dilemma is only "solvable" by "double vision" – by being aware of one's assumptions and expectations and at the same time approaching each situation as if it were a totally new one (see Chapter 10). The temptation to make quick and simplistic assumptions about a situation based on one's own prejudices is very strong, particularly for a practitioner who is under pressure to take action.

In spite of these difficulties we believe that there are particular advantages in using direct observation as a method of data collection, in particular because it relates well to the complex processes of professional practice. In this section we first give some ideas about how to prepare to observe, we then turn to making records of observations and then to using others as observers of your practice situations.

Preparing to observe

Observation always involves selecting from a stream of events. So that this does not become a matter of chance, consider in advance the *what*, *why* and *when* of observation:

- *What* are you going to observe? Is it the sequence of events, a pupil's behavior or one specific aspect of your own behavior? The more limited the focus of observation, the more precisely it can be observed. However, the more limited the focus of observation, the more likely it is that the outcomes will only shed light on a small, possibly even minor, aspect of the original research question.
- *Why* are you carrying out the observation? What are the assumptions and expectations on which it is based? Observing is not merely registering what you see and hear, it is also a theoretical reconstruction of a situation. The observer's assumptions and expectations are theoretical tools for this reconstruction. They are his/her "pre-judices" (pre-judgments), but striving for objectivity in observing does not mean that prejudices can be completely avoided; rather they should be clarified as far as possible, so that the part they play in producing an understanding can be taken into account at the stage of inter- pretation.
- *When* will the observation be carried out, and how long will it take? It is particularly important for an action researcher to decide beforehand when it is likely to be possible to devote attention to observation.

The simple method suggested below is a useful way of preparing to observe, both to increase sensitivity and to focus the observation on a chosen research question.

M21 GETTING TUNED IN TO DOING OBSERVATIONS

1 First, write down the focus for your observation (for example, "the level of pupils' oral participation" or "the client's physical demeanor during a counselling session").
2 Write down what you would like to see in relation to this focus. (What kinds of evidence do you hope to get?)
3 Write down what you suspect you will probably observe (e.g. "Only A – if anybody at all – will ask a question without being asked"). In doing this try to be as precise as possible (e.g. "B is going to call out an answer without putting up her hand" instead of "B is going to behave badly").
4 Choose one of the expectations listed above that relates closely to your research question and that you expect to be able to observe during the time you have chosen.
5 Decide what is the best way of writing notes of some or all of your observations (during the lesson or afterwards).

Recording observations

The main problem in direct observation is keeping a record for later use. The record can be made either during or after the observation.

KEEPING A RECORD DURING THE OBSERVATION

Time is a rare commodity for practitioners. It may save time to use an *observation schedule* with predefined categories. In the observation each relevant event is then assigned to a category and thereby recorded.

Here is an example of what we mean:

As part of evaluating a new hospital-based clerical role (inter-professional care coordinators (IPCCs)), many of the staff, including the IPCCs, expressed an interest in a researcher shadowing the IPCCs at work, in order to find out what activities they were involved in and look at the similarities and differences in practice between the four IPCCs. I observed three IPCCS for three days each, using an unstructured record writing down as much of what I saw and heard as possible. A second researcher was then allocated to observe the fourth IPCC and I wanted to make sure that comparisons would be possible between our records of observations. So I looked at my records for patterns and saw that a series of implicit questions had guided many of my observations:

- *Which IPCC?*
- *Who are they interacting with?*
- *Who initiated the interaction?*
- *What sort of interaction is it? Telephone? Face-to-face? Documentation?*
- *What are they talking about?*
- *What activity is the IPCC engaged in? E.g. giving information, gathering information, giving orders, taking orders, and making decisions?*

(After Bridges et al. 2001)

A second example is of a teacher who kept a record of her interactions with her pupils.

A teacher thought that she might be paying more attention to pupils in certain sections of the classroom than to pupils in other sections. She decided to keep a record of the pupils she called on and to note in each case whether or not they had given any signal that they wanted to be called upon. She made a plan of the seating arrangement in the class and marked a sign against the name each time a pupil was called on (e.g. a "+" for "called after having given a sign" and "−" for "called without having given a sign"). After a while a pattern began to emerge on the plan. During the observation she was already becoming aware that she called on some pupils more often than others. She responded by distributing her attention more evenly. Although this "distorted" the result it served the purpose of her investigation.

This example illustrates the essential elements in using an observation scheme of this kind:

- Categories must exclude each other: e.g. calling a pupil with/without a signal.
- There needs to be a protocol or instrument of some kind on which observations are recorded.
- There have to be rules for recording observations. In the example given above the rule was: whenever the teacher called a pupil she marked a sign against the name on the class-seating plan.

The categories in the example can be related to the observed situation quickly and with a minimum of interpretation. This is very important if observations are to be recorded reliably without unduly disturbing the progress of a lesson.

Pupils can be asked to help with simple observation tasks. For example, an English teacher asked one of his pupils to mark each pupil's utterances on a class list during ten lessons. Afterwards the teacher compiled the results and found that the number of utterances during these ten lessons varied from pupil to pupil between 12 and 107. He was then able to talk to the three pupils with the lowest number of utterances and try to identify possible reasons and develop ways of increasing their participation.

There are a large number of schedules for direct observation (see Hook 1995).[1] However, we believe that it usually works better for action researchers to design their own schedules, matching them closely to the purpose and subject of their observation. The existing schedules are generally designed for use by observers who are not practitioners and do not have to cope with any other demands in the situation. Consequently, they are often extensive and may require observers to be trained in how to distinguish categories correctly. By designing your own observation schedules you can avoid these disadvantages. However, as the examples show, observation schedules provide only relatively thin information. They are most useful for an initial survey, which is then followed up by other methods (e.g. memos of the observation, see Chapter 2).

MAKING A RECORD AFTER THE OBSERVATION

It is usually much easier for action researchers to make a record of the observation after the event, even though this may mean that some details will be lost. In most cases you will not be able to write a full record immediately after the observation. However, the most important observations should be recorded as soon as possible, at least in the form of brief notes (perhaps in the form of a data summary, as described in M32) to make it possible to produce a fuller reconstruction at a later time.

One of the most important methods for recording observations is the "memo" (see Chapter 2). If the observations recorded after a lesson do not relate to single events but follow a research question over a longer period of time they will develop a diary-like character (see also Chapter 2). Other methods are suggested later in this chapter.

M22 VIGNETTES

A vignette is a story about an event that is striking or surprising. Here is an example told by a secondary teacher:

I decided to investigate the quantity and level of difficulty of homework given to members of my class (11-year-olds) and began talking to Benjamin in "tutorial time" one day. He was considered one of the less able children but he became very animated telling me about making "sugar volcanoes" in Science: "We got . . . some aluminum foil . . . and we made a column cone-shaped with a pencil . . . put it like a hole inside, the shape of a volcano, and poured some sugar into it and put them under the Bunsen burners . . . and like lava come out! It was all different colors". But he was worried about Science homework: "I don't know if it's effort . . . it's hard to finish all my homework and that . . .". I asked if he could turn to anyone for help and he said he sometimes asked his Dad, but really his Dad expected him to get his homework done himself. When he came in from playing at about 9 pm he tried to do it in the bedroom he shared with his older brother who always had the TV on. It seemed that although he enjoyed Science, the work was too difficult for him, especially as his home background was not supportive. But then he said something else: "If I get homework before break I do it at break, or I do it at dinner time. So I don't have to do so much homework at home. I get confused and that if I get a lot of homework. Like the last two lessons at the end of the day, I can't do that at school, so I take that home and do it. . . . I get confused. . . . I remember quite a lot of it then, at school, see it's not so long away from that lesson. See when you've been out at play and that you forget some". Suddenly I realized that I had completely misunderstood the nature of his problem. It wasn't so much that he couldn't understand the work as that he couldn't remember what he was supposed to do. What I needed to do was to help him write down his homework and get him to practice reading it aloud before he went home.

Vignettes usually arise from surprising experiences rather than planned observations. Sometimes these are referred to as "critical incidents". The term "critical incident" originally comes from history where it refers to some significant turning point or change in a person, institution or social phenomenon (Tripp 1993: 29). In reference to one's practice, critical incidents are "mostly straightforward accounts of very commonplace events" that are critical in the sense that they are "indicative of underlying trends, motives and structures" (Tripp 1993: 25).

Because things have not happened as expected, the experience, or critical incident, stands out from the stream of familiar events. There is a discrepancy between expectation and reality that can help us to develop a new practical theory as the basis for changes in our practice. (See the discussion of discrepancies in Chapter 3 and M2.) Recording a surprising event as a vignette saves it from oblivion and makes it available for further analysis and discussion (perhaps in your research group, with your critical friend or with pupils, clients or patients). Writing vignettes is not difficult and is a good way of recording first hand experiences by describing situations and kinds of behavior.

A vignette should contain the following:

- a description of where and when it occurred and the people concerned;
- enough background information to give the context of the event;
- an account of the event: it should be written in a narrative form; important utterances (statements, answers, questions) made by the main participants should be quoted exactly in order to retain the authenticity and immediacy of the situation. The sequence of actions should be clear so that they can be easily imagined in their context;
- some commentary giving the observer spontaneous understanding of the situation. It is important that this is clearly distinguished from the account of the event.

M23 SELECTIVE OBSERVATION USING TOPIC CARDS

This method of recording observations is directed by carefully chosen questions:

1 Write down on about ten separate cards some issues about which you want to collect data.

2 At the end of the day shuffle the pack and deal two or three cards. Reflect on what has happened during the day in relation to these issues and write observation notes for each in your research journal. This should take no more than 10 to 15 minutes.
3 On each subsequent day deal a further two or three cards until you have written observation notes about each issue. Then start again from the beginning, possibly reshuffling the pack so that you take the issues in a different order.

What is special about this method is the combination of systematic and random elements of observation. During the day you know all the issues that may become the subject for observation notes, but you do not know which ones will be chosen when the cards are dealt at the end of the day. This serves to raise the level of readiness and sensitivity in observing. As time goes on connections emerge between observations. Some issues can be dropped if they prove unproductive and new ones can be included, for example, by splitting some of the existing issues into two (see Hook 1995).

Using other people as observers

As paradoxical as it may sound, most people know too much to make good observers in their own situations. Observation requires a certain "naivety", a "stranger's view" (Rumpf 1986), an ability to see the unexpected and uncommon in daily routines and in what is considered "normal". As an action researcher you need to distance yourself from the situation.

Every practice situation can be seen from different perspectives:

- *The practitioner's perspective* – the practitioner is responsible for organizing what goes on in the classroom, clinic or office, and will tend to want to judge his/her work as more or less successful, according to particular aims.
- *The pupils', patients', or clients' perspectives* – they may see themselves in a number of roles, for example as partners (or opponents) of the practitioner in organizing and enacting what goes on.
- *Another person's perspective* – an outsider will want to experience the situation and understand it.

Knowing the perspectives of others helps practitioners to distance themselves from the situation. By acting as an observer, someone from your research group or a critical friend can provide a new perspective on your situation, if only by having different "blind spots" from you.

In addition, someone who is not actively involved in the practice at that moment is able to observe more precisely, having time to do it without any responsibilities. Such an observer has access to information that is not easily accessible to the action researcher and that may, on occasion, be hard to handle. For that reason you need to choose an observer you can trust. Once trust is established you should not be content with trivial comments but ask the observer to describe in detail what he/she has seen. If you ask specific questions and/or define your expectations before the observation (e.g. What does A do in the course of the lesson?, or, I expect A will only write down calculations copied from the blackboard) it is easier for the observer to focus attention on the events that are important to you and write observation notes that will be genuinely useful.

Ask the observer to give you written notes as soon as possible, and take time to look at these and consider what additional information you need. Writing notes requires the observer to impose an order on impressions and some things may have got lost in the process. If you talk to the observer about particular points, keep a certain distance and don't apologize for things that were "bad" in your opinion, or try to justify yourself. If your perception deviates from the observer's, don't engage in any arguments (except perhaps to provide counter-examples without any comment) because the purpose is not to win an argument but to understand and learn as much as possible about another person's observations and interpretations. You may find it useful to look at the rules for analytic discourse (M9).

M24 NOTES ON OBSERVATIONS

What is important in writing good observation notes? Here are some suggestions, modified after Grell and Grell (1979):

1 Describe what happens as precisely as possible:

   - what people say – use quotations;
   - what people do – be as precise as possible.

2 Use abbreviations for words that occur frequently (e.g. we use T = teacher, P = pupil not identified by name, PP = several pupils, initials for identified pupils, B = blackboard, HW = homework). If there are more than a few people involved draw a sketch of the layout of the room and where people are located. Label the people and items so that you know who and what they are later.

3 Check your notes after the observation in order to correct mistakes, make things clearer and add additional remarks. Possible additions are:

- your feelings about specific events (friendly/unfriendly, encouraging/discouraging);
- ideas that came into your mind, e.g. things that might have been done differently.

4 Intensive observation for more than 30 minutes is very exhausting, so it is a good idea to alternate intensive phases with phases that demand less attention (e.g. 5 minutes trying to note as much as possible followed by 5 minutes taking brief, summarizing notes). One way of changing the demands on your concentration is to change the focus (e.g. observing one person in depth and the rest of the group more cursorily).

5 There's a need to distinguish between descriptive and interpretive reporting. Descriptive reporting describes the behavior "as it is" (what has been said and done) with as little explanation, judgment, and evaluation as possible. This kind of reporting refers to the lowest step of "the ladder of inference" (see M18). Interpretive reporting clarifies the effect of an event or a piece of behavior on the observer (the feelings that were evoked, how he/she understood it, etc.)

6 A helpful way of ensuring that you record both descriptions and interpretations is to fold your paper down the middle and use the left-hand side for descriptions and the right-hand side for interpretations and personal responses.

M25 QUICK METHODS FOR DATA COLLECTION

There are many different ways that you can quickly collect data from participants (students, clients, patients and so on) during or at the end of an activity or session. These include the "2+2" (see Chapter 3), the "Plus – Minus – Question Mark", the "Minute Paper", the "Muddiest Point" and the "RSQC2". We briefly describe each below, followed by a method for debriefing the information.

- 2+2 Participants are asked to briefly jot down on a piece of paper two compliments about the activity or session, and two suggestions for improving it.

- *Plus – Minus – Question Mark* Participants are asked to make individual notes to three questions (3–5 minutes).

  PLUS
  - What did I like?
  - What did I learn?

  MINUS
  - What did I dislike?
  - What was hard to understand?

  QUESTION MARK
  - What was left open?
  - What kind of questions arose?

- *Minute Paper* The Minute Paper is often used at the end of a class. The teacher asks pupils to answer these two questions: "What was the most important thing that you learned in this class?" and "What important question remains unanswered?" (Angelo and Cross 1993).
- *Muddiest Point* The Muddiest Point can be thought of as an abbreviated Minute Paper. Participants are simply asked to respond to the question, "What was the muddiest point in the class?" (Angelo and Cross 1993: 29).
- *RSQC2* This technique consists of five steps: Recall, Summarize, Question, Connect, and Comment. At the beginning of the class or session the participants are asked to make a list of what they recall were the most important, meaningful, or useful points from the most recent session. They are then asked to summarize as many of the points as they can into one sentence. The next step is for the participants to write down any questions that remain or have come up from the previous session. In the fourth step the participants are asked to try to connect their list of main points with what they believe is the major goal of their participation in the sessions. Finally, they are asked to write an evaluative comment about the class or session. It helps to provide them with sentence stems to complete, such as "What I liked the most/the least was . . ." or "What I found the most useful/least useful was . . ."

  (Angelo and Cross 1993: 396)

Debriefing the data collection activity

The easiest thing to do after the participants have completed the data collection activity is to collect their answers and analyze them later. You may, however, find it more useful to debrief with the participants immediately following the activity. The method that we suggest for doing this provides relatively detailed feedback and stimulates participants to reflect on quality criteria. It also guarantees a kind of anonymity because only group results are communicated. You should allow at least 25 to 30 minutes to tap the potentials of this method.

- *Phase 1* Participants are asked to exchange their notes with two to four neighbors and to identify and discuss similarities and differences (*c.* 5 to 10 minutes).
- *Phase 2* From each of these small groups one member communicates the results. It is advisable first to call up any positive statements, whereby each group names only one. After several rounds of positive statements, the negatives are called up and finally the neutral statements or suggestions. The session leader writes them on the blackboard or makes personal notes. In this phase the statements are not commented on.
- *Phase 3* The session leader asks for clarifications if necessary and comments on the statements.

M26 SHADOW STUDY

When an observer works alongside a practitioner there is the opportunity of carrying out a more precise investigation by using some additional methods of data collection, for example *shadow study*. In a shadow study the observation is concentrated *on* one individual or a small group and carried out over a longer period of time. Alternatively, the observation can be concentrated *on the experiences that an individual or small group encounters*, so to speak looking at the world through their eyes. The observer shadows an individual or group of pupils, patients, or clients, colleagues or the action researcher, for perhaps a day or more. An example of a shadow study from health care is given below.

In another example, Robinson (1984) observed a child during her first three days at school from 20 minutes before school started until 20 minutes after the end of the last session, and made detailed notes. His study showed that at first the child was keen to start "working" from the first minute of the day, but because she was made to do "admin" and boring repetitive tasks her enthusiasm quickly cooled. According to Robinson's interpretation: "Alienation begins as soon as pupils arrive at school." The study resulted in the headmaster and teachers restructuring the beginning of the school year.

While carrying out a shadow study the observer should be as close as possible to those being observed without being seen as a part of the group and without being involved in the pupils' work. However, a shadow study does not need to be carried out covertly. There may be occasions, for example, when observing small children, when the observer may wish to remain "hidden", but in many cases it is more ethical to discuss the study beforehand with the person to be shadowed and seek permission. This may also open up opportunities for a post-observation interview.

Audio-recording observations

Audio-recordings capture the sounds of a situation. Compared with direct observation some information is lost in an audio-recording: in particular, the surroundings and all non-verbal communication (movements, facial expressions, gestures, etc.). However, a more complete record is made of the sounds than is possible in direct observation. There are two ways of using audio-recordings:

- recording complete activities or sessions, to give an overview or to help in identifying possible research questions;
- recording interactions that are narrowly limited in time, and carefully selected to throw light on a chosen research question (e.g. a teacher explaining a concept to one child, a health care professional explaining continued care with patients, a session with the whole class revising a concept taught in a previous lesson or a small group carrying out an investigation).

An example: a recording of a pupil-pupil interaction

After having dedicated three maths lessons to the topic "movement tasks" a teacher wanted to investigate how pupils grapple with such problems on their own. The joint work of two pupils on a set of relevant tasks was audio-recorded. In the following transcript two students (Anton and Bernard) are working on this problem:

Peter has to travel 16 km to the next village. His speed is 4 km/h and he leaves at 8 o'clock. Peter's grandfather has left half an hour earlier, as he can only walk half as fast as Peter. Where is Peter going to meet him?

B: *Hmm, difficult, isn't it?*
A: *That is, Peter and grandfather . . .*
B: *and Peter*

A: *v, t,* and *s.* Speed of Peter was 4, the grandfather walks half as fast, therefore 2, the time . . .

B: is *x.*

A: half an hour before Peter . . . grandfather is *x,* Peter is normally *x;* Peter is *x+* . . .

B: *x+?*

A: +30 plus 1/2, plus 1/2 . . . and the distance?

B: 16.

A: But you don't know that. It's *s.*

B: Why?

A: You do not know the stretch, where he meets him.

B: But the stretch that the grandfather . . .

A: Where is Peter going to meet him? We don't know that. Or do you know that? I don't know it. (5 sec.) Hmm. I must think it over. Now you say something!

B: That is not correct. The stretch is 16.

A: But how do you know that?

B: The stretch is always 16. That's what the text says.

A: Look, why does it say, "Where is Peter going to meet him?" Well, the point where he is going to meet him, the time, that is what we would have to determine more exactly. Hmm. (5 sec.) Now let us think it over. You know what we could also calculate? Let's calculate how long – yes, that's it – let's calculate how long it takes Peter to go these 16 km per hour, these 16 kilometers. We have already got that. Now let us calculate how long grandfather, yes, it must take him twice as long

B: 16. It takes Peter 4 hours, the grandfather 8 hours.

A: Exactly. Yes, yes.

B: Mmm.

A: and the what's-his-name, Peter and the grandfather . . . speed is 4 and 2. The time . . .

B: Er, is *t.* We have got that, the time.

A: We already know the time he meets him. Eight hours the grandfather, so it takes Peter 4 hours. Seven and a half hours it takes the grandfather.

B: He has left half an hour earlier.

A: And the way was 16 km. So, when did he meet him? After 4 hours, so after 4 hours Peter met him.

B: But he could have met him before yet.

A: No, after 4 hours he met him. Look, this is A and this is B. A and B. 16 km. (A draws.) Half of it is 8 km, and 8 km there as well. Now let us have a look whether he would have met him before or after those 8 km. So if he walks 8 km, it takes Peter 2 hours. It takes the grandfather 4, 3 1/2 hours. (Murmur.)

B: Aha.

A: So 8 is grandfather's way and Peter's way. But they do not walk towards each other. If they had gone towards each other, we would have had it. . . . 2 km per hour, time is half of it, and so the way is . . .

B: 2 times 1/2 is . . .

A: s = v x t, two times 0.5 is . . .

B: 2

A: . . . 6 minutes. It takes him 6 minutes for half an hour. But that's not correct. He walks 6 km in half an hour.

B: 1 km.

A: But if he walks 18 then . . .

B: In half an hour he walks 1 km.

We recommend that you take a second look at the transcript so that you can see the richness of information it contains. As an illustration we put together some conclusions that we arrived at from reading the transcript (further information on the analysis of such texts can be found in Chapter 6):

- The pupils do not even try to find out what the task is about exactly.
- They concentrate on irrelevant information instead (e.g. the length of the whole trip) and carry out routines such as "You know what we could also calculate?" without checking if they are useful for the solution of the problem.
- They do not succeed in keeping separate the procedural steps, therefore they fall back to the same moves again and again, even if they have proved not to be useful.
- They seem to have difficulties in differentiating the concepts of time, distance and speed (at least with respect to the relationship between meaning and symbol), e.g. "grandfather is x, Peter normally is x".
- In some passages they appear to have difficulties with very common understandings such as "He walks 6 km in half an hour" (which "obviously" is impossible).
- Common understandings and formulas learned in school (everyday logic and mathematical schemata) seem to get in each other's way.

Usually, people only remain conscious that they are being recorded for a short time, especially if it happens frequently. However, they are likely to be a bit less communicative than usual at first. The extent to which a situation is changed by an audio-recording also depends on how the pupils, patients or clients have been prepared in advance, how important they believe the recording to be and whether or not they think the purpose is worthwhile.

Technical suggestions

At the time of writing, small and inexpensive digital audio-recorders have appeared on the market. They take up very little room and their sound quality is excellent. The quality of the recording is important and it can be improved greatly with the use of an external microphone. An audio-recorder can be slipped into a pocket of the action researcher or someone else participating in the activity, and the microphone can be clipped to the person's shirt. Audio-recorders can be moved around with the researcher or placed on a table near the group to be recorded. To record the whole event rather than particular individuals, we recommend that you use a high-quality microphone, perhaps suspended from an overhead light.

Much of what we do in our practice is unique to the time and place so it is important to make sure that the recorder is working (batteries fresh or charged and microphone switched on). Afterwards, if using a tape-recorder, label the tape immediately (place, date, class, topic). You may find it useful to write a brief note to yourself highlighting the main points of interest so that you can locate this tape quickly when you need it (see M32). If using a digital recorder, we recommend that you record a brief introduction stating the date, time, location and other main points of interest. You should download the digital recording to your computer as soon as possible and give the file a name that clearly identifies it. It can help to create folders for similar recordings.

Suggestions for transcribing recordings

It is easy to make an audio-recording and it actually takes very little time. The problems only start afterwards when you try to make use of the information. If you decide simply to listen to the recording, you will need to play it to yourself two or three times (preferably making brief notes) before you will be able to make any sensible use of the data.

For detailed study it is worth transcribing parts of the recording, although this is very time-consuming. Good-quality recorders with head-phones and foot-operated switches (transcription machines) for playing the tape help to save time. There is free or inexpensive software that mimics tape transcription machines, which facilitates the transcription of digital recordings. Because it takes so long, only relatively short extracts should be transcribed unless you are lucky enough to have some secretarial support. Recently there have been great improvements in the accuracy of voice recognition software, which could aid in the transcription process.

M27 PARTIAL TRANSCRIPTION OF RECORDINGS

An economical way of making good use of audio-recordings is to transcribe selected passages. We recommend the following steps:

1 Listen to the whole recording to get an overview.
2 Listen a second time and make brief notes of the structure: give each individual scene or phase of the recorded situation a catch-word and note the corresponding numbers on the counter so that you can quickly relocate the passages.
3 On the basis of these notes select the sections that are important and relevant to the research question and transcribe these fully.

There is the tendency for people to leave out the first and, some-times, the second of these three steps under time-pressure. How-ever, these "savings" can cost a lot of time afterwards and reduce the quality of the research. The first two steps are an important part of the process of constructing theory from the data. They also structure the work and enable sensible choices to be made about how best to reduce the effort expended on transcribing.

It can save a lot of time and space to use abbreviations and annotations when transcribing recordings. If you are using a computer to transcribe, you may even want to use features such as AutoText to automate the typing of common words or phrases. Here is a list of examples of abbreviations and annotations we use to save time and space when transcribing. You could adapt these as convenient to you. What is important is to have a system that is quick to use and consistent, so you know exactly what abbreviations mean when you come to read the transcript.

T	teacher
Ca	Caroline (named pupil)
P	unidentified pupil
PP	several pupils
(inaud.)	inaudible
(Let's add the 3?)	words guessed because difficult to hear
(surprised)	transcriber's note of non-verbal data (e.g. tone, laughter) or summary of an untranscribed passage
(. . .)	words or phrases omitted
. . .	short pause
(pause, 6 secs)	long pause (in this case 6 seconds)
this point	emphasized by stressing the word
as – a – result	spoken slowly

M28 OBSERVATION PROFILES

In an observation profile notes are recorded on a two-dimensional chart using criteria that closely refer to the research question(s).

The example in Figure 5.2 was drawn up by a teacher who was researching how to organize role-play. The profile has a horizontal axis, dividing the lesson into phases chronologically (before, start, rehearsal etc.). The vertical axis sets out the things you are interested in looking at (children's activity, concentration level).

Profiles like these help with recording observations after the lesson, as the blanks on the profile stimulate the memory. Observation profiles can also be useful if another person takes the role of observer. By giving a profile to the observer, a teacher can indicate what he/she considers to be important. Profiles can also be used when analyzing transcripts of lessons and interviews.

Photography

"A picture paints a thousand words." This is an exaggeration, at least in relation to action research, but nonetheless photographs capture aspects of situations that, although they can be observed, are more fleeting and more easily missed than verbal utterances.

What is the value of photographs for action researchers?

We have already discussed photographs as part of M14. However, they can be used throughout an action research project in a number of ways:

- to supplement observation notes or audio-recordings of a situation: photographs bring back a holistic impression of what took place and where;
- as an aid to studying non-verbal aspects of situations and events;
- as a means of raising questions and stimulating ideas to find a starting point for research.

Photos are most valuable when used in conjunction with other sources of data (especially interviews and audio-recordings). They can also provide access to other data – for instance, photographs make good starting points for interviews – participants may be stimulated to talk by the concrete character of pictures. "Tell me about what you were doing when this photograph was taken" has the advantage of being a fairly specific question while not being a leading question.

	Before	Start	Rehearsal	Performance	Discussion	Clearing up
My activity	Informal chat. Some direction of activity re collection of equipment.	Semi-didactic discussion/ lecture to ascertain the comprehension of particular part.	Helping with ideas and problems with equipment. Conveying information. Encouraging activity among those reluctant.	Watching. Helping with odd equipment and queries. Altering what happened by passing written messages to particular people.	Adding to ideas already brought up by Ros. Encouraging new ideas from kids. Helping to take vote on idea for next week.	Seeing that equipment put back, that room left tidy. Listening with half an ear to other ideas.
Children's activity	Seating themselves. Talking. Making enquiries as to the nature of the afternoon's activity. Moving about. Slow flow of children into classroom.	Some listening. Some restlessly whispering. Some quietly carrying on with written work.	Heavily involved in preparing their ideas physically and mentally.	Watching with a high degree of intensity. Acting out their ideas. Janice and Susan acting as a link. Using me and Ros to confirm ideas. Acting on messages.	Quiet, controlled but very lively interest and contribution.	Some taking equipment back, some helping to clear up. A milling around and breakdown of activity.
Noise level	Fairly high	Low but mumbly	Very high	Extremely quiet except for actors. Quiet talk at breaks	Moderate	fairly high
No. of children	–	20 rally involved. 6–7 uninvolved	All except 3–4 opters out	All – either as audience or actors	All	

Figure 5.2 Observation profile

Source: Adapted from Walker and Adelman (1975: 22–3)

Taking photographs in a practice situation can be disruptive, but this can be minimized. It may help if the action researcher – or one of the participants – takes the photographs, rather than a visitor. Clearly, everyone in the practice situation needs to know why the photographs are being taken, and how they will be used. Eventually they will come to see being photographed as a routine. Making the photographs available afterwards and discussing them with participants can further reduce any nervousness. If the photographer is not the action researcher it is very important for him/her to explain the purpose of the photographs carefully beforehand.

We began this section with the saying, "A picture paints a thousand words". In actuality, a picture evokes not only many words, but also many interpretations of what it illustrates. We suggest, for photos that you believe have special meaning or significance, that you make explicit which "thousand words" you believe the picture "paints". You can then compare your interpretation with those of members of your research group or your critical friend.

Technical suggestions

The quality of photographs mainly depends on the quality of the camera. It is important to be able to take photographs unobtrusively and without any delay. The ease of use of most digital cameras makes them ideal for use in action research and allows for you and your pupils, patients or clients to see the photographs instantly. Flash, whether with traditional or digital cameras is obtrusive and should be avoided. A fast film can be used without flash with a traditional camera, but with a digital camera it may be best to use a tripod to avoid "camera shake".

As soon as possible after taking the photograph a data summary should be made (see M32) including a brief description and comments on the situation in which the photograph was taken. This contextual information is essential because the "frozen frame" nature of a photograph provides no information on what came before and after. After being transferred to your computer, photographs should be labeled immediately (place, date, class, topic) and any necessary additions or changes made to the data summary.

Making video-recordings

At first sight video-recordings combine the advantages of audio-recording and direct observation as well as providing a record of movement. However, they also combine the disadvantages of both. The main advantage is that a relatively holistic record is made of the situation – seen from the perspective of the camera. By representing the sequence of events in time video-recordings can make the context and causal relationships more accessible than other methods of data collection. Behavior patterns become visible, including the relationship between verbal and non-verbal behavior (audio-recordings are actually better for analysis of verbal patterns alone). Video-recordings are also an excellent way of presenting a situation to others to open up discussion.

Video-recordings can be misleading because they give the appearance of being a complete record of events when in fact they are highly selective (the camera has been pointed in one direction and there is no indication of periods of time when it has *not* been recording).

Making good use of video-recordings takes a lot of time. A careful analysis concentrating on events that appear to be essential in terms of the research question requires repeated playing of the tape. Transcribing extracts (see M27) is more time-consuming and technically ponderous than transcribing audio-recordings because pictures and sound together contain a lot of information and this makes it necessary to spend time sifting useful data from much of which is irrelevant.

If someone is operating the camera it is possible to use a range of shots, including close-ups and panning. However, it is usually counter-productive if an attempt is made to imitate the conventions of television. For the action researcher a broader view of the situation can be much more informative than a face that fills the screen "as on TV". Sometimes a fixed camera is sufficient, positioned on a tripod at the (window) side of the room and allowed to run for the whole session without pause. It can be focused on a whole area of the room, on a group of participants or on one participant. Recordings of this kind make rather boring viewing for people not involved, but they provide a more complete record of the session for purposes of analysis or discussion.

Sound is also a problem with video-recordings. The radius of the camera microphones is usually too small to record a lesson involving a whole class, so an additional high-quality microphone is necessary. The positioning of the camera will depend on what is being researched, e.g. focused on a group of pupils if group work is the subject of investigation. Afterwards the tape should be labeled immediately (location, time, subject, topic of investigation) and a data summary made, as with audio-recordings.

The ethical considerations discussed later in this chapter, which are always important in collecting data, are more sharply focused when using video, because the apparently more holistic and authentic record of events increases the chances of invading the privacy of individuals and representing them in a way that goes against their interests.

INTERVIEWING

Interviews have developed from everyday conversation. They give access to other people's perceptions, including crucially the thoughts, attitudes and opinions that lie behind their behavior. Behavior and its manifestations are ambiguous. Behaviors of our pupils, patients and clients may mean something quite different to them from what it does to us. Questioning, orally or in writing, offers more direct access to their meaning than other methods.

However, even this access is limited. The interview, at its best, only brings to light what the interviewee *thinks* – his/her interpretations at the time and under the circumstances of an interview. Even interviewees who wish to tell the "truth", will in some sense misinform the interviewer by "withholding" information: they cannot be conscious of all the motives for their behavior and are engaged in their own process of reconstruction in answering the questions.

Interviews as a relationship among people

Interviews are communications that aim at getting to know points of view, interpretations and meanings in order to gain greater understanding of a situation. The key precondition for the success of an interview is to make it clear to the interviewee that what he/she has to say will be important in at least one of two respects:

- What is important for the interviewer: the interviewee should feel that his/her views will "count" for the interviewer.
- What is important for the interviewee: the interviewee should believe that the outcomes of the interview may be useful for him/her.

How can we set up the right preconditions for an interview? Watzlawick *et al.* (1980) distinguish between two levels of communication: the level of content and the level of relationship. These levels influence each other: the relationship between two persons (e.g. mutual trust) influences their understanding of what is said (the content). Vice versa, the interpretation of what is said influences the relationship. The interviewer can exert influence on both levels, but only to a limited extent. If a teacher interviews a pupil the interdependence of the two levels can cause problems: teacher and pupils do not just build up a relationship during the interview, but have already developed various attitudes towards each other (on a continuum of trust and mistrust, affection and animosity). The same is true for social worker and client or nurse and patient. This framework of relationships provides the context in which the interview starts. It influences the way in which the interviewee understands what the interviewer says. For example, if the pupil sees the teacher as someone who is interested in answers to questions only insofar as they demonstrate what has been learnt (repeating what the teacher already knows), the interview questions will be viewed in that light: i.e. the pupil will not assume that the teacher really wants to know something he/she does not yet know, for example the pupil's own personal perceptions. This problem can be partly overcome by asking a third person to do the interviews (for example, someone from your research group or your critical friend) – someone the interviewee does not know, or know well, and who will therefore have a better chance of building a new relationship during the interview.

If relationships between the action researcher and his/her pupils, patients or clients are strained or difficult, a third person acting as interviewer can be indispensable in getting access to their perceptions and views. But, ultimately, the action researcher should do the interview him/herself. Although action research usually starts from the practitioner's research interest, in the course of time it should become a common concern of all participants in the practice situation. We do not only suggest this for ethical reasons, but also because it is our experience that the quality of understanding and potential for development are greatly enhanced if teachers and pupils, nurses and patients and social workers and clients become research partners. An important side effect of establishing the kind of relationship needed to have good interviews is almost always a permanent change in the relationship between the practitioner and participants, which is likely to be supportive of the goals of the practice.

Preparing for an interview

The aim of an interview is to learn from one or more people what you do not yet know, but consider to be important. So you need to reflect carefully on what you want to know and why. The aim is to decide upon the issues that will be the focus of the interview. We recommend that you formulate questions that are either central to the research question, or that will enable you to reflect more deeply on sensitive issues. While it is important to have preformulated questions, you need not follow your interview protocol exactly. In fact, there are instances when preformulated questions can take your attention away from the interviewee and the dynamics of communication.

Most people are familiar with the highly structured interviews used by pollsters. These interviews have very specific questions and are followed exactly according to the protocol. They are done this way for several reasons. One is that they are looking for consistency across many interviews conducted by many interviewers. Second, by asking all interviewees, the same questions it greatly reduces the complexity of the data analysis. A third reason is that some pollsters are influenced by politics or a particular ideology and construct their questions in ways that will give them the answers they want. Therefore, it is imperative that their interviewers follow the "script".

There are also interviews that are almost completely unstructured. They may begin with a prompt like, "Tell me about your day" or "What was the most interesting thing that happened in your practice this week?" The interview then follows in the form of a conversation, with one person, the interviewer, tending to ask questions about the interviewee's responses (Seidman 1998). While there are reasons why an action researcher may want to use an unstructured interview, we find it more useful to do interviews that are *semi-structured*. A semi-structured interview begins with a set of preformulated questions. However, the interviewer can stray from the protocol, and more importantly, can ask follow-up questions that probe what the interviewee was saying. For example, the interviewer can paraphrase what he/she thought the interviewee meant by a comment and ask whether he/she got it right. In this way interviewers can check and recheck their understanding of the interviewee's statements. In this chapter we will only discuss semi-structured interviews. Semi-structured interviews are examples of what Hron (1982: 119) calls a focused interview. These interviews ask for perceptions and interpretations of specific events or beliefs.

Remember that both the researcher and interviewees will be very familiar with interviews on the radio and television that vary from being confrontational to "cozy" and often have the explicit purpose of getting quotable "sound bites". It is easy to slip into these familiar patterns, so careful preparatory work is important to make the purpose of the interview explicit to both parties.

The choice of the interviewee depends on the research question. For some questions it is important to interview several people who somehow differ from each other. For some questions individual interviews are more appropriate, for others group interviews. The group interview is a more normal situation for many people: the social pressure to talk is lower for the individual because of the presence of others, and if one person talks this can stimulate comments from the others.

A group interview is often called a *focus group*. In a focus group participants are free to talk with other group members about the questions. A focus group allows action researchers to gather data in a more natural setting than a one-to-one interview, and can be used to get information about how pupils, patients, or clients relate to one another. The major drawback of a focus group is that because it allows for participants to interact with one another directly, the interviewer can lose control of the conversation (Marshall and Rossman 2006: 114–5).

The choice of place and time for the interview also depends on the research question as well as on opportunity. Secondary teachers may be able to interview pupils during a free period if a colleague is prepared to release them from class for a short period. Primary teachers may be able to carry out interviews with the support of a colleague in a team-teaching situation. Sometimes interviews can take place during teaching sessions by setting tasks that require students to work independently of the teacher, either alone or in groups. Patients and clients can be interviewed during office hours or scheduled at other times.

M29 PREPARATION OF AN INTERVIEW PROTOCOL

An interview protocol is a document that gives information about the structure of the interview and the set of questions that will be asked. When preparing an interview protocol you should keep in mind that any kind of data collection, but especially interviewing, is an intervention into a situation. If you interview colleagues, senior people, administrators, clients, parents or pupils, specific approaches regarding the content, formulation and sequencing of questions may be important in order to gain their cooperation.

When you prepare the interview protocol you should pay attention to the following considerations:

1 *Sources for questions*

- Brainstorm developmental and research interests with your critical friend or research group, if possible.
- Review your research journal and other data sources.
- Consider documents and research or professional literature.

2 *Structure of the interview*

- Structure the interview with headings.
- Have both primary and secondary questions.
- Distinguish between necessary and dispensable questions.

3 *Sequence of questions*

- Which sequence of questions is advantageous? (E.g. warming-up, open questions first, important questions not at the end);
- Introduction (e.g. purpose of the interview, ethics, warming up);
- Conclusion (e.g. thanks, agreements);
- Critical questions (rather near the end of the interview).

4 *Preparing materials*

- Layout of the guidelines (well structured, manageable checklist);

- Possibly preparation of illustrative material (e.g. time line, documents, pictures)
- Preparation and test of equipment (audio-recorder, batteries, cassettes).

5 *Test of the protocol*

- Try out the protocol with persons who are comparable to the persons to be interviewed later and who are willing to provide detailed information on weaknesses of the design of the interview, such as your critical friend or a member of your research group.
- Revise the protocol based on your test.

Carrying out an interview

Starting the interview

It is important to explain the purpose of the interview at the start and enlist the interviewee's help. This does not take long and is recommended for.

- *Ethical reasons* It is not ethical to use the information from the interview for any purpose without the knowledge of the interviewee.
- *Reasons relating to quality of the information* An interviewee who knows what it is all about is more likely (in most cases) to be able to give the information the interviewer needs;
- *Motivational reasons* An interviewee who is treated as an equal and fully informed (becoming a kind of partner) is more likely to confide in the interviewer.

It is essential for the interviewee to be clear that the interview situation is different from other question and answer sessions with the practitioner. If they perceive the interview as a kind of exam they will probably only say what they believe the interviewer wants to hear. We recommend audio-recording interviews for two reasons:

- the record of what was said will be more authentic,
- you will be able to concentrate fully on the interview and not be distracted by having to take notes.

It may not be possible to audio-record: interviewees' permission should be asked and may be refused. If the interviewees are minors you will need permission from their parents or guardians. On some occasions the audio-recorder may make interviewees so nervous that continuing will adversely affect the quality of the interview. In this case the best strategy is to take brief notes during the interview and use these to write more detailed notes later. It may help during the interview to use one half of a folded sheet for catchwords and the other half for quotations, as this makes the subsequent reconstruction easier.

Listening

It takes two people to generate the information: one who tells and one who understands what is said. Communicating honestly about complex matters requires particular qualities of the listener: empathy, disciplined imagination, sympathy, attention, patience, distance, a feeling for truth, and willingness to understand (MacDonald and Sanger 1982)

During an interview listening is as important as asking questions. Non-verbal messages communicated by the interviewer's manner of listening are as important as the questions in indicating to the interviewee whether he/she is being taken seriously as a partner in the interview. These are some of the ways of showing seriousness and respect:

- by not interrupting trains of thought;
- by accepting pauses as a natural part of reflection;
- by accepting whatever is said, however unexpected and regardless of the interviewer's own views. This kind of neutral attentiveness can be difficult for many people: they may not be used to accepting statements with which they do not agree or, on the other hand, withholding approval when the interviewee meets their expectations. Both approval and disapproval of utterances can show the interviewee that the interviewer does not want to know what they really think but only wants confirmation of previously held views. This can lead to inter-viewees trying to gain the approval of the interviewer, perhaps by guessing what he/she wants to hear. Approval and appreciation should not refer to what is said, but to the interviewee's willingness to communicate.

Asking questions

The questions should make clear what the interviewer wants to know, while at the same time helping the interviewee to explore his/her mental space. The beginning of an interview is particularly important because it establishes a relationship between the interviewee and the interviewer. It indicates to the interviewee what the "real" intentions of the interviewer are.

A good beginning may be to recount an event and ask: "Why do you think that happened? What do you think lay behind it?" A personal approach of this kind shows that the researcher is interested in the interviewee's opinion. It is important to ask open questions, especially at the beginning of an interview. They allow the interviewee to shape the answer and take responsibility for structuring the information. By telling the interviewee the issue and asking for comment he/she is free to decide on the best linguistic form for presenting the ideas. This is another way of showing that it is what the interviewee thinks that counts.

Closed questions (where the format and structure of the answer is already predefined) could tell the interviewee (irrespective of what has been said beforehand) that the prime purpose of the interview is to confirm or disconfirm the interviewer's expectations, or that the interviewer is not interested in any details. Closed questions are only useful if the interviewer knows exactly which answers are possible for a question and wants to cross-check possible interpretations. But if such questions (for example, expecting yes/no answers) open the interview the whole discourse can become a "(short) question and (short) answer" game. This can be avoided if you ask why they are responding in that way, or for examples that support their answers.

However, openness can also go too far, for example, if a bundle of issues is packed into one question. This may seem very open to the interviewer, but the interviewee will more likely regard it as a request to be superficial and get the impression that the interviewer wants to know a little about a lot, but nothing in depth. It is better to focus on one issue at a time.

Answers to questions can be either more descriptive or more interpretive. The balance is partly determined by the way the interviewer asks the questions. It may be best to shift the direction as time goes on. At the start of an interview, it is often better to ask for matter-of-fact and descriptive information, leaving room for more personal and interpretive comments when the necessary confidence has been built up. Questions should not be suggestive and interviewers should not prompt to elicit particular opinions. Leading questions have negative consequences for the interview, as they undermine the credibility of the interviewer. Transmitting the interviewer's expectations to the interviewee (sometimes without either of them being aware of it) is one of the most common pitfalls in carrying out an interview.

Expansion and clarification

The process of expansion and clarification is one way of showing the interviewer's interest in what the interviewee is saying. It demonstrates a desire to learn about details, clarify apparent contradictions and so on. There are many ways of doing it:

- Repeat what the interviewee said in your own words to find out whether your understanding is in line with what he/she wanted to communicate ("What I'm hearing you say is. . . ."). This is especially important if the interviewee has difficulties with self-expression.
- Ask the interviewee to give an example as illustration.
- Ask for interpretations of causes, reasons or aims.
- Ask for clarification of contradictions.
- Have a pen and paper to hand and ask for diagrammatic representations of some ideas.

There are some pitfalls. Attempts to expand and clarify can give contradictory messages: a request for more details can be interpreted either as a strong acknowledgement of the importance of what has been said, or as an indication that you are questioning its truth. When expanding and clarifying, it is important to make clear that you are neither interested in finding fault nor in confirming your own prejudices, but in understanding.

After the interview

The most important task after the interview is preparing the data for further analysis. If the interview has not been recorded on tape, the interviewee's statements should be reconstructed as literally as possible with the help of the notes taken during the interview (the sooner this is done the better as it is remarkable what you can remember within 24 hours). If the interview has been recorded you should label the tape or the audio file (interviewee, place, date, topic) and write a data summary (see M32). Sometimes it is useful to transcribe some sections of the interview (see M27).

Some suggestions for learning how to interview

Interviewing is not very easy to learn as it depends more on developing an approach that helps to build a relationship with the interviewee than on learning a set of techniques. One good idea is to study interview transcripts and analyze how the interviewer and interviewee influence each other. Video-recording and analyzing interviews on television or radio can also help. The most important way of learning, however, is through preparing, carrying out and analyzing your own interviews. M30 contains some suggestions.

M30 FIRST ATTEMPTS AT INTERVIEWING

1 Write notes on issues or questions that spring to mind from your own practice: pleasant or less pleasant experiences, hopes and fears, wishes and plans.

2 Ask a pupil, client, patient or colleague with whom you have a good relationship to let you interview him/her.

3 Explain to the interviewee that you want to research and develop your practice, and for that purpose you need to see things from his/her point of view. Tell him/her that you want to record the conversation on tape because otherwise you would have to take written notes. Remind the interviewee of his/her rights as a participant in your research.

4 Give your interviewee your own impressions of the part of your practice situation that is relevant to the interview. Then remind him/her of one or two events that took place recently that had pleasant and/or unpleasant features.

5 Ask the interviewee to tell you his/her impressions of the situations.

6 Be careful not to interrupt the interviewee while he/she is talking and to give him/her time for pauses. If he/she stops talking repeat his/her last statement and ask for more details (or for an example), but leave sufficient "wait-time" so that he/she can think about his/her responses.

7 If you have time for more questions you might ask him/her what he/she thinks your aims are in the situation, and how he/she views them or what kind of difficulties he/she (or others) experience in your practice.

8 Thank the interviewee at the end and ask him/her for suggestions of whom you might interview next.

9 Write brief notes of your experience in this interview and what was striking about what you found out.

10 Listen to the tape several times when you have time to relax. Try to get a feel for your own contributions, for their influence on the interviewee and for how his/her statements influenced your questions. Make notes on what you have noticed (rather than on all the good intentions that come to mind!). Compare these notes with the ones you wrote immediately after the interview (has anything changed?).

11 Now have a critical look at the suggestions for interviewing earlier in this chapter and compare them with your experience.

12 It can also be helpful to play the interview to a colleague and ask for comments. Probably by now you will notice much more than

your colleague, but in spite of that, someone not directly concerned may be able to see things you have failed to notice. Make sure that you pay attention to promises of confidentiality.

13 Invite someone else from your practice to be interviewed and reread your notes on the first interview again before you begin.

M31 STANDARD QUESTIONS FOR THE ANALYSIS OF CLASSROOMS

These questions can be used for interviews with teachers and pupils, or for lesson observations, as follows:

- to start a discussion on teaching without pre-empting the outcomes in any way
- to explore ideas about teaching before deciding on a clearly defined research question or starting point;
- when trying out interviewing for the first time.

If you are interviewing a teacher these are 'standard questions' that you might ask before a lesson:

1 *What are your aims in this lesson?*
2 *What do you expect to be problematic in this lesson?*

You can also ask the teacher these questions after the lesson (What were the aims? The difficulties?). Or you can adapt them for pupil interviews:

1 *What were your teacher's aims today, do you think? What did your teacher want to get out of this lesson?*
2 *Were there any parts of the lesson when you got lost? Or bored? Were there any parts of the lesson that you particularly enjoyed?*

These apparently simple questions often lead to profound discussions of teaching because they are quite open and allow the interviewee plenty of opportunity to explore ideas. They can, of course, be easily adapted for other situations.

Example interview protocol used in a nursing action research study

This interview was developed by a group of five nurses who wanted to improve the discharge preparation process for children with respiratory problems. Part of their method was to interview parents about their perceptions of the discharge process. They developed the following interview, which they gave face-to-face with local parents and by telephone for those who lived further away (Suderman *et al.* 2000).

INTERVIEW QUESTIONS

1 *Can you tell me how you (your family) managed after (child's name) came home from the hospital?*
Probes:

   a *Could you tell me more about that?*
   b *Did you have some help?*
   c *Who helped you?*
   d *What concerns or questions did you have over this time?*
   e *What were you feeling?*

2 *When you think about the time when (child's name) came home, what things do you remember most?*
Probes:

   a *What was most demanding?*
   b *Did you change your routine? How?*
   c *Did you have the supplies you needed?*
   d *How did that make you feel?*

3 *Were there things you wished you had known more about?*
Probes:

   a *Where did you learn about these things?*
   b *Who told you about these things?*
   c *Was that easy or hard to learn?*

4 *How is (child's name) today?*

5 *Is there anything else you would like to comment on? (Suderman et al. 2000: 4)*

There are several things that we'd like to point out in this interview protocol. First, it is short – there are only five questions. If an interview has too many questions the interviewee may feel harried or harassed, and speed through the answers without giving them much thought. Second, three of the questions have probes – these are supplemental questions that the interviewer asks in case the needed information did not come out as a result of the main question. If the information does come up, there is no need to ask the probing questions. Third, we believe that all interviews should end with a question like number 5. A variation of it that we prefer is, "Is there anything else that you would like to tell me about that you think is important but which I haven't asked about?"

Example interview protocol used in a social care action research study

The following interview was developed by Jinny Hay as part of her social work practice to gain information from clients about the ease or difficulty in receiving help, and the quality of the services that were provided.

1   *How did you find out about the Social Services Dept?*
    (Friends, family, neighbors, previous contact, other organizations, phone book etc.)
2   *How easy was it to make contact with them?*
    (Was phone number easy to find? Did you have difficulty getting through? Were you dealt with quickly? Passed to another person? Did you leave a message? Did they call you back?)
3   *Were you able to ask for help easily?*
    (Were you reluctant to seek help from the agency? What made you decide to make the contact?)
4   *How were you able to make your concerns/situation understood?*
    (Did you feel you were being listened to? Did you understand what you were being asked about yourself and why? Were the questions you were asked relevant to you? Was your urgency understood and noted?)
5   *Did you feel you were clearly told about and understood what would happen next?*
    (Referral to Assessment Team – and time scales?)
6   *What help and information did you get at this stage?*
    (Was it appropriate?)
7   *What did you do with the information?*
    (Was it followed up?)
8   *What help did you get from the organization/service you contacted?*
9   *If you did not follow up the advice/information did you contact the agency again?*

This interview is a bit longer than the previous example but is still quite short. One of the things that we would like to point out is that the probes in this interview are suggested and will not necessarily be asked by the interviewer. That is, if the initial question elicits the type of response sought, then there is no need to ask the follow-up, probing questions. The inclusion of optional probes in this interview suggests that the interviewer has more latitude in changing the interview than in the preceding one. That is, if the interviewee makes a comment that is interesting or unexpected, the interviewer could invent new questions to probe more deeply into the interviewee's ideas, beliefs or conceptions.

Sources of misinformation in interviews

A basic criticism of interviewing as a technique is that what people say they do is not always the same as what they do, or what they intend to do (either consciously or subconsciously). If intentional misrepresentation is excluded, there are many other reasons for misinformation, for example: selective memory, rationalization, difficulty of the topic, personality, and status of the interviewer, the presence of an audio-recorder and the social and environmental framework in which the interview takes place (often very different from normal conversation).

Some of these problems can be addressed as follows:

- When people contradict themselves it often indicates a tension in their thinking. Talking about the contradictions can sometimes resolve them.
- Pauses indicate that the speaker is thinking or that something is being left out. Careful questioning, without interrupting the train of thought, can help to stimulate the interviewee's memory.
- An important method for avoiding distortions is to ask for details. (What did you do? What did you say?) Because of our background knowledge, we can easily jump to the wrong conclusion and fail to ask any further questions, believing that we already know the answer.
- Misinformation can be reduced by confronting interview data with other data (e.g. observation notes), or by comparing accounts given by different people (see "Triangulation" at the end of this chapter).

There is also a deeper reason for distortions in interview accounts: interviewees are not always sure how to interpret situations, or why they have done certain things. The interview can be an opportunity for them to understand the situation better. This illustrates a more general point: interviews are not only about collecting data, they constitute a more or less meaningful, more or less conscious learning process for interviewees. The interview creates a framework within which the interviewee is made to think about a situation or issue and interrelate experiences, thereby potentially gaining a deeper understanding. Collecting data in this way can contribute to a change of attitude and indirectly to a change in the situation itself.

THE WRITTEN SURVEY

The written survey is a kind of formalized interview. The most important difference is that in a survey the interviewer cannot respond immediately to the answer or specify new questions.

Sample questionnaires

Roger Pols (undated) used a simply structured questionnaire to investigate how his pupils (10-year-olds) were coping with group work.

Questionnaire on group work

Please underline the answer you want to give. If you are not sure, underline the answer that comes closest.

1   *How much of the lesson did you enjoy? All of it /Some of it /None*
2   *How much do you think you learnt? Nothing /Something /A lot*
3   *How much did you understand? Most of it /Some of it /Nothing*
4   *Could you find the books, information and equipment you needed? None / Some of it / Most of it.*
5   *Did other people help you? A lot /A little /Not at all*
6   *Did other people stop you working? A lot /Sometimes /Not at all*
7   *Did the teacher help you? Enough /Not enough*
8   *How long did the lesson last? Long enough /Too long /Not long enough*
9   *What was the lesson like Boring /Interesting*
10 *Did you need anything you could not find? Yes /No*
11 *Where did you get help from? Teacher /Group /Someone else*
12 *How did you find this work? Easy /Hard /Just about right*
13 *Write down anything that made it hard for you to learn.*
14 *Write down anything you particularly enjoyed about this lesson.*

Roger's aim was to learn how the pupils assessed (1) the task, (2) their success with it, and (3) the conditions (material, time, help from the teacher and classmates, distractions). His immediate purpose was to improve the planning of the next lesson. In the long term, he wanted to find out which changes, if any, take place when group work is done more frequently. He asked the pupils to complete the questionnaire (in about 5 minutes) after each group work session. The quantitative analysis took him half an hour. One of the findings was:

> *At first 63 per cent said they were only hindered a little compared with 48 per cent at the end, while none said at first they were hindered a lot, but by the end this had risen to 16 per cent.*

Roger commented on this result:

> *Left to their own ideas, some children are not capable of working without direction and become a distractive influence. They therefore need direction – but in a large class inevitably some children must wait.*

One of his long-term conclusions was:

> *There is a need for a careful plan and structure as well as resource material for the less-able children to keep them from frustration if they are unable to cope with the tasks.*

Suggestions for the design and use of questionnaires

Compared to interviews which are often seen as difficult, hard to organize, and time-consuming, questionnaires seem to be a quick method of collecting data, easy to develop, and administer without any problems. This widespread impression is not quite correct. The usefulness of a questionnaire depends principally on the quality of the questions, as follow-up questions are only possible in a limited way, if at all. There is a tendency for action researchers to think of a survey or questionnaire as a first step in data collection. As we have already noted, good data is difficult to get unless you have good questions. There are obvious pitfalls to be avoided like asking "double questions" where it will be impossible to interpret the answers. For this reason a questionnaire should always be piloted with a small number of people who resemble those who will be surveyed as closely as possible.

It is also often difficult to get people to complete questionnaires. For example, we found that putting survey forms in colleagues' mailboxes results in so few completed and returned that we may as well have put them straight into the recycling bin! Therefore, we suggest that you ask respondents to complete questionnaires or surveys when they are "captured" in some situation like a staff meeting or class. What this also suggests is that it can be difficult to ask the same people to complete a second questionnaire. For these reasons we suggest that you carefully plan out your questionnaire based on your data collection needs before you ask others to complete it.

Even if the questions have been well-formulated so that they are understood as intended, the insight gained with the help of the questionnaire is often much smaller than expected. In general, the more structured a method of data collection is, the more formal and meagre in content are the answers. In spite of this basic problem, questionnaires can be useful to action researchers. The following suggestions should be helpful. (For further information, see Hook 1995.)

Before starting work

Effort spent on thinking through the problem you want to investigate before developing the questionnaire saves a lot of time and effort in subsequent analysis of the data. Consider in detail why you are asking these questions, what answers you expect and what you are going to use them for. The more precisely you know your intentions in advance, the better structured the questionnaire can be. Vice versa: the less you reflect beforehand, the more open the questions will be and the more difficult and time-consuming the analysis will be.

Formulating the questions

A questionnaire can consist of open or closed questions. If closed questions are used, the informant chooses the answers that apply to him/her; with open questions, the informant must formulate answers. In both cases a number of decisions have to be made when constructing the questionnaire.

DECISIONS ON CONTENT

- Is the question really necessary? How useful are the expected answers likely to be in solving the problem?
- Does the question cover the topic? Will you need further information (more questions) to be able to interpret the answer? Be careful not to ask "two questions in one" as this makes the answers difficult or impossible to interpret.
- Do the respondents have the information they need to answer the questions? If you have doubts, no useful answer can be expected.
- If you ask for subjective information (opinions, attitudes), have you followed this up with a supplementary question asking for factual information? For example, the question, "How informative was the debriefing for you?" can be followed by another question asking exactly what happened in the session.
- Questions concerning very personal, intimate, or taboo topics, or topics where personal interests or social pressures are dominant, tempt respondents to give an expected answer or one that will show them in a good light (if the question is answered at all). If you need to ask questions on these topics, it is useful to begin with a more general question. This situation comes up often in the health and social work fields, but can also be of concern to teachers. For example, a teacher may want to ask, "What, in your opinion, do most pupils think about the new dress code?" before asking the student what he/she thinks about it.
- Does the way you have constructed the questions restrict the range of possible answers? For example, check that you have asked for both negative and positive experiences.

DECISIONS ON THE WORDING OF QUESTIONS

- Could the wording be misunderstood? Are the concepts easy to understand for all possible respondents?
- Does the wording suggest a particular answer?
- Are there any emotionally loaded words? These might have negative consequences for the validity of the answers.

- Does the question ask for a factual account or subjective opinions? Either is quite valid, but it's important to know precisely what you are asking for in each question.
- Which is more suitable – a direct or an indirect question? Direct questions ask about a person's opinion on an event or situation, for example, "Did you enjoy the lesson?" Indirect questions ask for reactions to other people's opinions, for example, "When he was talking to Sanje about group work Peter said, 'I don't bother to do much in group work because the others do the work anyway.' What do you think of Peter's statement?" Your choice between these two types of questions will be a trade off between possible bias and the efficiency of asking a question directly.

DECISIONS ON THE FORM OF ANSWERS

- Should the questions ask for "multiple-choice" answers, short answers (closed questions) or freely worded answers (open questions)? Combinations of open and closed questions are often possible, e.g. "Do you prefer working on your own – with a classmate – or in a group (please underline your choice)? Why do you prefer to work in the way you chose?"
- In multiple-choice answers, are all the alternatives useful in relation to your research question?
- In multiple-choice answers, are all the choices clear and distinct from one another, and are all the important options covered? Notions like "generally" and "well" are ambiguous and difficult to interpret.
- Is it clear what kind of response is expected? For example, in multiple-choice answers is it clear whether only one or more than one alternative should be chosen?

DECISIONS ON THE SEQUENCE OF QUESTIONS

- Will the answer to the question be influenced by the content of the preceding questions?
- Does the sequence of questions allow the respondent to move gradually into the topic of the questionnaire? Factual questions should come at the beginning and questions asking for attitudes, feelings, etc. should follow later when the respondent has had a chance to focus as fully as possible on the situation.

Advantages and disadvantages of questionnaires using predominantly closed questions

The questionnaire can be a useful method of data collection for action researchers. Its most important advantages are:

- It is easy to distribute to people involved in your practice situation including colleagues and family members.
- It need not take much time to fill in.
- A large number of individuals can answer the questions simultaneously.
- The impersonal nature of the questionnaire and the possibility of answering anonymously make it easier to be completely honest.
- The social pressure on the respondents is not as strong as it is in an interview, which makes it easier for respondents to reflect on the questions before answering.

However there are also disadvantages:

- There is no way of ensuring that questions are understood as intended. This problem can be reduced by testing the questionnaire in an interview situation before it is handed out, or by including more than one question on the same topic (to enable answers to be cross-checked).
- Questionnaires are not always taken seriously by everyone, particularly if the topic is not important to the respondent. This can also show up in the formal answers, for example:
  - in that yes/no or true/false questions are more frequently answered "yes" or "true";
  - in selecting "middle of the road" answers rather than those that express clear views.

- Answers may be distorted by factors of which the respondent is not at all or only partially aware. Attitudes and emotions are closely linked to self-image and self-esteem. This can lead to a sub-conscious tendency to paint a positive picture of oneself, or at least to avoid giving a negative impression.
- When questionnaires are not returned anonymously there may be a tendency for the respondents to confirm the researcher's expectations (for example, in questions asking for information about an action researcher's own practice).

These problems are equally true of the interview but are more easily recognizable through the personal contact between the interviewer and the interviewee. One important way to reduce these disadvantages is to win over the respondents to the aims of the research. For example, if the patients understand the reason for the research and are interested in its outcomes, a questionnaire can produce very reliable data and, at the same time, make a contribution to improving the situation. A questionnaire can also raise patients' awareness of issues for further research.

Surveys and questionnaires can also be administered through the Internet. However, it is important not to send out questionnaires without any prior agreement from the survey group, as unsolicited emails are regarded as a nuisance and may either be ignored or classified as spam and bring your research into disrepute. At this time there are companies that provide the resources for developing and administering web-based surveys for a small fee. Some even offer a no-cost option for short surveys with small numbers of respondents.[2]

COLLECTING DATA AS PART OF DAILY PRACTICE

Data is also available from practitioners' daily practice. In health care one of the first things done is to take a patient's case history. It can also be easy to adapt regular practice to generate relevant data. Open essay questions can be used to collect pupils' perceptions in the course of classroom work. For example, after an unpleasant argument with pupils as a result of disappointing work on a project, one teacher asked his pupils to write their reactions to the lesson for homework. The resulting writing was the most important source of data on this lesson, as these three examples indicate:

He (the teacher) practically roared. He asked every single pupil what she had done for the project. I said: "Questions" and he wanted to know "Which ones exactly?" Of course I couldn't remember exactly and didn't say anything. He said (loudly): "Well, this is great – saying nothing and then moping." I was very angry because I wasn't moping. But I hid my anger and didn't say anything, and I was sulking on purpose. I wanted to tell him what I thought to his face (Alexandra).

First I was very angry. How could he talk to us like that? He shouted at us and called us "schemers" and other names. I'll show him! But after a while I realized that the conflict was our fault too, not only his . . . (Kerstin)

I got angry when we were called "idiots of this day and age" – lacking in character, lazy, scheming, deceitful, mean, and whatever. That we would never find a job because we lacked character. Of course we realized that we had not done everything we should, but was it necessary to threaten to keep us back a year? (Sabine)

Commenting on his pupils' essays the teacher wrote, among other things:

I was surprised at the words I had used according to my pupils. I was not aware of having used some of these words. I was also surprised that they had evoked such strong emotions. It was my intention to make them think about it and maybe even to hurt them. After all I felt hurt by their lack of work. But in fact I had only caused helpless anger and put many pupils into a situation where they had to reject me, because some of my expressions had damaged their self-respect.

(After Schindler 1993)

One way of collecting data regularly on pupils' perceptions is the pupil's journal. Entries in a journal can be answers to open questions, for example, "What happened at school today that made you think?" One primary teacher used journals both as regular homework for her 6-year-old pupils and a source of data for research on her teaching. She also started a dialog with some pupils by writing short comments after their entries.

A COMBINED METHOD: TRIANGULATION

One of the ways to increase the quality of action research is to use a method called *triangulation*. The term derives from the use of trigonometry by surveyors and navigators to locate objects. For example, let's say that a hiker is lost in the forest and makes an emergency radio call. One of the ways of locating the hiker is to use triangulation. One rescue worker, observer A, may determine that the hiker is to the south-west, while another rescue worker, observer B, may determine that the hiker is to the north-east. The hiker will be at the intersection of the two 'lines of sight' (see Figure 5.3).

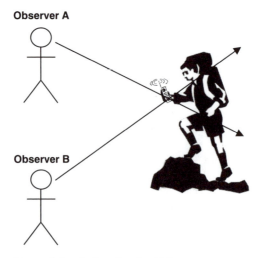

Figure 5.3 Using triangulation to locate a lost hiker

We can use the same strategy in our research. By combining different methods of data collection and/or data provided by someone else (e.g. a member of the research group or a critical friend), we can better "locate" the meaning of our data. For example, triangulation may consist of a combination of observation and interview to the get the perspective of our pupils, patients or clients (Figure 5.4). It is important to note that for triangulation to work to locate the hiker, the two observers must know their locations. In the same way, the different data sources shown in Figure 5.5 should pay attention to the context of the practitioner's situation.

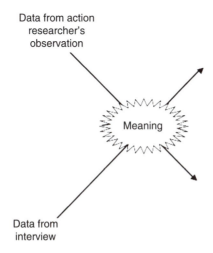

Figure 5.4 Using triangulation to better ensure the accuracy of our interpretations.

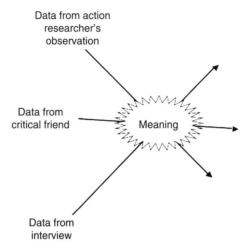

Figure 5.5 Adding an outside perspective increases the likelihood that we have 'located' an accurate interpretation of the data.

When the perspective of the person who is outside of your situation is added, then there is even more reason to believe the meaning that you have attributed to your data (Figure 5.5). See Sands and Roer-Strier (2006) for an interesting example of the use of triangulation in social work in their interviews of mothers and daughters.

An example of triangulation

As teacher in charge of information technology in his school, Vince Moon (1990) wanted to try out and evaluate the use of computers and a video camera in a "Newsdesk" project with his class of 10-year-olds. "News" from a simulated press agency was printed out by the computer at random intervals (using the Newsdesk program). The children had to work in groups to handle the writing (on other computers), presenting and video-recording of a television news broadcast. The project was set up as a special activity taking a whole day. Jon Pratt, Vince Moon's critical friend, helped with data collection. The teacher and the critical friend planned the day together, deciding on the aims of the activity and drawing up a list of concrete issues and questions and the focus for data collection. (They started with the "standard questions", see M31).

They decided to use three different data sources:

1 On the day the critical friend observed the activities, spending part of the time taking notes and part taking photographs.
2 A short time later the critical friend interviewed three pairs of pupils chosen by the teacher, using the photographs as a way of starting the discussion, as well as the original issues and questions.
3 After the lesson the teacher used the issues and questions as a framework for writing detailed notes of his perceptions of the day.

In this way they arrived at three sets of data: the views of the six pupils (as a partially transcribed interview), the teacher's perception (in writing) and the observer's notes. The data were then juxtaposed, enabling a comparison of the three different points of view to be the focus of the analysis.

The results were fed directly into plans for a second Newsdesk Day with a parallel class. The value of having three points of view became clear in analyzing the extent to which the teacher should structure the day: initially it was the teacher's view that more structure had been needed to enable the groups of pupils to work more effectively, but the pupils felt it had been important that they had been allowed to organize themselves. The critical friend was able to contribute his view that at one point an intervention from the teacher had come too soon and may have impeded the group's decision-making.

Advantages and disadvantages of triangulation

Triangulation is an important method for contrasting and comparing different accounts of the same situation. Through identifying differences in perspective, contradictions and discrepancies can emerge that help in the interpretation of a situation and the development of a practical theory (see Chapter 3). In addition, where the different perspectives agree with each other, the interpretation is considered more credible (Sands and Roer-Strier 2006).

Triangulation has the following advantages:

- It gives a more detailed and balanced picture of the situation.
- The contradictions that are often hidden in situations become visible, enabling a more profound interpretation.
- It breaks the "hierarchy of credibility", which limits our understanding, by giving equal status to people from different ranks. "Hierarchy of credibility" means that individuals of a higher social rank are more credible (reliable) than individuals of a lower social rank: the nurse is more reliable than the patients; the doctor is more reliable than the nurse; and so on. Triangulation regularly shows that pupils are able to help explain a situation by providing relevant information hitherto unknown to the practitioner.

But triangulation also has its disadvantages:

- Many practitioners see it as threatening. It obviously demands a high degree of self-confidence to confront your own perceptions of a situation for which you feel responsible (and which you feel is a "part of yourself") with other people's perceptions, and in doing so to question them. It seems that a neutral observer's perception is seen as less threatening than the people whom we feel responsible to and for. For example, John Elliott (1978) recommends teachers new to research not to begin with triangulation, but to start with less threatening methods of data collection such as free observations recorded in a research notebook, or audio-recordings of lessons.
- A further disadvantage of this method is the amount of effort required to set it up: a neutral observer has to be invited into the classroom and data on the same situation collected from three different sources. However it can be helpful to focus data collection within a relatively short period of time – particularly as triangulation provides very rich data that are likely to take some time to analyze and interpret.

It is important for us to note that "triangulation" has a specialized meaning in the field of family therapy. In the model of family therapy developed by Murray Brown, triangulation is the process of including a third person when tension and anxiety become uncomfortable between two people

(Bowen 1978). While the idea of multiple viewpoints is common to both meanings of triangulation, its use in research is very different from its use in family therapy.

CRITERIA FOR GUIDING THE QUALITY OF ACTION RESEARCH

We believe that there are four primary objectives in action research:

1 to develop and improve practice through research in the interests of all those concerned;
2 to develop the knowledge and practical understanding of those involved in the research process;
3 to develop the professional knowledge of practitioners in your field as a whole;
4 to develop and improve your practice field (e.g. education, nursing or social work) as a discipline (see Chapter 10).

Each of these objectives has a directionality to it. That is, we have a vision and goal for the direction in which we want the practice and knowledge of our colleagues, other research participants and ourselves to develop and improve. In the same way, we have a vision and goal for how we would like our field of practice to develop and improve as a discipline. Given this we can talk about different quality criteria of action research based on how our action research helps us to move towards those visions and goals. We believe that it is during the data collection process that we should especially pay attention to criteria that can help us do high quality action research.

Before we turn to those criteria, we want to point out a significant difference between objectives 1 and 2 and objectives 3 and 4. The former refer to the practice situation while the latter have a wider-range focus which includes all practitioners in your field and your practice field as a whole. Because objectives 1 and 2 refer to the local practice situation, their quality criteria are, in a way, less demanding than those for objective 3 and 4. Once we begin to construct knowledge that will be used beyond our own situation (objective 3) we need to be able to convince others that our claims have meaning and usefulness beyond our classroom, clinic or community. The same is true for objective 4: if we want our action research to have an effect on the practice field as a whole, then we need to be able to produce strong arguments and evidence that we can use to convince others of the usefulness and veracity of the outcomes of our action research.

In a way what we're talking about here is the validity of the research. Many action researchers have rejected the use of the term 'validity' because of its association with quantitative research that uses statistical analysis of measurements. Given that these methods are seldom used in action research, it makes it very difficult to use criteria that are based on them. The idea of validity is also rejected because in many fields researchers try to ensure validity by making their studies repeatable and unbiased. Because action researchers are very much a part of the situations they study, it is impossible to remain objective in order to make one's research valid. And because action research is done as part of ordinary practice, there is no way to develop action research studies that are repeatable in the same way as those in the hard sciences or some of the social sciences. However, there are other ways of defining validity. This definition, for example, can be used as a basis for the assessment of the quality of action research:

> An account is valid or true if it represents accurately those features of the phenomena that it is intended to describe, explain, or theorize.
>
> (Hammersley 1992: 92)

We believe that it is possible for action researchers to do research that is of high enough quality for it to be considered "valid" according to this definition, and that, if that is done, we can meet all the objectives for action research that we listed above.

We now want to put forward four wide-ranging criteria that you can use to guide your action research so that it can meet your goals and achieve your vision. Here again we see the way that action research proceeds through a series of mini-action research cycles. You shouldn't expect that your initial research design will fulfill all these criteria. As you collect and analyze your data and take action in your practice situation, your starting point and research design will change. It is important to make sure that you are conscious of the way it is changing, and that as you make decisions about what actions to take or how to change your research design you pay attention to these criteria. We state them in the form of questions to facilitate their use in this way.

Considering alternative perspectives

Have the understandings gained from research been cross-checked against the perspectives of all those concerned and/or other researchers?

Why do we believe considering alternative perspectives is an important criterion in judging the quality of action research? In traditional empirical research, objectivity, reliability and validity are usually regarded as central criteria for judging quality. (Altrichter (1986a) presents a detailed comparison between the methods of empirical science and other forms of research.)

These three quality criteria in empirical research are derived from the basic idea of making close comparisons. By "repeating the research" (e.g. having different people looking at the same event, using different research methods – interviews, classroom observations, etc.) it is possible to make a detailed comparison at each stage. Discrepancies can be identified as they would be if a second photograph were to be superimposed on the original one. Any such discrepancies in the research process are interpreted as indicating quality deficits, and conformity as indicating quality.

These quality criteria are also important for action research, although some of the procedures for testing them, developed for research in experimental settings, can hardly be applied to action research in naturalistic settings:

- *For practical reasons* – (see also the section on practical compatibility) Complex procedures for testing validity require time, effort, and resources that are not available to a teacher-researcher. Even considering alternative perspectives by drawing on a second observer may give rise to insurmountable difficulties in some cases.
- *For theoretical reasons* – in action research reliability is only possible in a very restricted sense. Naturally occurring situations are usually changeable: it is seldom possible to observe comparable situations at different times because the situation will have developed in the meantime. In addition, the action researcher sets out to destabilize a situation by developing and putting into practice action strategies to change and improve it (see Chapter 7).

However, the quality criterion "consulting alternative perspectives" is in the spirit of the central idea of the traditional quality criteria of empirical research, namely that the quality of research can be raised by "repeating the research" in order to discover discrepancies. Action researchers can discover weak points in their research and raise its quality, if they confront their findings with alternative perspectives of the situation. If discrepancies arise, these can be used as starting points for further reflection and development.

In practical terms there are several possible sources of alternative perspectives:

- *Other people's perspectives* – our own understanding of a research situation (as it emerges for example after clarifying the starting point of research, or after the first activities of data collection and analysis) can be confronted with other people's views. Clearly this is an important role of people in your research group or your critical friend. It can also be people who are directly or indirectly involved in the situation (e.g. pupils, patients or clients, colleagues, family members, or supervisors) or people who are relatively uninvolved (e.g. external observers).
- *Perspectives developed in other, comparable situations* – these can lead to the discovery of flaws in our own research process. Other practitioners'

accounts, research papers and books and the action researcher's own experiences are all sources of alternative understandings of the situation being investigated.
- *Perspectives drawn from other research methods* – triangulation with another research method or data source is obviously a way to get another perspective.

One of the results of seeking alternative perspectives is that we may find discrepancies among the accounts and explanations. Discrepancies can have three main causes:

- They can result from the way research methods were used. For example, our own observations of a situation can be different from an external observer's observations. This calls for three possible courses of action. First, we can identify and correct mistakes in our own observations, or, if there is no way of knowing which data are more reliable, we can provide alternative interpretations that express the ambiguity. Second, we can learn from this experience and adapt, or add to, our research methods. Third, we can try to reconcile the two accounts through analysis of both and synthesizing a new interpretation based on the combined observations.
- If discrepancies cannot be explained by re-examining the research process, they may be caused by different perspectives inherent in the situation being researched (see Chapter 3). In this case, the practical theory emerging from the research will need to be extended to explain why the situation is seen differently from different perspectives. This is illustrated by the following example.

  A teacher begins a lesson by asking questions. In an interview he explains his intention: The questions are meant to stimulate the pupils to think about the subject matter and discover links between different ideas. But he is not satisfied with the results. To him the pupils' answers show very little "thinking" and no "links between ideas". During a group interview with the pupils it emerges that they interpret the teacher's questioning as a test. In this situation they want to give an answer that is "correct", and that "reflects the views they believe the teacher holds". They do not want to take any risks. In this case the reason for the discrepancy between the teacher's and the pupils' views cannot be explained in terms of the research methodology. The discrepancy "is inherent in the situation". It will be important to explain the existence of the divergent explanations in the practical theory of the situation, for example, by saying:

  - The teacher interprets the situation in terms of his immediate motives for action.
  - The pupils do not perceive the teacher's motives in this situation,

but interpret his action in terms of their own experiences of similar situations in the past (their socialization as pupils).

- ○ The result is the observed "misunderstanding".
- ○ This finding does not suggest any different interpretation of the teacher's motives. However, if he takes seriously the pupils' understanding of the situation from their socialization in the classroom, he will have to take into account ways in which, over time, he can improve the effectiveness of his questioning.

- Discrepancies may also be caused by different ideologies or beliefs that shape the "windows" through which we gather data. It is possible for two people to observe exactly the same set of events and yet attribute different meanings to them because of their prior experiences, knowledge and beliefs. For example, one social worker could react to a client's erratic appointment keeping by attributing it to irresponsibility on the part of the client. Another could attribute it to the client's possible lack of resources that makes it difficult to keep appointments without the possibility of losing his/her job or leaving his/her children without care.

Testing through practical action

Have the understandings gained from research been tested through practical action?

How can we know whether our new knowledge or understanding is valid? That is, how can we tell if it accurately describes, explains or theorizes? One way to answer these questions is to test our knowledge and understanding through practical action. When we apply our new knowledge and understandings to our practice we construct practical theories. Practical theories can be the source of hypotheses that we can test through actions that we take in our practice. In Chapter 7 we show some of the ways in which our practical theories can be tested by putting them into practice.

3 Ethical justification

Are the research methods compatible with both aims of our practice field and democratic human values?

There is the stereotype of the dispassionate scientist, locked away in his laboratory, pursuing science so pure that he need not be concerned about its effects on humanity. While there may be some scientists who still believe that they are in this exalted position, there are few who are unaware that their discoveries will have some effect on society. This can be seen in the review criteria of the National Science Foundation. As one might expect, they ask reviews to examine the intellectual merit of the proposed activity; i.e. "How important is the proposed activity to advancing knowledge and understanding within its own field or across different fields?" But they also ask reviewers to examine the broader impacts of the proposed activity, including how well it promotes teaching and learning, broadens the participation of under-represented groups, and the benefits of the proposed activity to society (National Science Foundation 2004). However, what many scientists do not consider are the effects of society, such as their own beliefs, politics, religion and gender, on their research. This is contrary to the findings of those who study the working of scientists who have found that there is a dynamic interplay between the culture in which the science is being done and the research questions asked, the methods used and the conclusions drawn. What all this suggests is that even those researchers in the most traditional sciences need to pay attention to ethical and political considerations of their work. While these considerations have not become part of the accepted criteria for the validity of traditional research, we believe that they should be for all research, and especially research that is concerned with humans and other living beings.

Action research as we define it is research involving those people whose problem it is and who want to do something about it to improve the way they work with other human beings (Hay, personal communication). Action research, therefore, always interferes with social situations – it always has an effect on other human beings. And other human beings always have an effect on the action researcher, the methods used and interpretations of results. Therefore, when we carry out action research it is very important that our activities abide by ethical quality criteria. We examine some of those criteria below. However, as the practice professions like teaching, nursing and social work have become increasingly regulated, ethical codes of practice have been developed by professional associations and state and national regulatory agencies. In addition, many institutions have their own rules for if and how research can be done in their setting. Those institutions that routinely do research with human subjects (e.g. universities and teaching hospitals) have Institutional Review Boards (IRBs) that review all proposed research using ethical standards. Therefore, it is important for action researchers to be aware of the rules and regulations that govern the research process in their practice situations.

Given this, we have two main quality criteria for action research:

1 The research should be compatible with the aims of the situation being researched, rather than working against them. For example, data

collection based on competitive tests would be incompatible with the educational aim of fostering cooperation between pupils. Similarly, methods that kept patients unaware of all their medical options would be contrary to the aim of increasing patients' rights.

2 Action research is based on the belief that effective change in practice is only possible in cooperation with all the participants in the situation – it cannot be achieved against their will. Therefore research methods should help to develop democratic and cooperative relationships. Chris Argyris (1972) shows convincingly that many research designs do not contribute to democratic and cooperative responsibility. Action research tries to overcome this problem (a) by being governed by ethical principles; (b) by negotiating an ethical code; and (c) allowing all aspects of the research to be open to negotiations among the participants and the researcher.

a The research methods are governed by *ethical principles*, in particular:

- *Negotiation* Research techniques may only be used with the consent of all those concerned. What does this mean in practice? In classroom research the pupils are told the aims of the investigation and are asked for their cooperation. If the effects are likely to go beyond the classroom, fellow teachers, administrators, and community members are similarly approached. This process of informing and asking for cooperation is repeated at every stage. If the methods of data collection are not acceptable, alternative procedures have to be negotiated. Before an interview, the participants are told what use will be made of the data, and afterwards they are given the opportunity to think over what they have said and asked if the data can be used in the research. If they refuse permission this has to be accepted (e.g. by handing over the tape to the interviewee). In our experience it is very rare for participants to refuse to cooperate if they believe a project is important for them and they have been asked for their cooperation explicitly. They usually want their views to be considered. It is worth noting that the rather vague category of "all those concerned" is likely to include both those immediately involved and others whose significance may emerge only after the research begins (for example, a fellow teacher who taught the class in a previous year – see Posch 1985).
- *Confidentiality* The data are the property of those from whom they originate. Data have to be treated confidentially and may not be passed on to others without permission. Research reports and case studies must not be published without giving participants the opportunity to comment: this may lead to changes being

made or to the comments being incorporated in the writing. If individuals can be identified they must be asked for permission before the report is passed on to others. Making data anonymous by leaving out or changing the names is often not good enough. Most action research is local research and it is easy to identify the location and participants.

- *Participants' control* – those who participate in the situation keep control of the research. This ethical principle is of great importance in building trust between an action researcher and external facilitator, or between teacher and pupils. Lawrence Stenhouse (1975) argued convincingly that control over research and any changes resulting from it should be in the hands of those who have to live with its consequences. This principle is of special importance to outsiders who facilitate action research. They must make sure that they support but not dominate the action researcher.

b The ethical principles are set out in an ethical code. When action researchers collaborate with external facilitators, it is important to draw up an ethical code defining the rights and duties of all parties. This should be discussed with participants beforehand and revised if necessary. Some external facilitators sign a contract with the action researchers setting out their aims and principles for democratic collaboration. An ethical code of this kind will always need to be negotiated among all those concerned, so that it is tailored to the particular context. Again, it is important to determine what rules and regulations govern the doing of research in your situation.

c The conduct of the research remains open to negotiation. Even if those concerned have been fully informed from the start, and principles for collaboration have been written down, misunderstandings and conflicts can emerge in the course of the research. Therefore "negotiation" continues to be important *throughout the entire research process* and, in the event of conflict, existing agreements must be open to further negotiation (see Johnson 1984).

4 Practicality

Are the research design and data collection methods compatible with the demands of practice?

Practitioners are very busy people. It is possible that action research activities can get put on the back burner or are left in the "next things to do pile". If action research is to be of high quality, it needs to be compatible with the work and life of the action researcher. By compatible, we mean that the research design and individual research methods should be:

- compatible with the temporal and spatial flow imposed by the practitioner's main responsibility. What we mean by this is that unlike traditional researchers who can collect data and then spend months or even years analyzing it, action researchers need to have results from their research almost immediately. While it will help a social worker in future years to know how best to work with a client, the need is immediate if he/she is going to improve the ongoing situation both for the client and for him/her. To help accomplish this, action researchers should develop as many ways to embed the research process within their regular practice as possible. For example, a discharge interview can be both an opportunity for patients to learn what they need to continue to regain their health, and it can be a means of collecting data on a research question. A group session can be therapeutic and also provide data on how best to run the sessions. It is also important for action researchers to be aware of their professional and personal lives. An honest assessment of demands could suggest that it may not be the right time to do an in-depth action research study and that it should be put off to a later date.
- compatible with the professional culture of the practice field. Sometimes people who engage in action research choose a problem to investigate that is interesting to themselves and to others, but is tangential to their practice. This can easily occur if an outside facilitator puts his/her agenda ahead of the teacher's. In short, the focus of the action research should match the actual concerns of practitioners, and help them to understand their practice situations and to improve their practice.

Chapter 6

Data analysis

Our purpose in this chapter is to help you answer the question "How can I make the best use of my data?" For the most part, this chapter – like the one on data collection – is a kind of toolkit. It contains a variety of analysis methods to make the best use of data. In it we will show you ways in which you can analyze your data so that your understanding of your situation becomes clearer, and more reliable as the basis for planning action.

MAKING SENSE OF DATA

Human beings look for meaning. One of the ways that we do this is by ascribing meaning to what initially appears to be a jumble of information. We sort, characterize, group and separate. We analyze and synthesize; inventing categories that help us to ascribe meaning to chaotic events. This is one of our most important abilities. It helps us to see the world as a network of interrelationships, coherent and predictable. The more we refine this ability the more we feel at home in our environment. A very old example of the human need for meaning is mythology. Here is an Australian aboriginal myth:

> Walu, the sun goes down into the sea every night and becomes Warrukay, the big fish, in order to swim beneath Munadha, the earth, and come back again to the proper place in the morning.
>
> (Isaacs, 1980:144)

For the inhabitants of the coastal region, the sun sinks daily into the sea and emerges again on the other side of the world. It must have come to the other side somehow. It is certainly plausible to suppose that the sun could only do this in the shape of a big fish. This myth resulted from an *analytic process* in which observations were selected, put into relation with each other and interpreted. The explanation seemed reasonable to the people: it corresponded with their understanding of the world, confirmed and expanded it. It was emotionally balanced and made them feel secure.

In another example, meaning is also ascribed to events:

> While a teacher is explaining a point she is observing the classroom. She watches the behavior of some of the under-achieving pupils, among others Susie, who from previous experience she does not expect to pay much attention. She notices that Susie is listening, who then asks a sensible question. The initial impression is intensified and is accompanied by interpretations and feelings: e.g. "Susie is participating"; "perhaps she is having a good day"; "maybe I've been underestimating Susie". But the teacher is still unsure. "Is she really on task? Or is she only pretending? After all she isn't taking notes." The teacher wants to be sure and asks Susie a question that she should be able to answer if she has really been listening. Susie answers the question and the teacher gives her an approving smile.

One of the purposes of analysis is to find explanations that "fit" our understanding and therefore seem plausible. The teacher in the example above searches for an interpretation of the situation that seems right to her and serves as a secure basis for action. However, plausible explanations cannot necessarily be trusted. Sometimes they are the product of prejudices and wishful thinking and fail to stand up to examination. Another of the purposes of analysis is to check on explanations and test them. As a result, what seems to be plausible at the end of an analytic process often differs from the assumptions that seemed to be valid at the beginning of the process.

The example above illustrates the most important analytic procedures:

- Events are observed.
- The focus of observation is selective. The teacher pays more attention to the low-achieving pupils.
- Events are organized to present a coherent mental picture, that is, a theory of the situation. The teacher relates different observations to each other (e.g. Susie listening, Susie asking a sensible question).
- The situation as perceived is interpreted: the teacher draws conclusions: "Susie is participating", "she is having a good day", "maybe I have underestimated her".
- The practitioner's understanding of the situation is examined critically. Not only is a theory constructed, based on the perceived events, but also it is subjected to critical questioning. The critical part of the analysis goes hand in hand with the constructive one. In the example this takes place through internal questions ("is she only pretending?"), through observations that at first seem to contradict the interpretation ("she isn't taking notes") and through definite actions (asking a question).

Rather than being clearly separated from each other all these procedures are interconnected and enable us to cope emotionally, intellectually and practically with our daily routines. This kind of analysis of daily routines allows us to react quickly to an initial understanding and use it as the basis for action (e.g. praising Susie). Its disadvantage is that it all happens very quickly so that we can only process a very limited amount of information and carry out a small number of testing procedures. It is therefore insufficient for understanding any major discrepancies between our expectations and our perceptions of the situation. This requires greater distance from the events and a certain amount of time to concentrate on the analysis.

Data can be an important prop for your memory when you want to withdraw from the stream of events and give yourself time for careful analysis; with the help of data, memories can be reconstructed more vividly (e.g. by listening to the tape-recording of a lesson), and be more available to critical questioning, making it possible to correct false interpretations.

The analysis of both data and direct experiences should result in a deeper understanding of the situation, and a "new" practical theory that can extend existing understanding. Through analysis, data and experiences are restructured and practical theories elaborated. In this sense analysis, theorizing and restructuring are the same. But, can this be called research? Is the teacher, nurse, social worker or other professional practitioner who does the analysis a *researcher*? A sharp line cannot be drawn between analysis in research and everyday analysis. The more systematically an analysis is carried out (based on theoretical and methodological knowledge), the more critical the process (tested against conflicting data and interpretations), and the more communicative it is (the process and the results made public), the more it deserves to be called *research*.

The results of the process of analysis are preliminary and hypothetical, and require further testing through reflection and examination in practice. Results are the interpretations, practical theories and conclusions that we draw from our data. We use data analysis methods both to *construct* and *critique* our findings. The constructive data analysis process – how we formulate our findings – can be represented in a cycle of four steps:

- *Reading data* – data are "read" (closely scrutinized) in order to recall the events and experiences that they represent: What was done? What was said? What really happened?
- *Selecting data* – important factors are separated from unimportant ones, similar factors are grouped, complex details are sorted and (where possible) simplified.
- *Presenting data* – the selected data are presented in a form that is easy to take in. This can be in the form of a written outline or a diagram (see Chapter 4).

• *Interpreting data and drawing conclusions* – relationships are explained and a practical theory (or model) constructed to fit the situation that has been researched. This theory or model should relate to the research focus.

We represent this process as a cycle because the interpretation of data to draw conclusions and construct findings can require several revisits to the data. It may also lead us to collect more data, do additional research activities or even reformulate our starting points for research.

These activities do not only take place during a separate stage of analysis, but during the entire research process, with the result that decisions made in each phase have consequences for what follows. This is especially clear with respect to data collection: decisions have to be made about which aspects of events are observed (selection), in what form the data is stored (presentation) and so on. Figure 6.1 looks very much like Figure 1.1 in which we first represented the action research process. This reminds us that almost every aspect of action research can be seen in itself as a mini-action research cycle.

We do analysis to make sense of our data. This construction of meaning is accompanied by a *critical examination of the analytic process*. Critical does not mean being negative in this sense. Each stage of the analysis is tested. Do the data bring the event to mind? Has the data selection focused on the central issues? Does the data presentation clarify the relationships between events and stimulate further analysis? Does the interpretation

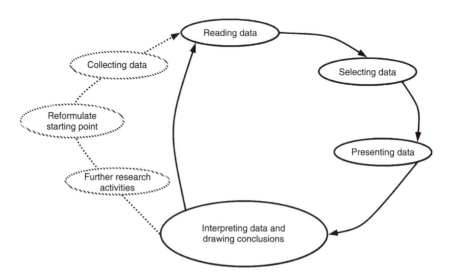

Figure 6.1 The constructive analysis of data

Source Miles and Huberman (1994: 12)

explain the data satisfactorily? This critical examination often occurs at the same time as the constructive activities, but sometimes it is useful to create a separate stage in the research process specially for testing.

The critical element of analysis should consist of two activities: checking the reliability of any evidence that substantiates a finding, and searching for any evidence *against* it. Both activities are important in testing the trustworthiness of findings. Both also contribute to their development: the first by enriching and enlarging them, the second by restricting and defining them and therefore clarifying and sharpening understanding.

It is important that the findings should be clearly formulated before this critical process begins so that they can be either confirmed or disproved by the data. This means relating interpretations to observations (e.g. using "the ladder of inference", see M18). The reality represented in the data must have the chance to "speak for itself" – even if the action researcher's main interest is in finding supportive evidence to reduce the amount of work required, or to validate a chosen course of action. It is important to remain open to data that, rather than confirming your theories, question them, and therefore encourage further reflection. In the long run this is an important part of justifying your confidence in your own practical theory. It does not imply denying your own convictions and judgments, which is impossible for practitioners (and is only an illusion for professional researchers). But it does imply a readiness to step back from your assumptions, look at the data and be open to any evidence that is counter to your assumptions.

The critical analysis of findings is not primarily a question of procedures. More important is intellectual integrity and the determination to be honest with yourself and others. All researchers are under pressure to be successful, especially when implementing and evaluating something new. The feeling that you have to prevail over your own insecurity and other people's skepticism can threaten your willingness to accept unexpected results. It is nevertheless an important part of learning to become a researcher.

Testing the reliability of results is essentially a never-ending process and there can be no such thing as absolute reliability. Nevertheless, the research must stop somewhere. One indication that it is time to finish is when it appears that collecting any additional data would yield nothing new in either a positive or negative sense. This situation is called *saturation*. There is, of course, also a pragmatic limit arising from a practitioner's responsibility to act. Because the research is intended to be useful to practice, there is not always time to wait for saturation. In any case, the critical process is not completed with the end of data analysis, but continues as ideas are translated into actions (see Chapter 7).

We want now to present practical methods that an action researcher can use to try to make sense of data. We will begin with elementary methods for the constructive and critical stages of data analysis – a kind of basic toolkit for the action researcher (avoiding repetition of the methods of analysis described in Chapters 2, 3 and 4). We then will go on to present two complex methods combining elements of these basic methods: pattern analysis and dilemma analysis.

CONSTRUCTIVE METHODS OF ANALYSIS

M32 MAKING DATA SUMMARIES

It is helpful to review data immediately after they have been collected (audio-recordings, observations notes, documents) and write a summary, both to provide easy access to the data later and to get an overview of what they offer concerning the research question (Miles and Huberman 1994:51). The data summary might contain answers to the following questions:

1 What is the context in which the data were collected? Why were they collected? Why in this particular situation? Why use this method of collection?
2 What are the most important facts in the data? Is anything surprising?
3 About which research issue are the data most informative?
4 Do the data give rise to any new questions, points of view, suggestions or ideas?
5 Do the data suggest what should be done next, in terms of further data collection, analysis or action?

It is a good idea to cross-reference each answer to relevant passages in the data to audio-recordings or transcripts. Summaries of existing data are also useful. A data summary should not take more than two pages or it begins to lose its value as a quick point of reference.

DEVELOPING CATEGORIES AND CODING DATA

One important method of getting "conceptual leverage" on data (see Schatzman and Strauss 1973) is organizing them into *categories* (coding them). Imagine a room in which a large number of toys have been left lying around and it is your job to create order. You will probably begin by walking round and having a look at things. According to your interests and the characteristics of the toys, features will come to mind that help you to order them: for example, color, size, shape, state of repair, the age group for which they are suitable and so on. Then you will choose two or more features by which to begin to sort them. Something similar happens when a researcher wants to create order from a quantity of data. Categories (features) need to be chosen that are relevant to the research question and at the same time partially express the contents of the data. Using these categories the data are sorted: for example, by ascribing a suitable category to each passage of a text. This process is called coding.

There are two well-recognized methods of coding data. According to the *deductive* method categories are chosen from the researcher's theoretical knowledge and the data is then searched for relevant passages: in this case the development of categories is independent of the data. According to the *inductive* method categories are chosen during and after scrutinizing the data: in this case the categories are "derived" from the data (see M15).

In action research it is probably most useful to use a mixture of both methods, capitalizing on what you already know but remaining open to the surprises the data can contain. As the inductive method is less common we will describe one possible approach to carrying it out in M33.

M33 INDUCTIVE DATA CODING

Develop the categories by grouping concepts that belong together. This is a two-step process. First you give conceptual labels to parts of the text. Then the concepts are grouped together into categories. This gives some structure to the whole by suggesting connections among individual categories (see M15).

Coding of data using the inductive method

1 Read through the text you want to code (e.g. the transcript of an interview). Underline or highlight each passage that seems to you important (interesting, surprising, unexpected) in relation to your research question. This will give you a broad overview of the contents of the data through the marked passages.

2 Go through the text a second time looking only at the marked passages, and decide upon a conceptual label (one word or a short phrase) for passages that express its contents.

3 Now look for ways to group conceptual labels into broader categories and list them on the category sheet.

4 For each category write down the passage(s) it refers to, giving the following information:

   • the name of the file you are coding;
   • the page number of the text;

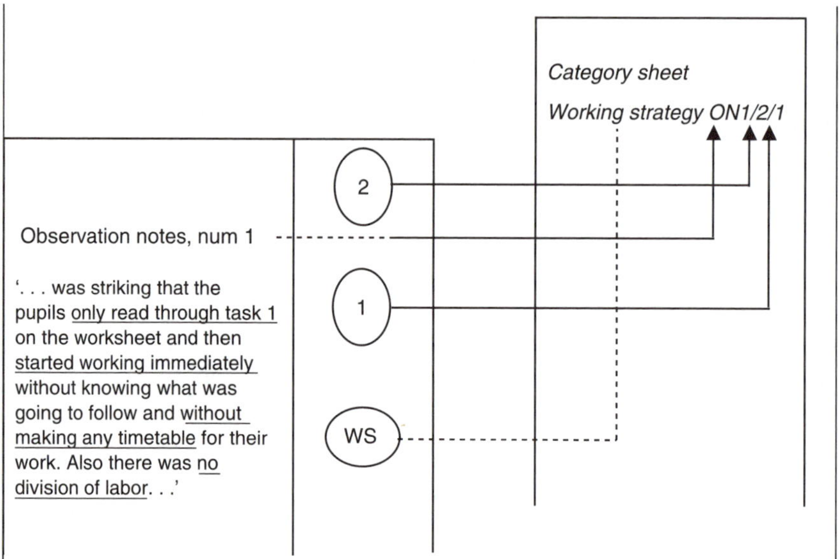

Figure 6.2 Example of inductive coding

- the margin number of the marked passage (each marked passage is given a serial number in the margin, starting with 1 on each new page). For example "ON 1/2/1" in Figure 6.2 means that a passage in the Observation Notes, no. 1, on page 2, with margin number 1 has been ascribed to this category. A coding system of this kind is important as it enables much more information to be written on the "category sheet", which ensures that you can retain an overview.

5 Also write the category in the margin beside the passage it refers to. For example the short form "WS" in Figure 6.2 stands for the conceptual label, "Working strategy".

This figure shows a section from page two of Observation Notes No.1 (ON1) on a group of pupils working together to solve mathematical problems. In the Observation notes interesting passages have been marked by underlining, and given a margin number at the right hand side of the page. The coding of the passage is noted both on the category sheet and in the right hand margin of the Observation Notes (in an abbreviated form).

It is also possible to do coding with the use of computer software. If the text is in word-processing software you can use mark-ups and comments, highlighting and so on to annotate the text. There is also qualitative analysis software that will partially automate the process of coding.[1]

A few practical tips for coding

In the process of coding you begin to hold a reflective conversation with the text. You check whether the categories correspond with what is in the text and relate to your research question, and change them if necessary. When you have gone through the text a second time you will have a categories sheet containing all the categories you have ascribed to the marked passages on the text, with one or more number codes written beside each category, making it easy to find the relevant passage quickly. The text will also list the categories in the margin beside the marked passages.

It is a good idea to write *definitions of the categories* that you can refer to. A definition expresses your theoretical understanding of the category and gives it a meaning independent of the data. Definitions are useful particularly if you continue to elaborate and refine them in the course of your work, in relation to both new data and your own developing understanding. It also helps to provide exemplars of the categories. Exemplars are data that illustrate the definitions.

Here are a few other tips:

- Data should be coded as soon as possible, while your direct experience of the event is still fresh. Coding can also be helpful in suggesting ideas of what to do next in your research.
- Categories are key concepts that form the nuclei of ideas. Time spent working on them is well invested. To develop and test your first categories we recommend that you write a short piece to try out how easily you can use them. Some categories give rise to a number of ideas and suggest possibilities for action, whereas others remain sterile.
- It is an advantage in action research (in contrast to traditional empirical research) if the action researcher does the coding, so as to make use of relevant background information not accessible to non-participants in the situation. This implicit knowledge of everyday, self-evident things can however lead to "blind spots". Therefore, we recommend that you talk about the categories, and how best to structure them, with your research group or critical friend who can help you to become aware of any blinkered assumptions that stand in the way of your understanding.

M34 CATEGORIES FOR QUESTIONNAIRE OR SURVEY DATA

Surveys and questionnaires can produce *qualitative* and *quantitative* data. M34 will focus on the analysis of quantitative data. Here we want to show how qualitative textual data that comes from surveys or questionnaires can be grouped and categorized to reduce it to make it more manageable. We will illustrate this through an example.

Jeff Kenney, a middle school science teacher, had early on in his career recognized that it was important to "connect" with each of his pupils. By connect he meant that he wanted to have a relationship with each pupil in which they – Jeff and the pupil – saw each other as a distinct human being. Jeff felt that he was usually good at doing this with his pupils, but as a result of the reconnaissance that he did to develop a starting point for research, he realized that there were pupils who for some reason did not respond to his attempts to make this connection. Rather than single out these pupils as subjects of his research, he chose to survey all of his pupils to find out what in their teachers were important to them. He asked them to complete the following sentences:

1 The thing that I like most about my favorite teacher is . . .
2 I feel really good when a teacher . . .
3 I hope that next year's teachers will . . .
4 I really like teachers who . . .
5 I have trouble getting along with teachers who . . .
6 It makes me angry when a teacher . . .

In reading through the surveys he grouped the pupils' responses into a large number of concepts. Here, for example, are the concepts that he developed for question, "The thing I like most about my favorite teacher is . . ."

A He/she has a sense of humor. (25)
B He/she is nice. (21)
C He/she helps me. (13)
D He/she makes work fun. (9)
E He/she understands me. (7)
F I can talk to him/her easily. (4)
G He/she encourages me. (4)
H He/she gives us freedom. (4)
M He/she doesn't yell. (1)
N He/she is easy to understand. (1)
O He/she lets us do experiments. (1)

P He/she relates to us. (1)
Q He/she is laid back. (1)
R He/she is happy. (1)
S He/she smiles. (1)
T He/she won't let me fail. (1)
U He/she listens to me. (1)

As a result of this initial coding, Jeff found that found that many of his students responded that they wanted their teachers to be "nice" and not "mean". Jeff gave the students a second, quick survey that asked them to explain what they meant by "nice" and "mean". When that information was combined with his original results, he had nearly 500 responses to his questions, with typically more than 20 different conceptual labels for each question. To make sense of his data he then grouped the concepts into categories. Figure 6.3 shows the result of the grouping that he did with his critical friend.

He used the method described in M33 to develop categories. For the most part the categories described positive or negative behaviors of teachers. For example, one of the categories that he developed was "Positive teacher disposition". This included student responses to Prompt 1 such as "He/She has a sense of humor", "He/She is laid back", "He/She is happy" and "He/She smiles".

Another category that he used to sort responses to prompt 6 was "Teacher's actions are negative towards student". Examples of conceptual labels to Prompt 6 that he included in this category were "Doesn't listen to me", "Pays no attention to me", "Doesn't sympathize with me" and "Embarrasses me in class".

Categorizing survey or questionnaire data in this way can be a powerful means of data analysis. This can be seen in Jeff Kenney's analysis in which the students put much more emphasis on the teacher actions and characteristics that concern the relationship between the students and teacher than on the quality of teaching methods. While this may have been evident in the original list of data, the coding, categorizing, and representing of the data in a table make the difference much starker. Before we take significant action based on this finding, it would make sense to look critically at Jeff's analysis. For example, there the difference is due to the way that the prompt was worded, rather than any fundamental aspect of the educational situation. Also, there is the possibility that the large number of responses in any one category (for example, "Positive teacher disposition") could be due to it being very broad.

Prompt	Type of student comment	Number of responses	Percentage
1 The thing that I like most about my favorite teacher is …	Positive teacher affect.	43	45.7
	Teacher's relationship to student is positive.	30	31.9
	Teacher's actions make classroom environment positive.	13	13.8
	Quality of teaching methods.	8	8.5
	Total responses	94	100
2 I feel really good when a teacher …	Teacher's actions that relate to students' feelings.	45	60
	Teacher's actions that help students.	20	26.7
	Teacher's actions make classroom environment positive.	10	13.3
	Quality of teaching methods.	0	0
	Total responses	75	100
3 I hope that next year's teachers will …	Positive teacher affect.	45	54.9
	Teacher's relationship to student is positive.	18	22
	Teacher's actions make classroom environment positive.	16	19.5
	Quality of teaching methods.	3	3.7
	Total responses	82	100
4 I really like teachers who …	Positive teacher affect.	36	43.4
	Teacher's relationship to student is positive.	27	32.5
	Teacher's actions make classroom environment positive.	19	22.9
	Quality of teaching methods.	1	1.2
	Total responses	83	100
5 I have trouble getting along with teachers who …	Negative teacher affect.	32	49.2
	Teacher's actions make classroom environment negative.	19	29.2
	Quality of teaching methods.	14	21.5
	Total responses	65	100
6 It makes me angry when a teacher …	Teacher's actions are negative toward student.	41	74.5
	Teacher's actions make classroom environment negative.	10	18.2
	Quality of teaching methods.	4	7.3
	Total responses	55	100

Figure 6.3 Categorizing qualitative survey data

M35 WRITING THEORETICAL NOTES

At any stage in the research process – e.g. when formulating questions or analyzing data – ideas and theories are likely to come to mind relating to the research question: what certain data mean, how observations could be explained, how an important concept could be defined, etc. Such ideas should never be wasted even if they are not needed at the present stage of the research, but should be recorded in the form of a *theoretical note* (TN).

Theoretical notes help us to move beyond the detail of events to a conceptual level, to develop theories, uncover relationships and find significance. Writing them only takes a few minutes and is a quick way of capturing emergent ideas during the research process. Writing theoretical notes usually gives some immediate satisfaction, as they offer access to your own ideas that may have been hidden, or partly hidden, up to this point.

Theoretical notes should always be dated and labeled with a suitable catchword so that they can easily be found again. It's a good idea to make a brief note of the data or event that gave rise to the ideas. This short section is intended only as a reminder. Further information on this quick and economical first form of analysis has already been given in Chapter 2.

M36 QUANTIFICATION

To quantify something is to measure it (OED 1989). In classical social science research the measurements are typically used in ways that aggregate the features of many events or cases and, as a result, it often represents too little of the holistic structure of practice. In action research we recognize that some elements of quantification are of great importance in people's thinking about practice. For example, when we say that something is "significant" or "common" we often have come to this judgment by counting, comparing and weighing up. Intuitive counting is often a precondition for developing categories. It is important to become aware of the close connection between our judgments and quantitative aspects of our experience, and to quantify consciously whenever it is useful and gives a good return for effort.

Quantification can be useful in the following situations:

1   *To provide information that helps you to describe your situation*
     Numerical data can be used descriptively in many different ways.
     One of the simplest is to keep track of attendance of some sort. It
     could be class attendance or attendance in therapy sessions.
     Another use is to keep track of how you use your time. Allan
     decided to do that to find out what was happening to his time
     after he told one of his doctoral students that he only had 25
     minutes to speak with her about her dissertation proposal. In
     reflecting on that comment, he realized that this was dissonant
     with his desire to be a good mentor to his students. He wondered
     what it was that was wrong with his practice that caused him to
     have little time for his students. He decided to note down how
     he spent his waking time for one week. The results are recorded in
     Figure 6.4.

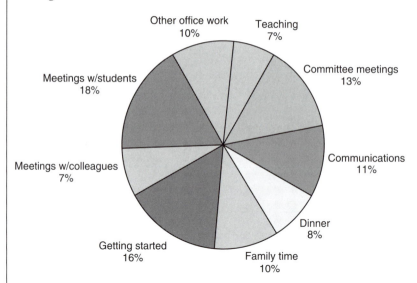

Figure 6.4 Percentage of Allan's waking time spent in different activities

2   *To carry out a preliminary survey and get some data quickly*
     For this purpose you can make use of the fact that numbers are
     much easier to handle than words. For example, Shelly Bathe
     was a case manager for university students with psychological
     and/or medical disabilities. As a way to better understand her
     practice she developed a ten-item questionnaire to try to under-
     stand her clients' beliefs about successful case management.
     Five of the items used a Likert-type scale (Likert 1967). This
     scale gives the respondent a range of five choices from strongly
     disagree to strongly agree. These choices can then be associated

with numbers, for example, from 1 to 5. If a respondent chose Agree for item 7 (she agreed that a comfortable rapport between student and case manager contributes to successful case management), then that would be recorded as a 4. If she had chosen Neutral, it would have been recorded as a 3, and so on. Shelly could have put the values for all the respondents onto a spreadsheet and found the average response, the spread of responses and so on. She also could have used the spreadsheet to make a table or graph of the responses (Bathe 2000).

3 *To reveal prejudices*
This function of quantification is important because of the key part played by intuition in action research. There are moments when you feel a sense of revelation and everything seems to fall into place. The only problem is that you can be wrong. Observations that do not fit your own expectations may have been ignored. In situations like this quantification can be helpful to check the reliability of intuition.

Grayson DeWitt (2000) had just started teaching in a new school. In his previous school he had been concerned that there was inequitable participation in his classes. He wrote, "As I got more familiar with my surroundings, and had some time to reflect on my performance, I again felt that girls were not participating in class to the same extent as the boys". To check whether his "gut feeling" was accurate, he audio-taped several lessons and counted the number of times that boys and girls participated. He also kept a tally during other lessons, making simple marks on a piece of paper every time a student participated (see Chapter 5 on observation). Grayson found little difference in his classes. Although this confirmed that he was meeting his goal to have equitable participation along gender lines, it opened up several other questions: "Even with this confirmation I was still unsatisfied. How were students participating? What was the quality of student responses?" (DeWitt 2000: 9). He then went on to gather data to examine these questions in his second cycle of action research.

4 *To explore the generalizability of findings*
Sometimes results relating to only a few people (or a single case) have more general validity and this can be confirmed by quantitative methods. An example of this is the amount of time between when a teacher asks the class a question and when he/she expects students to answer. In the early 1970s Mary Budd Rowe, while studying elementary school lessons, found that elementary science teachers allow an average of one second for a response to a question, and follow a pupil response by a comment within an

average of nine-tenths of a second. She also found that extending this "wait-time" to 3–5 seconds had profound effects on the pupils. For example, the pupils increased the complexity of their responses, more pupils volunteered to answer questions and pupil confidence increased (Rowe 1972). While this effect was observable in one teacher's classroom, Rowe's quantitative studies showed that increasing wait-time could have significant effects in all classrooms.

METAPHORS IN RESEARCH

The movie *Il Postino* (Radford 1994) is a fictionalized account of Pablo Neruda's exile to a small island off the coast of Italy. Mario, the only island inhabitant who is literate, becomes the postman. As he interacts with Neruda he becomes worldlier in many ways. One interaction centers on the meaning of metaphor. In this scene, Mario has delivered the mail and then waits for an opportunity to talk with Neruda about the meaning of his poetry. Their conversation becomes an exchange of lines from Neruda's poetry. It soon becomes clear that Mario does not know what a metaphor is. To help him to understand, Neruda asks him if he knows what it means if he were to say that the sky is weeping. When Mario replies that it means that it is raining, Neruda tells him that is a metaphor.

As Mario learned, a metaphor is a figure of speech in which a word or term is used in place of another to denote an analogy. Metaphors go back to the roots of language. Originally there were only words for things that can be perceived sensually and these had to be used to convey abstract ideas as well (see Reiners 1961: 317). For a name to be transferred from one thing to another there must be something in common that allows a comparison: tears fall from one's eyes and rain falls from the sky. What make metaphors interesting are the ramifications of their meaning including their emotive connotations, all of which are transferred to the new object. We can see this by comparing Neruda's metaphor with this one: "A tap in the sky is open". "Weeping" has many associations that are not present in the open tap. If the sky is weeping, does that mean the sky is happy/ sad? Who is weeping and why? A metaphor therefore provides the opportunity to see something freshly, offering a new perspective on the concept, object or event to which it is applied.

Metaphors generate meaning

In the example above we can see how metaphors can transfer meaning between objects, events or feelings. Metaphors can also generate meaning.

There are countless examples in education, such as those that preservice teachers come up with when asked to find a metaphor for "teacher", e.g. a teacher is like an orchestra conductor, an actor or a coach. In these metaphors, the preservice teachers transfer the aspects of the other profession onto the role of the teacher. The conductor strives to make sure that each musician knows his/her piece and that all the musicians together sound harmonious. The teacher wants each student to learn and excel, and wants the class to work together to create positive opportunities for learning. But there is more to these metaphors than one may see at first glance. The conductor is in front of the orchestra on a stand directing it. Implicit in this metaphor is a separation between pupils and teacher that is both physical and hierarchal. The separation is even greater in the metaphor of teacher as actor. While the conductor is expected to have direct effects on the performance of the musicians, the actor is on a stage in front of a darkened hall and generally looking for reactions and appreciation from the audience. The coach metaphor suggests a stronger relationship between student and teacher, with both physically on the same level, and, given the media image of coaches, some type of "tough love" interaction. Metaphors act similarly in other practices. In medicine patients are treated differently if their care providers think of them as human beings rather than as illnesses.

Our point in these examples is that metaphors help us to understand new situations and roles, but they also have a generative character that affects the way we see the world. In recent years the metaphor of the marketplace has become a powerful ideological tool to shape social policy. Politicians in some countries argue that parents and children should see themselves as customers of schools and shop around for the best one. Market forces would then cause schools to compete for "customers" and those that are not successful would close, just like a business that does not have enough customers. This metaphor is also being used to reshape the medical and mental health professions.

Sharon Lowenstein, a divorce mediator, has paid careful attention to the ways that metaphors can shape the negotiations between adversaries. She describes the way that she does this in the following metaphorical manner:

> Rather than relying on the metaphor of *war*, which dominates the language of our political and legal systems and thus that of conflict in general, in mediations metaphors should *bridge* differences, *cut to the chase* and put everyone *on the same page* so that negotiations can proceed in a *constructive* manner . . . Mediation puts clients in the *driver's seat*; litigation is a *gamble, a roll of the dice* that takes control from them. I frequently suggest that clients take *one bite of the elephant* at a time in order to avoid *indigestion*. And, of course, regardless of the amount of

fault each assigns to the other, nearly everyone will respond knowingly to the statement that it *takes two to tango*.

(Lowenstein 2006: 1, original emphasis)

Lowenstein's advice to mediators shows how language conveys more than the meaning of specific words. It also conveys attitudes, mindsets, and perspectives. The way in which we use metaphors shapes the way we think about the world and influence the decisions that we make about what we choose to do. As another example of this generative character of metaphors (Schön 1980), we will contrast two different metaphors for teaching and learning: teaching and learning as banking of knowledge, and teaching and learning as construction of meaning.

Teaching and learning as the "banking" of knowledge

The banking model of education was first described by the Brazilian educator, Paolo Freire in his book, *Pedagogy of the Oppressed* (Freire 1989). Freire wrote that in this model, education

> becomes an act of depositing, in which the students are the depositories and the teacher is the depositor. Instead of communicating, the teacher issues communiqués and makes deposits which the students patiently receive, memorize, and repeat.

(Freire 1989: 58)

This metaphor transfers the idea that teaching and learning is similar to banking: knowledge is "deposited" into pupils' brains and pupils can withdraw that knowledge for tests or other assessments. This metaphor is extended further in many classrooms in which teachers use a "point system" for grading. When pupils complete an assignment, teachers "pay them" with "points". Depending on how many points a pupil has amassed, he/she can "buy" a higher or lower grade (Feldman *et al.* 1998).

Freire provides examples of how this metaphor generates teachers' and pupils' behaviors and norms. They include:

a   The teacher teaches and the students are taught.
b   The teacher knows everything and the students know nothing.
c   The teacher thinks and the students are thought about.
d   The teacher disciplines and the students are disciplined.
e   The teacher chooses and enforces his choice, and the students comply.
f   The teacher chooses the program content, and the students (who were not consulted) adapt to it.

(Freire 1989: 59)

Teaching and learning as the 'construction' of meaning

This metaphor carries the idea that learners themselves frame their process of learning and "construct" new knowledge, using the experience and knowledge they already have. This metaphor is similar to photosynthesis where the plant builds organic matter from inorganic matter with the help of light and chlorophyll. The pupil is seen as an active constructor of knowledge who "understands" facts by reconstructing them using his/her own resources. This attitude generates different norms of behavior:

- The teacher should "start from where the pupil is at" because the pupil's existing knowledge provides the materials for constructing further knowledge.
- The teacher should encourage pupils' independence if he/she wants to exploit their maximum potential for learning.
- The teacher should build on pupils' interests because they will provide the energy and motivation necessary for learning.
- The teacher should offer a variety of activities to cater for the differences in pupils' prior experience.
- Mistakes, rather than harming the learning process, will provide an opportunity to reflect on learning strategies and improve them. The teacher should encourage the pupils to monitor their own progress, and support them in doing so.

The metaphors of teaching and learning as "banking" and as "construction" call for totally different, even contradictory courses of action. For a pupil to turn to a classmate and ask a question may be seen as an unwelcome disturbance in terms of the first metaphor, but as a useful part of the learning process in terms of the second.

Metaphors and the action research process

Identifying, constructing and analyzing metaphors can help action researchers in several ways. The process widens horizons and enables a better understanding of the practitioner's situation. Metaphors provide alternative approaches to reality, like mirrors reflecting different facets of the same complex event. The more facets there are, the deeper the understanding of a situation can be, as each facet reflects different aspects of reality. For example, the metaphor "learning as banking" emphasizes the curriculum as presented to the pupil and disregards the processing of the curriculum by the pupil. The metaphor "learning as construction" emphasizes the dynamics of the pupils' activities and disregards the cultural and social conditions of learning.

Metaphors are good at communicating complex matters as they carry a lot of information in a few words. They are – despite consisting of words themselves – the pictures (images) of language. The metaphor of "banking" evokes a number of associations that can remain unspoken as the reader already knows them from familiar areas of experience. On the other hand, misunderstandings can result from metaphors, as a language full of images is not very precise. Differences in people's experience can conjure up different associations. This is especially true of the feelings evoked by metaphors.

Metaphors open up new action strategies. Strategies of action often seem normal and obvious only from the point of view of the generative metaphor they are based upon. As soon as the metaphor changes new strategies of action become relevant. Schön illustrated this with the example of a research team that was trying to develop paint brushes using synthetic fibres (Schön 1980). The team was having little success in getting the synthetic brushes to apply the paint as smoothly as natural bristles until one of the researchers began to think of the brush as a pump to move paint from its container to the canvas or wall. This new metaphor generated new ways for the team to think about what they were trying to accomplish, which led them to come up with different designs for the brushes.

Schön also made clear that while research and problem-solving can be facilitated by the construction of new metaphors, there are pre-existing, tacit metaphors that shape the way we think about our practice situations and shape our behaviors. Therefore, it is important for us to become aware of the metaphors that we live and work by, so that we are not manipulated by the images they create in our minds. Understanding the generative character of metaphors can also help action researchers to distance themselves from the apparent obviousness of daily routines. If you know that you see reality only through the "glasses" of metaphors (a metaphor again!) it is easier to change them – and new strategies of action become possible (see Chapter 4).

M37 RESEARCHING WITH METAPHORS

Metaphors are of a generative character. They cannot replace the analysis of data, but they can stimulate new directions for analysis and in this way enrich the research and development process. Although some suggest that metaphors are only valuable if they come to mind naturally, and that it is no good searching for them consciously (Reiners 1961: 335), we suggest several different ways to use and construct metaphors in your research.

Miles and Huberman (1994: 252) provide the following advice:

- Stay aware and become aware of the metaphors that you use in your practice and in your research.
- Avoid trying to find overarching metaphors too early in your research. They can cause you to narrow your focus too early and too much.
- Handle your data playfully. For example, you could ask yourself, "If I only had two words to describe this situation, which ones would they be?"
- Talk about your data with your research group, critical friend or colleagues. Conversation in a relaxed atmosphere may spawn new and unusual perspectives.
- Know when to stop pushing the metaphor. "When the oasis starts to have camels, camel drivers, a bazaar, and a howling sandstorm, you know you're forcing things" (Miles and Huberman 1994). On the other hand, pay attention to when the metaphor falls apart – that can open up new ways to think about your situation.
- Take up metaphors that are in the data (e.g. in interviews) and elaborate playfully upon their possible meanings for the data. For instance, if a school principal refers to his role as leader as "father of a family" ask who are the "distant relatives" and who are the "naughty children".

There are also specific methods that you can use to construct metaphors. One is called "A walk in the woods". We're all familiar with stories about people solving problems or coming up with new ideas when they turn away from their work and do something relaxing, like taking a walk in the woods. You can increase the likelihood of producing an "aha moment" by writing yourself a note about your situation and putting it in your pocket. Most likely you will forget about that note after a while, and then later on, when you put your hand in your pocket and find a folded piece of paper, the surprise of re-encountering the problem can help you to create a metaphor. It would also help to have some other paper and a pen or pencil to jot down the ideas that you get so that you don't forget them as you hike back home.

We suggest that you do the following:

1 Construct a metaphor for your practice. You can do this by following Miles and Huberman's suggestions (see above) or by taking "a walk in the woods".
2 Push the metaphor. Stop pushing either when the metaphor no longer pertains to your research or when "the oasis has camels, camel drivers, a bazaar, and a howling sandstorm". How do the details of the metaphor correspond or map onto your practice situation or research?

> 3 Ask yourself, "Why doesn't the metaphor work anymore?",
> "What do the differences between the metaphor and my practice/
> research tell me about my practice situation?" and "What I am
> trying to learn and improve?"

Another way that you can use metaphors is to "remodel the problem". In Chapter 5 we looked at the example of the nurses who wanted to improve the discharge preparation process for children with respiratory problems. This problem – how to make sure that the children and their parents follow the proper procedures at home – could be remodeled into a simpler problem, like "How to take care of the new puppy". Once the new problem is remodeled, you can brainstorm a list of things that you would need to do to take care of the new puppy. This could include making sure that it has the right food, taking it for walks, making sure that it gets the right vaccinations and so on. Once you have that list, you can "back map" – ask, "What is the equivalent to taking the puppy for walks in the discharge preparation?" In this way, a metaphor – puppy care – is used to make a more complex, unfamiliar problem simpler and more familiar.

CRITICAL METHODS OF ANALYSIS

In Chapter 5 we discussed the issue of quality of action research. We presented a definition for validity that asks whether our representation of a phenomenon is accurate. We use critical methods of analysis to try to ensure the accuracy of our representations, conclusions or findings. In Chapter 5 we suggested several ways of doing this. They included: (1) considering alternative explanations; (2) testing through practical action; (3) ethical justification; (4) practicality; and (5) the use of triangulation. We now turn to two specific methods to test the accuracy of what we believe we have learned from our research.

> ### M38 TESTING THE FINDINGS
>
> Stearns *et al.* (quoted in Miles and Huberman 1994) suggest a procedure for formulating and critically analyzing findings.
>
> 1 Write a series of sentences on cards, each expressing one important result of the analysis (one sentence per card). The sentences are freely based on your experience, taken from notes (e.g. your research notebook) or taken from hypotheses or analytical notes developed while coding data (e.g. M33). You may be tempted to

do this using a computer but we find it more useful to have cards that can be physically manipulated. Some people do find it effective to use software that allows you to look at relationships intuitively, such as *Inspiration (www.inspiration.com) or N-Vivo (www.qsrinternational.com)*.

2   The sentences (cards) are sorted into sets according to the issues they refer to.

3   Each set of cards is then laid out in a way that makes them easy to survey and clarifies the relationships between them.

4   Each card is checked against the available data. Any data that seem to relate to the sentence are cut out and placed beside the card. At this point it actually may be more worthwhile to group cards and data using a computer.

5   In the light of the selected data, look again at the sentences and expand, modify and illustrate them, either by writing additional sentences and adding these to the layout of cards or by rewriting the original cards. In this way the sentences and data make up the "backbone" of a written report, and if this procedure is followed with every single sentence, the report will be rich in detail and grounded in the data.

The following example is taken from action research into the support given to students on teaching practice. Mentor teachers, university teachers and the teacher education students all wrote case studies that were analyzed as a group exercise during a seminar. The analysis took place as follows: each participant wrote three statements from their findings on cards (step 1). The cards were arranged in an order (step 2) and relationships between cards were identified (step 3). Then, relevant arguments for and against the statements were found in the case studies (step 4). After examining and developing each statement (step 5), a report was "put together" analyzing and recommending ways of supporting students on teaching practice. The following passage was taken from one group's report:

Statement (developed from a sentence on a card):

> *The first few days of teaching experience in the introductory course to school practice are too soon to decide on a starting point for a case study, since students are too busy with the basic problems of their school practice.*

Evidence for (+) and against (−) the statement, using data from the case studies (CS):

> *A student's statements (CS22/1):*

+   *"It didn't seem to make sense to me that I had to write a case study at the beginning of the term."*

+   *"What could I use as a focus for a case study? Why can't I think of anything?"*

Mentor teachers' statements:

−   *"(. . .) Case studies help to make problems in teaching become visible"* (CS20/6).

−   *"Asking students to write case studies gives structure to lesson observations, practice teaching and reflection, and has become a useful tool that enables me to get away from the arbitrary jungle of talking about lessons"* (CS20/7).

M39 COMMUNICATIVE VALIDATION

Communicative validation is a method for checking the validity of an interpretation through establishing a consensus view between the researcher and a participant of the situation being researched, e.g. between an interviewer and interviewee. Practitioners use this method when they tell a pupil, patient or client their interpretation of what has been said. Concurrence is seen as an indication of the validity of the practitioner's interpretation.

Member checks can be used to seek communicative validation. In a member check the researcher tests his/her data, interpretations and conclusion with research participants (Lincoln and Guba 1985). For an action researcher, this would mean discussing with pupils, patients, clients, family members, colleagues and so on who inhabit your professional situation the meaning you have derived from your data. Member checking can be done informally during your interactions with participants, or it can be done more formally by arranging meetings with participants individually or in groups. When done informally it provides the opportunity to check what the participant's intention was in saying or doing something. Rather than rely solely on your own interpretation of what you saw or heard, you can ask the person why he/she made the particular statement or action. It also provides the participant with the opportunity to add to his/her account, or to correct your mis-interpretation (Lincoln and Guba 1985).

The amount of agreement indicates the validity of the results of the analysis. However, as in all other cases, the validity that emerges through this communication process is fragile and temporary.

The problem of power relations due to age, gender, and status differentials can cause participants to say what they believe you want them to say. There is also the possibility that the participants are honest in their beliefs, but that their perceptions are skewed by societal beliefs or myths, or by the limitations of their own experience. Disagreement in interpretation, on the other hand, does not in principle devalue the result, but challenges the researcher to face the differences of opinion and explain them (see the example in Chapter 5, p. 146).

COMPLEX METHODS OF DATA ANALYSIS

We now turn to two more complex methods of data analysis: pattern analysis and dilemma analysis.

Pattern analysis

Patterns are "regularities of behavior" or "forms of interaction that occur over and over again". This is a working definition (see Ireland and Russell 1978), which we hope will be deepened and extended by the example that follows. This is a translated transcript of part of a tape-recording of a lesson on Germanic Literature for 14-year-old pupils in Austria (Sorger 1989).

Extract from transcript of a lesson (18 April 1989)

T: Well, first of all, here are some new worksheets ... You will get these worksheets for each chapter in literature from now on; on the left side you can always see what happened in literature at a given time. I've underlined the facts you should particularly try to remember. O.K? That's work that you actually should have done yourselves. On the right hand side I've listed things that are characteristic for that time. Now, I have a question: What kinds of things are listed on the right? Who can explain to me what I've put there? Yes, Bernhard?

Be: Historical facts.

T: Well, historical facts! Is there anything else? Something special?

PP: (inaud.)

T: Well, not only historical facts, but cultural facts.

PP: Dates, religious events, books.

T: Yes, that too, there is a system! That's one part.

P: First of all dates.

T: First of all just historical facts.
P: Then culture . . . then comes art.
T: Then art. I will present that in a similar way on each sheet from now on. Is that clear? On the left is literature, German literature. On the right historical events, cultural events, art, music and literature that is not German, if there is any. O.K?

(Lesson continues)

A very simple and repeated pattern is the sequence of alternating speech by the teacher and the pupils: each time the teacher speaks this is followed by a pupil speaking, and this in turn is followed by the teacher. This is called the T-P-T pattern. This example shows some characteristics of patterns:

1 *Patterns select data* – from the data as a whole, only the data connected by patterns are selected. In doing this certain data are emphasized, and other data unrelated to the pattern remain in the background. Even selected data are only seen from a certain perspective in relation to the pattern.
2 *Patterns structure data* – they organize the contents of the data. The order is *discovered* and at the same time *constructed*. This depends on the contents of the data but also on the prior knowledge, expectations and ideas (theories) of the person who identifies the patterns. Patterns are segments of the dense network of interrelationships existing in the data or emerging from it.
3 *Patterns interpret data* – they are presumptions (hypotheses) about the nature of teaching and learning:

   - Each pattern presupposes that there could be an underlying order that is a key aspect of the teaching process.
   - Each pattern presupposes deeply rooted attitudes (e.g. of the pupils/teacher towards their roles, etc.) that are keys to a better understanding of teaching.
   - Each pattern also assumes that it has effects, that it transmits messages that have influences (e.g. on attitudes).

Looked at on a more basic level, patterns indicate what is routine and habitual. They are usually largely unconscious, controlled by tacit knowledge hidden in unspoken routines.

How is pattern analysis done?

We want now to show how pattern analysis is done. We break up the process into five stages:

1 identification of patterns;
2 significance of the patterns;

3 effects of the patterns;
4 relationship between the pattern and the practitioner's intentions;
5 new actions.

STAGE 1 IDENTIFICATION OF PATTERNS

During this first stage it is useful simply to describe patterns, starting from intuitive hunches and then trying to elaborate their characteristics and relationships (see Figure 6.5). One pattern has already been identified above. We called it the T-P-T-pattern. It consists of a pupil's utterance in between two utterances by the teacher. When we take a closer look at what was actually said, we can see that there are several different ways in which this pattern can be played out. The extreme form of it, which is really T-T-T, is where the teacher asks a question, waits almost no time and then answers the question him/herself. Another type is the "sentence completion pattern", which can be seen in the extract from the transcript below:

T: If they had no writing . . . literature that hasn't been written down
      normally gets lost . . . in theory . . . I could imagine? . . . Rudolf?
Ru: Oral tradition.

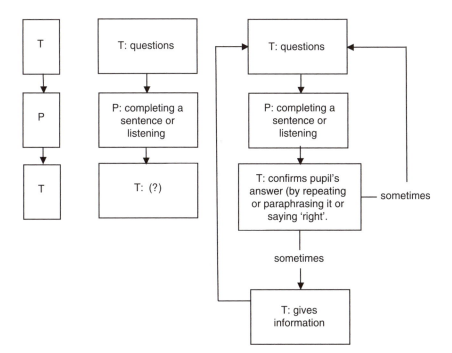

Figure 6.5 Development of the T-P-T pattern

In parts of the transcript that we have looked at so far the teacher responds by "revoicing" the pupil's response, repeating or rephrasing it to use the "correct" language. Sometimes the teacher will also evaluate the student's response. This sequence is known as IRE because it consists of teaching initiation, student response and then teacher evaluation. According to Cazden (1988) it is the most common pattern of classroom discourse for all grade levels. This is illustrated in the following excerpt from the transcript:

T: So a ritual is an action taking place according to certain rules. That means, normally everyone knows what he/she has to do at each stage of it, right? You might know of some rituals in everyday life today, can you think of any? Veronika . . . Sandra?

S: Daily meals.

T: Yes, daily meals. . . . Totally right!

Another type of sequence is IRF, which consists of teacher initiation, pupil response and then teacher follow-up. This sequence begins with either the teacher asking a question or introducing a topic. After a pupil responds, the teacher then uses the response to move the conversation forward. This sequence tends to be rare in classrooms. Rarer still are what we may think of as authentic discussions in which the classroom discourse becomes more of a conversation among participants than an exchange mediated through the teacher. The patterns for these discussions may be T-P-P in which there are two or more pupil responses to one teacher question. In this pattern the teacher may call on pupils without commenting on the previous pupil's response or intervening in the flow of ideas. There is even the possibility that a pupil could initiate the conversation with a question or comment and this is responded to by other pupils, again without teacher intervention (P-P-P).

Although the examples that we have here are from teaching situations, patterns of behavior can be identified in any type of professional practice. This kind of regular pattern, whether it is between pupils and teachers, nurses and patients or social workers and clients, is usually the result of unconscious routines that have been established through experience. Routine behavior should not be discounted, but it is important to ask to what extent these routines reinforce our aims and values, and what consequences they have.

STAGE 2 SIGNIFICANCE OF THE PATTERNS

We can end our analysis with the identification of the patterns, and depending upon their effects, either change our behaviors or not.

However, it is also useful to think of the patterns as being the surface features of our assumptions, skills, intentions or even fears. For example, what does it mean if a teacher embeds the pupils in his/her train of thought in the way expressed by the T-P-T pattern? First, it means that the teacher controls the way in which pupils respond to the subject matter. The most important control mechanisms are the questions the pupils are asked and the comments on their answers. If we look closely at the transcript it appears that the teacher's aim is to get the students to come up with ideas that fit his own thinking: he asks the questions in such a way as to maximize the likelihood of the pupils producing answers that meet his expectations. If a pupil does not give the answer he expects, or fails to answer, the teacher ignores "the wrong answer" and rephrases the question to another pupil.

Remember that if we are investigating our own practice the transcript will in fact be a transcript of ourselves interacting with our pupils, patients or clients. In this case, although we can attempt to reflect deeply on the meaning of the patterns, say through journal writing, it helps to have a conversation or be interviewed about our actions. This can be done as an analytic discourse in our research group or with our critical friend. The teacher in the transcript was interviewed about the lesson and here are some of his thoughts.

"I need some subject matter which I can examine."

"If they are afraid of being asked a question they pay attention."

"They have to know how they will be graded in the exam . . . I am finding it more and more difficult to give grades."

"(Because I have so few periods with them) I can't afford to waste any time in the lessons."

"The pupils like it because it reduces the risk for them (of failing) . . . If I asked questions in the exam which required interpretation of literature, I am afraid that some of them would fail."

"I like to separate the things that really matter (i.e. their ability to respond to literature) from preparation for oral exams."

The next step would be for you, along with your research group or critical friend, to try to make sense of your statements in relation to the lesson. Here are some of the teacher's assumptions that were inferred from the interview:

- He thinks that these patterns enable him to examine the pupils' knowledge in a way that is fair and not too stressful.
- He thinks that these patterns are good for discipline and ensure that the pupils pay attention.
- He thinks that this kind of teaching is expected of him and makes the best use of the time available.

The interpretation placed on a pattern should be plausible in the context and fit in with the analysis as a whole. This is the best way of deciding whether or not a possible pattern is of value. We recommend that you read relevant passages of a transcript several times looking closely for emerging associations. In this way you can pick up important clues as to the pattern's meaning and its importance to you and the part it plays in your professional self-image. It is not a good idea to discount too quickly those patterns you or others do not like, because they nearly always have some significance and you rarely gain anything by ignoring them. Equally, before changing routine patterns you should at least partially understand their meaning and the part they play in the complex system of your practice (see Chapter 4, pp. 74–5).

STAGE 3 EFFECTS OF THE PATTERNS

Your analysis of the transcript could end with the uncovering of your assumptions and intentions. However, an important part of professional practice is the effects that our work has on our pupils, patients or clients. Even an analysis of the complete transcript of this lesson does not tell us much about the effects of the patterns on the pupils. Those pupils who took an active part appear to have accepted the pattern, been able to work with it and even seemed to force the teacher to stick to it. However the majority of pupils did not take part, so it is conceivable that they did not accept the pattern and as a result did not volunteer answers or reply to the teacher's questions. As a way of delving into the pupils' beliefs and feelings about the pattern the teacher interviewed three of the pupils about his way of asking questions. Here is his summary of their answers (Sorger 1989):

- The way questions are asked makes it relatively clear to the pupils what is expected of them.
- The pupils feel involved in the lesson, even if only through the "risk of being caught out if your mind wanders".

For the pupils these patterns of interaction with their teacher obviously offer a clear framework in preparation for the examination, both in terms of subject matter and the format of the exam. Let's speculate on other possible consequences of the T-P-T pattern:

- What effect does it have on the atmosphere in class? Is the teacher right in his assumption that the pupils are satisfied with it? Are they all satisfied? On what does he base this belief? When an analysis is done of the complete transcript it is apparent that at least six pupils made oral contributions and in addition there were times when several pupils were talking at once. This indicates that a number of pupils appear to be happy with this teaching method, but the data do not tell us how many. We get some indication of the general atmosphere from the number of voluntary contributions made by pupils (without being asked by name). The percentage is about 70 per cent of all contributions (although this is difficult to judge from the transcript).

- What effect does it have on learning? It is even more difficult to get clues from the transcript as to how much the pupils were learning. According to the teacher the pupils were adequately prepared for the exam, which means, they learnt what he wanted them to know in the exam. Although we have no transcript of the oral exam, it can be assumed that the same patterns occur, so that the lessons can be seen as training for oral exams.

- What consequences does it have on teaching? Teaching that uses this pattern could be described as "close guidance". The teacher decides on the learning task by asking the questions, he decides on the subject matter and its organization by the format of his questions and he defines the quality of pupils' answers by his comments, which at the same time allow him to give additional information. A strength of close guidance of this kind is that information can be tailored to the pupils' needs (or, at least, to the needs of those who contribute). A further strength is that it helps the students to prepare for — and the teacher to plan — the exam. A weakness is that knowledge acquisition is implicitly defined as answering set questions. This kind of teaching would be unlikely to make a significant contribution to the pupils' ability to think independently.

Any pattern will have a number of effects. The effect of a pattern depends on the situation in which it occurs and on the personality traits and abilities of those concerned. For this reason we recommend that you always look for a number of possible effects, to prevent being blinkered by the first one that comes to mind. Sometimes some effects can be identified in the transcript itself, but normally you will need to collect more data.

STAGE 4 RELATIONSHIP BETWEEN THE PATTERN AND THE PRACTITIONER'S INTENTIONS

A close analysis of an example of your actual practice can illuminate the relationship between your intentions and the effects of your actions. For example, when discussing the transcript of the lesson the teacher said, "I'm not happy with using it [the T-P-T pattern]". It seems that the teacher has teaching aims that are not in line with the pattern. What are they? Does he want his pupils to move beyond the acquisition of facts to an understanding of concepts and theories? Does it bother him that the pattern might encourage them to learn for the sake of the exam rather than out of their own interest in the subject? The teacher's case study gives some clues (Sorger, 1989):

> . . . *only then did my real problem begin to emerge. I have to give grades, so I must teach things I can test, and (at the same time) I want them to know what is likely to come up in the exam; but, on the other hand, the aims that are important in studying literature and the kinds of tasks that would support those aims are very different. I just submit to the pressure of circumstances.*

This shows that the teacher feels under pressure and unable to achieve the aims that he "really" considers worthwhile. At this stage of the analysis it is important to consider these "real" aims, as well as the blocks to achieving them. Reflecting on these issues can give new perspectives that help in bringing about improvements.

STAGE 5 NEW ACTIONS

If the effects of the patterns do not match our intentions, what new action strategies should we develop? What strengths can we call on to improve our practice? One way to develop new action strategies is to identify and develop those patterns whose effects potentially match your intentions better than others. The teacher decided that he could respond to students in a way that would draw them out, using the IRF sequence described above:

T: so-called magical poetry, the magic spells. They are usually short spells – having what purpose? Martha? . . . Edith? . . . Rudolf?
R: Well, making people believe something!
T: I don't understand what you mean. I don't follow that. What do you mean by that?

Pattern analysis is a creative process in which a practitioner begins a "conversation" with the reality of his/her practice from transcripts of interactions with pupils, patients or clients. The process of pattern analysis does not consist merely in identifying existing patterns, but is an active process of constructing personal meaning by relating intentions to what is perceived to be happening in reality. On the other hand, this construction is not a purely personal matter, as the data (the transcripts) act as a frame of reference providing evidence of particular patterns and therefore making it possible to discuss them with your research group or critical friend.

M40 PATTERN ANALYSIS

The purpose of this activity is for you to try out pattern analysis of your own practice.

1 Audio-record a group interaction from your practice, e.g. a classroom, a committee meeting or a session with patients or clients.
2 Select a 10–15 minute extract to transcribe word for word (see M27) and number the lines.
3 Read and reread the transcript and highlight any pattern that repeats or that you know is repeated on other occasions.
4 Make a list of the patterns in neutral language that does not suggest that they are positive or negative. Refer each pattern to the line numbers in the transcript where it can be observed.
5 Discuss your pattern analysis with your research group, a critical friend, or other participants.

Dilemma analysis

A dilemma is a situation in which a person must choose one of two or more alternatives. As one might expect, practitioners, who work on a daily basis with other people, can find themselves facing major dilemmas. Therapists often find themselves in a situation in which they could give a client advice that they believe is good advice, but are reluctant to do so because it may interfere with the therapy. In the US, teachers and other care-givers are required by law to report instances of drug use or physical or sexual abuse. Often pupils, patients or clients will only confide in them if they are promised confidentiality.

There are, however, other dilemmas that are not so major that are inherent in practitioners work and can be made explicit through action research. Once explicit, they can be used to examine one's work in order to come to understand it better and to improve it. This data analysis method is called *dilemma analysis* (Winter 1982). Dilemma analysis is based on the notion that practitioners are continually faced with dilemmas that require professional decision-making. In most cases these dilemmas can be expressed in the following terms: "on the one hand . . . on the other hand. . .".

Here is an example of a dilemma:

On the one hand it is important to keep an overview of the classroom to ensure that every pupil is getting on with his/her work. On the other hand it is important to engage individual pupils or small groups in discussion, from time to time, so as to encourage them to think deeply about concepts and problems (which will require your full attention).

Another example comes from the collaborative action research done by a group of US physics teachers who were implementing a new curriculum (Feldman and Kropf 1999). The curriculum was designed to help students gain a deep conceptual understanding of a small number of concepts. The teachers liked the idea of having their best students use the curriculum because they would most likely study physics again at university. However, they found themselves in a dilemma with their other students who most likely would never take another physics course:

On the one hand, if they used the curriculum some students would really understand the physics that they learned. On the other hand, other students would not be exposed to many other topics in physics, which might have enticed them to study more physics.

Dilemma analysis is not as difficult as the name seems to indicate. As an example we will look at a short extract from the interview with the teacher of German literature. As you read it, see if you notice any of the tensions and decision points. We suggest that a good way of going about it is to work with your research group or critical friend: begin by reading through the data, individually, and mark any places where you note inconsistency, tentativeness or decisions; then talk over what you have found and, together, draw up a preliminary list of dilemmas.

I have just had the autumn exams. This time, when I was setting the questions, a lot of things had become clearer and I thought, what shall I do now? I could move away from teaching and examining factual knowledge more or less totally, and just work on the texts, and judge the students right from the start on the quality of their responses. But this is where my social responsibility comes in. If I did that, I could be accused of only wanting to create an elite. It would mean that those who are intelligent, who can make the links, who actually don't need me as a teacher, strictly speaking, but would learn anyway, would be favored and the others would be neglected. I have to take these things into consideration, because the ones who need my help to widen their mental horizons are more important to me than the ones who have a wide mental horizon already. And this is the reason for my emphasis on facts and testing facts – so that they can climb this mountain. But by doing this I narrow their chances of doing anything independently.

Everyone may find different dilemmas in analyzing any text, because there is a tendency to pick up on points that resonate with your own experience. Compare your own outcome with our analysis. We found the following tensions emerged from the interview:

- On the one hand, the teacher wants to get away from teaching and examining facts and would rather just "work on the texts". On the other hand, this would imply judging the pupils on the quality of their thinking and their responses to the text and would lay him open to the accusation of "creating an elite" and favoring those who need his help least.
- On the one hand, testing factual knowledge should help those who are unable to "climb the mountain" when working on texts. On the other hand, by doing this he restricts their chances of learning to work independently.

How to carry out dilemma analysis

STAGE 1 FINDING DILEMMAS

It is not difficult to find dilemmas. You will probably find there are quite a number. In carrying out dilemma analysis, data is selected, structured and interpreted so that contradictions come to light rather than commonalities. This method of analysis is easier when applied to data that interpret social reality and reveal its tensions (e.g. interview data) rather than data that focus on actions and events (e.g. observation data). It also helps to discuss your data with your research group or critical friend.

STAGE 2 FORMULATING AND EXPLORING DILEMMAS

Once you have found dilemmas in your practice the second stage of the process is to formulate them in a way that further exposes the conflict in the dilemma. One way of doing this is through the linguistic structure "on the one hand ... on the other hand..." that we illustrated in the above examples. Once you have formulated the dilemmas you can delve more deeply into trying to understand what effects they have on your practice. We think the following pragmatic approaches are helpful. They are drawn from examples taken from the interview quoted earlier in this chapter:

1 *Is the dilemma solvable?*
   Many dilemmas express contradictory and unavoidable aspects of situations so that they cannot be resolved by any course of action. An example is the contradiction between the desire for autonomy and the need to work within rules and structures. In this era of accountability most practitioners find themselves increasingly bound by rules and structures that restrict and constrain their practice. One example is the increasing use of high-stakes standardized exams in the US and elsewhere. Teachers find themselves bound both by the legal requirements and the ethical imperative that they prepare their pupils as well as

possible for the exams. This leads them to the conclusion that they must cover a lot of material and use drill and practice techniques. This conflicts with their desire to make their classrooms places where pupils can explore content in ways that allow them to gain deep conceptual understanding of the subject matter. This dilemma can be formulated as:

> On the one hand, I need to do my best to prepare my students for the high-stakes exams. On the other hand, if I focus on coverage and use drill and practice, my students won't have the opportunity to truly understand the subject matter.

2 *Is the dilemma related to the complexity of the situation, which makes it difficult to see what is happening?*
Many dilemmas result from having to act in situations where many factors are unclear, and causes and effects are only partly understood. This can result in the either/or representation of the dilemma when in fact there is a wide range of options available. For example, the dilemma that we described above becomes less dilemmatic when the complexity of the situation is exposed. It is possible for the teacher to use a variety of methods including those that both help prepare the students for the mechanical part of the exam (drill and practice) and help develop deep understanding (problem-based instruction, essay-writing and so on). It is also possible for the teacher to identify a few core concepts for more in-depth treatment and use the drill and practice techniques for the other topics. We call this "going around the dilemma" in the same way that it may be easier to go around the mountain than climb over it.

3 *Is the dilemma emotionally stressful?*
Emotional stress often results from believing that you have to take some course of action that goes against your instinctive judgment. Clearly the example that we gave above of the legal reporting require-ment can result in emotional stress. We want to help our pupils, patients or clients, but we cannot unless they confide in us. If they do, we must report what is said to the authorities. But if we don't promise confidentiality, they won't confide in us. Do we break the law so that we can help our pupil, patient or client, or do we stand by the law, not promise confidentiality and not have the opportunity to help them? Again, there is the possibility of resolving this dilemma by examining its complexities and seeking a way to negotiate a different set of con-ditions that allow you to get past the enormity of the mountain facing you by seeking an alternative route around it. We recognize that especially in this example, it is not easy to find that alternate route. But often we find ourselves faced with stressful dilemmas because we are missing information or because we have insufficient knowledge or

skills. In the same way that we would want the help of a guide when we travel in unfamiliar territory, it makes sense to seek the counsel of others, including members of your collaborative action research group, your critical friend and knowledgeable outsiders.

STAGE 3 WORKING ON DILEMMAS

We work on dilemmas to solve them if possible. Even if a dilemma is at first judged to be "unsolvable" we can still look for acceptable ways to cope with it. Just talking about a dilemma with your research group or critical friend may give rise to ideas for solutions. Unfortunately it is impossible to give any generalized explanation of how to deal with dilemmas. Instead, we will return to the case of the teacher of German literature as an example of how to understand dilemmas better, explain them and derive action strategies from them.

In comparing the teacher's statements with some of the things his pupils said, an interesting contradiction emerged: On the one hand, the teacher wants the pupils to respond to literature critically and become independent in their thinking. On the other hand, the pupils said in the interview that they pay better attention when the teacher asks them questions, because it is embarrassing for them being "caught" if they don't know something they are asked, and it is boring without questions like this. The teacher's and the pupils' aims seem to be clearly contradictory.

When we take a closer look at this dilemma it becomes even more complicated. The teacher's statement contradicts other statements he has made: he does want the pupils to acquire knowledge of facts. The pupils' statements are also not free of contradictions: in another statement they say that lessons in which you have to think for yourself and find things out on your own are much more interesting than other lessons. Obviously there are other reasons why the pupils work, as well as wanting to avoid embarrassment when caught not paying attention to the lesson.

It seems as if during lessons neither teachers nor pupils always do what they themselves consider valuable (taking a longer view). They are busy with "content oriented" learning, with passing on knowledge (teacher) and with remembering and reproducing knowledge (pupils). But they also want to support independent thinking (teacher) and think for themselves and discover things (pupils), i.e. defining and working on problems.

How can these contradictions be explained? One possible explanation could be that these two kinds of teaching and learning contain different levels of risk for both pupils and teachers. Problem-oriented work ("thinking for yourself") offers less security than the acquisition of knowledge. The pupil has to go beyond the information offered by the teacher and work with it using his/her existing knowledge. So there is a danger of not coming up to the teacher's expectations.

Under what circumstances will a situation like this be seen as a risk? Possibly when the pupil regards the lessons as a form of trade (grades for effort) and when, as a result, the economic principle holds sway (maximum results for minimum effort). In these circumstances the pupils become interested in making a good "deal" (as good a grade as possible, with as little effort as possible) and reducing the risk of poor grades. This may also be true for teachers in a similar way. They are interested in pupils who achieve something, take part in the lesson and are well behaved. They get achievements and good behavior more easily if they restrict themselves to asking only for the knowledge they have already given the pupils. In this way the risk of failure for teachers is also kept very low (Doyle 1992, Feldman *et al.* 1998).

Even in a case where a dilemma at first appears to be "unsolvable" analyzing it can help to understand it better and find an acceptable *modus vivendi*. We believe that a useful outcome of the analysis can be that you begin to accept the dilemma as something "normal" and this reduces any frustration resulting from it (e.g. frustration in feeling "whatever I do conflicts with something I believe to be important"). A dilemma can also be discussed with your pupils, patients or clients: for example, a teacher could check the extent of pupils' interest in problem-oriented work to find out how much support there would be for some work of this kind in the daily routine.

The function of dilemma analysis

Analyzing and working on dilemmas may be important in the following ways:

- *Valuing minority views* Views that are taboo or not discussed for other reasons (e.g. because those holding them do not have enough power) can be expressed in the form of dilemmas. By juxtaposing different views the common phenomenon of the "social hierarchy of credibility" may be overcome (see Chapter 5). Problems are presented in a way that is not too threatening, making it possible to discuss them and analyze them rationally. Minority views are not only a social phenomenon. Within each person's mind there are views that are devalued and repressed, but that nonetheless have consequences we are not aware of. Dilemma analysis can help in pointing out our personal minority views, which makes it possible to have a closer look at them and deal with them.
- *Reducing stress* Dilemma analysis is an alternative to searching for definite answers that can only solve one tension at the expense of increasing another one. If we accept that contrary perspectives can be

enriching, we experience emotional relief. Our energy is freed to search for ways of dealing with dilemmas that we can accept.

- *Enabling discussion* Winter (1982) developed dilemma analysis in order to introduce an egalitarian note to discussions between student teachers, their teacher mentors and college supervisors. Through dilemma analysis he was able to ascribe equal value to students' perspectives and the perspectives of those who had a higher status in the social context. In a similar way dilemmas can facilitate discussions between pupils, patients or clients, family members, and community groups, or between colleagues. The discussion is likely to be more stimulating and productive if the issues to be discussed are expressed in terms of dilemmas.

M41 DILEMMA ANALYSIS

The purpose of this activity is for you to try out dilemma analysis.

1 Choose a piece of your data that deals in depth with decisions that have to be made. It may be interviews with two or three people who share the same interest or work together but have different roles; an interview that a colleague has carried out on yourself about what you find problematic in your work; or some pages from your research notebook in which you have written in depth about something problematic.

2 Read the data carefully several times looking for indications that something is difficult to decide, creates tension or is problematic.

3 Clarify the issue by describing it in a short note using the phrasing, "On the one hand . . . On the other hand . . ." The idea here is to explain the reasons why you might take multiple courses of action. If you are looking at data from two or more people, you may find that they have different assumptions springing from their different roles (the power that they have).

4 Produce a discussion sheet in which you list all the dilemmas that you have found, being careful to express them in neutral language.

5 Hold a discussion between yourself and your critical friend, your interviewer, the colleagues involved in your analysis or your research group.

6 The aim of dilemma analysis is to clarify the understanding of those involved in the discussion of what the key issues are. In some cases this may assist in better decision-making. In others, it may be useful to know that there is no easy solution to stressful situations.

Chapter 7

Developing action strategies and putting them into practice

In this chapter we want to look particularly at developing action strategies and putting them into practice. As we have made clear in earlier chapters, in action research the knowledge generated about practice is used to improve your practice. Transforming the knowledge and insights developed through action research into practical action is also a way of testing the theories you have developed. It enables us to ask the question, "Does my practical theory about this situation stand the test of being put into practice or do I have to develop, modify or change it?" In practical terms, action researchers ask the following questions at this stage:

- How can I develop action strategies that fit my practical theories and that are likely to improve the situation?
- How can I select appropriate action strategies from the range of alternatives available?
- How can I develop and put into place the action strategies I want to try out?
- How can I monitor the effects of the action strategies and record the outcomes?

These are all questions that will be explored in some detail in this chapter. Before we do so, we want to remind you that we see action research as a more extended process that includes mini-cycles of refining starting points, collecting and analyzing data and taking action. You shouldn't feel that you need to progress through all the preceding chapters in order to finally get to the point where you will take actions as part of your action research. As a practitioner you are always taking actions within your practice situation. The mini-action research cycles allow you to use your ongoing research to positively influence your ongoing practice.

PRACTICAL ACTION AS AN INTEGRAL PART OF RESEARCH

In experimenting with using word processing as a tool for teaching writing, a teacher organized her class of 11-year-olds into groups and asked them to write stories collaboratively. Each group was asked to write a "long story", over a period of two weeks, and produce drawings and maps to go with it. Bridget (one of the authors of this book) found that the pupils were very highly motivated by using the computer and that this had an obvious positive effect in their interest in their writing. However, it also had an unwelcome side effect in causing increased tensions within the groups: some quarrels broke out and in two of the groups (one of boys and one of girls) there were tears. Using a range of data (a critical friend's observation notes, her own research journal (see Chapter 2) and a series of interviews with the pupils) she investigated these tensions. To her surprise, she found that they seemed to be coming about because the group members were trying to collaborate with each other much more closely than usual: everyone wanted to take a turn writing on the computer, so it was not possible for them to "escape" from collaboration by allocating separate tasks to each other and working individually. This led to two hypotheses: that the children might collaborate more successfully if they were shown that cooperation was valued by their teacher; and that they needed some teaching in how to collaborate – it would not happen automatically.

On this basis she decided on an action strategy to improve group collaboration: to introduce "collaboration" as the topic for a class discussion. During an hour, each group explained to the rest of the class the strategies they had been using to make group decisions. It became clear that one group, which was using the democratic principle and allowing the wishes of the majority to override the others, was experiencing a lot of tensions. An alternative suggestion, put forward by another group, was that you had to talk through each idea until everyone came to a consensus. In the process of putting this action strategy into practice (through listening to the children's discussion) Bridget realized that her two hypotheses – on their own – were too simple. Collaboration in group work is more difficult than she had thought – probably for adults as well as children. She realized that she would also need to alter the kind of writing task she was setting.

Thus, in putting this action strategy into practice she encountered some success, but also gained a new understanding of the problem. This resulted in rethinking her "new practical theory of the situation" (that the children needed to be taught how to collaborate and made aware that she valued collaborative work). What had been misjudged in her practical theory? Which important conditions had been neglected? What alternative action strategies would be possible? Such deliberations eventually led to a better understanding of the situation, and specifically to setting shorter written tasks for the groups working on the computer so that the pressures of time were reduced (Somekh 1985).

Action research is undertaken by practitioners to improve their practice in addition to coming to a better understanding of it. For practitioners it is not enough to develop theories about a situation: they also want to change the situation, as a result of their new knowledge, to improve the conditions for themselves and their pupils, patients or clients. To make it worth investing time and energy in research, which after all cuts across both professional and private life, teachers, nurses or social workers must go beyond the generation of new knowledge and theories and, in addition, make improvements in their practice situation. Developing action strategies in practice, however, means more than just making practical use of research results. It is itself a part of the research process. In planning action strategies, we formulate the outcomes of analysis as a preliminary practical theory. In developing action strategies in practice, we test the outcomes of analysis and thus, indirectly, test the preliminary practical theory (see Chapter 5). From the success or failure (most often a mixture of the two) of our carefully planned action strategies we can evaluate aspects of our practical theory, and find out in what ways it needs to be developed, modified or radically revised.

Action research is characterized by a close interrelationship of action and reflection (see Chapter 10). Another way of putting this is to say that using research results to improve practice, by means of developing action strategies, is an integral part of action research. The trustworthiness of research results is not established by clever analysis based on any specific theory, or by rigorously applying a set of validation procedures, but rather by a process of interrelating research and action. By continuously putting reflection into action, and subjecting action to further reflection, both the theories developed from reflection and the stock of action strategies are extended, subjected to analysis and improved.

Some people say that research is a "never-ending task". Is this also true of action research? It certainly applies to day-to-day professional reflection. Action research, however, is day-to-day reflection made more systematic and intensive. Thus, action research concentrates for a specific period of time on issues that deserve close scrutiny, but it will finish for pragmatic reasons, even if some questions are unanswered and need further investigation:

- because the researcher is reasonably satisfied with the outcome;
- because he/she has to cope with another task that will consume all available energy;
- because he/she simply needs a rest from extra demands.

In comparing action research with natural or behavioral science, Elliott

(1984a: 75) describes "the implementation and evaluation of action strategies as a form of hypotheses testing". In the same way that some other researchers develop hypotheses as concrete propositions based on their theories, action researchers design their action strategies on the basis, and as a consequence of, their practical theories. Developing action strategies in practice corresponds to the testing of hypotheses in traditional research.

In fact, trying out action strategies may be thought of as a kind of *field experiment*. There has recently been a call for educational research to be "more scientific" and to rely more on experimental methods. Those who favor this position have a particular understanding of the word "experiment". While they do not necessarily mean laboratory-based experiments, there is the understanding that an experiment should use random samples and highly controlled variables to test hypotheses. While we believe that field experiments are a way to test out hypotheses that are based on practical theories, we use the term experiment more loosely to refer to the systematic and reflective trying-out of practice strategies. Since professional practice is characterized by complexity, ambiguity and development (see Chapter 10) it is not possible to plan what will happen in any situation with any certainty.

WHAT ARE ACTION STRATEGIES?

Up to now we have used the term *action strategies* without defining it. Let us now give some examples. In the introductory example of this chapter a teacher tried to clarify ways of "improving group collaboration" when using a computer in teaching writing. She developed an action strategy, namely to "introduce collaboration as the topic for a class discussion".

In another case a teacher, Christa Piber, who had recently taken over a new class, felt irritated by the behavior of one girl who seemed to her to be unfriendly and sullen. After a while she became aware that she was beginning to dislike her. Their relationship seemed to be moving towards open conflict when she asked her critical friend to interview the girl. The interview revealed that the girl had been having some problems in adapting to Christa's more informal teaching style and, generally, to the change of teachers, since she had been one of the previous teacher's favorite pupils. The interview, however, also showed that Christa's impression (and fear) that this pupil did not like her or her teaching was utterly unfounded. As a result of this new information, she no longer had any reason to have a negative attitude to the girl. Her manner in addressing the girl changed and the tension went out of the situation. As Christa put it:

> *I look at Karen with different eyes now and I find it easier to approach her. I address questions directly to her if she doesn't volunteer any answers, and she is becoming noticeably more active and seems to enjoy the classwork*

more. She is still rather a quiet girl, but I don't interpret it as sullenness any more.

(This work is described in Posch (1985: 60))

In a third example a university teacher was attempting to develop her course on "Statistics in the social sciences", which, she felt, needed improvement (see Altrichter 1986b). A graphical reconstruction of the situation, after the first cycle of investigation, is set out in Figure 7.1):

Whenever she introduces a new concept she begins by explaining it in words (1). Then she does an example on the blackboard (2) and afterwards she asks the students to do another exercise in their books (3). Usually, the students have difficulty in understanding (4) because the concept is difficult and too much information is being given all at once. If she feels that she is not explaining things clearly, or the students show signs of not understanding, she can feel herself becoming tense and she tries to explain again. However, this makes her teaching become jerky and even less clear. When interviewed she said:

My behavior is "reactive." Whenever something unexpected pops up or I pick some sign that they are not understanding, I react immediately and abandon my lesson plan. I must learn to observe these things and store them away to think about later, without being put off my track.

(Altrichter 1986b)

On the basis of this interpretation of the situation the teacher decided upon the following action strategy (5) in Figure 7.1 below, among others: *to take a deep breath*. Whenever she felt that her explanation was becoming nervous, jerky and difficult to understand the teacher decided that she would "take a deep breath". In this way, she hoped to avoid these nervous

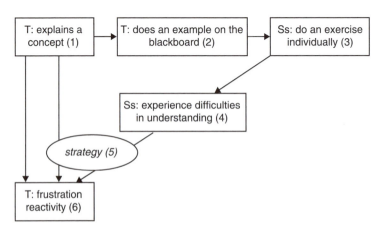

Figure 7.1 Excerpt from a graphical reconstruction – 'Course on statistics'

reactions. In the "breathing-space" she hoped to be able to think whether it was actually necessary to abandon her planned sequence of explanations. Through this strategy she hoped to break the vicious circle of quick and unthinking changes to her lesson plan that she was finding annoying and that she also thought were getting in the way of the students' learning.

We will return later to discussing why it is not always easy to translate a "good intention" like this into action (see later in this chapter). When an action strategy is developed from the analysis of practice it is important to be able to relate the strategy to a specific point in the analysis. You may find it helpful to draw a diagram, such as the one shown in Fig. 7.1, to show how it relates to your action research.

Let's use this example to explore some of the characteristics of action strategies:

- Action strategies are actions that are planned and put into practice by the action researcher in order to improve the situation or its context.
- Action strategies are connected to your aims. They are used to maintain or develop the quality of a situation. They are considered "successful" if the desired effects come about without unexpected, negative side effects.
- Action strategies are typically tightly linked to theories developed from practice as a result of action research into the situation. The diagram in our last example shows this clearly: it sets out the teacher's interpretation of the situation (i.e. her practical theory); her action strategies can easily be given a specific place in this diagram. Diagrams are not only useful as a technique for developing action strategies but also as a method of looking at them carefully. Diagrams quickly show the points in the practical theory at which no action is being taken. This leads to questions such as, "Why not?", "Will there be any side effects these aspects of the situation are neglected?" Diagrams also show whether action strategies are planned that do not actually arise from the practical theory. Sometimes this indicates a routine "*ad hoc* strategy" that cannot be justified by the analysis of the data. More often, however, such a "floating" action strategy points to some incompleteness in the analysis: the action strategy expresses intuitive knowledge about the situation that would not otherwise have been made explicit. Reflecting on the floating action strategy helps to extend the practical theory.
- Action strategies can be thought of as preliminary answers to the researcher's questions or "experimental" solutions to the problem he/she is investigating. In this way, they are always relevant to the theory because the process of carrying them out throws light on the practical theory of the situation.

- Action strategies may aim to make changes of very different scales: for example, one teacher might decide to make profound changes to her whole style of teaching to give the pupils much greater autonomy in learning, whereas the university teacher in our last example has basically kept her style of working but adapted it by making some slight changes in her behavior.
- The extent to which an action strategy is new can differ widely. By using the terms "change" or "improvement" we may give the wrong impression that only significant and radical breaks with existing practice count as action strategies. This is not true. Researching and analyzing a situation may just as easily lead to corroboration of existing practice and underlying theories. In some cases there may be no visible changes in terms of actions, although views and attitudes are greatly changed: for example, earlier in this chapter we described how a teacher came to "look at her pupil with different eyes", no longer feeling antagonized by her, and therefore able to act towards her without feeling tensed up. In other cases analysis of a problem may lead to quite new actions.
- When we speak of "improvement" or "solving a problem", we do not mean to imply that all the problems of professional practice can be "solved" satisfactorily. Sometimes the analysis of a problem shows that important, contributory factors lie outside the practitioner's sphere of influence (e.g. a patient's prior history, the resources of the clinic). "Solving a problem" in a case like this often does not mean making it vanish, but developing a different attitude towards the problem that helps to limit personal strain. Often a change in attitude makes it possible to make a number of small changes that are helpful, but that previously did not seem to be worth the effort.
- The term *action strategy* needs to be understood in terms of the following provisos:

  ○ Complex social situations are not changed by one single action. Usually, an action strategy will consist of a number of coordinated actions planned on the basis of the research.
  ○ Do not expect immediate solutions. Change is usually a long-term process, in the course of which several single elements of a system begin to move and action strategies have to be adapted and modified. Planning action strategically means being prepared to learn from the outcomes of the "first wave" of a change strategy and using this to inform the "second wave" (see Kemmis and McTaggart 1982: 24).
  ○ In any social situation actions usually have unforeseen side effects. These unexpected outcomes have to be judged in terms of our aims. We do not simply ask "Did we achieve the ends we set?" but rather

'Do we like what we get?' (Schön 1983: 141, see Argyris *et al.* 1985: 218, Atkin *et al.* 2005).

In what follows we will put forward some ideas and methods for coping with the kind of practical difficulties likely to arise from developing action strategies and putting them into practice.

HOW CAN I FIND A VARIETY OF SUITABLE ACTION STRATEGIES?

Where do we look to find suitable action strategies? The most important source is our *new understanding* gained from analysis of the situation. Understanding an issue, by uncovering the network of interrelationships, does not only lead to a new awareness of the situation, but usually also offers a wealth of ideas about possible action.

A second important source is the actual process of *data collection*. Simply finding out the attitudes of our pupils, patients or clients may be enough to suggest possible solutions (see the example earlier in this chapter). Indeed, the interview may itself be an action that changes a situation.

A third important source is our own *aims, objectives and values as practitioners*. What exactly ought to be different? How should a relationship change to make it more satisfactory for our pupils, patients or clients and for us? How should our practice situation be organized to provide all participants with worthwhile learning experiences? Debating what we really want is a part of the process of clarifying the issue, which becomes more and more important as the research progresses. In the course of problem analysis and data collection the action researcher's aims become more practical and realistic as he/she is better informed by knowledge of the situation.

Fourth, ideas and suggestions for suitable action strategies may come from *external suggestions*, for example from conversations with your research group, critical friend, or colleagues, information about how other people have coped with similar situations and ideas in books and articles. We have deliberately left this fourth source to last because it is most useful, in our experience, when used in conjunction with other sources. No advice from an experienced colleague and no book can replace your own analysis of the situation, an understanding of its complexities and a clear view of what you are aiming for. But both sources may yield valuable ideas if they fall on fertile ground: that is, if you have already developed an understanding of the situation and possible action strategies that can be broadened and modified by external suggestions. This is because such suggestions, instead of remaining discrete and separate, are integrated with your own conception of the situation.

Despite the large number of books available in all practice fields, it is not easy to find those that both provide good ideas relevant to your own specific situation and are written in understandable language. It is a great advantage for action researchers to have contacts with colleagues who are familiar with some of this literature, or to have contacts in higher education institutions. Reports and case studies written by practitioners are often particularly useful.

Developing action strategies is a constructive and creative activity that is interwoven with the action researcher's personality and the specific situation in which he/she lives and works. As a result, there is no one way of going about it, and we can only give suggestions that we hope will facilitate your search for action strategies:

- Don't be content with just one idea. You need to have the opportunity to choose between several possible strategies. In some situations this is particularly important: the more different strategies you think of, the greater the chance of unusual solutions coming to mind that may help you to escape from "vicious circles" and dead-end situations.
- Don't worry too much about feasibility to start with. First of all, these ideas are for broadening your awareness. They provide new perspectives and create the impression that it is at least possible to think of solutions. This may be an important starting point for constructive thinking. To start with it is more important to consider the potential opportunities offered by an action strategy than to think about possible difficulties (all solutions are bound to raise difficulties). This means that you can concentrate on your inner strengths and inspires some confidence. Don't reject a possible action strategy too quickly just because some difficulty occurs to you.
- Don't forget to consider existing strengths. When we talk about "improving a situation" or "solving a problem" it is part of our culture to think in terms of errors and mistakes. However, there is another way of looking at it. We can often bring about improvement by emphasizing strengths and building on processes that are already operating in the system (see our discussion of the systemic approach in Chapter 4). It pays to reflect on questions such as: What are (my, our, the pupils', patients', clients', etc.) strengths in this situation and how can I create the conditions to build on them? What processes are in operation that already tend towards an "improvement of the situation" and how can I strengthen them?
- Sometimes action strategies become obvious during the analysis of the situation, sometimes we have to search for them. When the latter is the case a group is usually better than an individual. A group supplies a wide variety of ideas from the varied experiences of its members. In addition, collecting and discussing action strategies for a particular

situation is often, not only illuminating for the practitioner who is looking for ideas, but also enriches the insight of other members of the group into similar situations.

Various methods can be used to identify possible action strategies. Diagrams, produced as part of the process of analysis, may also be used to identify potential action strategies (see M12). As in the case quoted above, every element and every relationship in a diagram gives rise to questions: Can I intervene constructively here? Which action strategies could I use to bring about some positive development at *this* point on the diagram? Another possibility is that metaphors developed during data analysis may lead to new ideas for action strategies (see M37). Brainstorming (see M5 and below) is another alternative, useful for collecting many different ideas from a group of people.

M42 INDIVIDUAL BRAINSTORMING

If you do not have access to a group of colleagues willing to reflect with you on your research situation, it is possible to brainstorm individually. This is a form of "reflecting through writing" (see Chapter 2). Set aside some time without interruption (approx. 15 minutes) and take a clean sheet of paper or a new page in your research notebook (you may prefer to use a computer, but for this exercise we personally prefer to use paper). Then, jot down all the associations that come to your mind when you think of the question "What can I do in situation x?" It is important to "go with" your associations and not to reject any immediately as unrealistic or trivial. Evaluation of the quality of the ideas takes place after, not during, this exercise.

HOW CAN I CHOOSE WHICH ACTION STRATEGY TO PUT INTO PRACTICE FROM THE RANGE OF AVAILABLE ALTERNATIVES?

In the process of analyzing a situation and searching for action strategies, a particular alternative sometimes becomes obvious. You feel that your understanding of the situation is changed and clarified through looking at it in this way, as if this course of action had become the obvious and natural thing to do. Usually, however, the path to deciding on a specific action strategy is not paved by such intuitive clarity. Then, you need to weigh alternatives carefully, judging their feasibility with respect to yourself and your practice, your pupils, patients, or clients, and your aims for your situation.

M43 CROSS-CHECKING ALTERNATIVE ACTION STRATEGIES

Deciding on an action strategy is a very individual process tailored to the specific circumstances of a situation. Subjective judgment often plays a more important role than any formal evaluation procedure. Nevertheless, the following criteria can often be helpful.

1 Usefulness

- How useful is this action strategy?
- Will it solve the problem? For how long?
- Might there be any additional positive effects?
- Might there be any negative side effects?

These questions may be answered with the help of the data you have collected or simply from your own knowledge of the situation. Sometimes, however, you will find you need additional information. This serves to show how many decisions in everyday life have to be taken on the basis of insufficient knowledge (because of sheer lack of time). But, bear in mind that it is impossible to foresee all eventualities before taking action, and that uncertainty and "mistakes" are therefore unavoidable. Being aware of this can give you the confidence to face problems as they come, accepting them as an expected feature of life as a practitioner. In this way you make problems accessible for development – instead of denying and repressing them.

2 Practicality

- How practical and feasible is this action strategy?
- What room for manoeuvre will there be when implementing this strategy?
- Can this be done alone or does it require the goodwill, support and cooperation of others?

Some ideas can appear to be very useful but are simply not feasible in this particular situation. They may take too much time. They may require the cooperation of other people (e.g. colleagues, family members) who are not willing to give it. They may need financial resources, which are either unavailable or out of proportion to the expected usefulness of the idea. Or it may be that you do not have the necessary knowledge and expertise, or the opportunity to acquire them quickly enough to make it worthwhile. In the light of the practicality criterion those action strategies are preferable that give you most room for maneuver

and are least dependent on other people and institutional structures. However, this does not imply that such action strategies are
useful or acceptable.

3 Acceptability

- Will this action strategy be acceptable to the practitioner(s),
  pupil(s), patient(s) or client(s), and others concerned?

An idea may be useful and feasible but it may not fit your
values, personality and circumstances, that of your pupils,
patients or clients or that of your organization or profession. Personal ownership of an idea is more important than its quality by
more objective criteria when it comes to many practice problems,
but particularly those relating to interactions between people.
This third criterion highlights the personal nature of a decision on
an action strategy. However, coping positively with problems
of professional practice also requires the other participants to feel
comfortable with the solution and be prepared to support its
implementation. Generally, this is more likely to be the case if the
chosen strategy gives them more room for maneuver and greater
responsibility.

A group, as we have said before, can be supportive at the stage of looking
for ideas, but this is seldom true when it comes to deciding which alternative should be put into practice. This is a decision that needs to be taken
by those actually concerned. As an action researcher you cannot allow this
burden to be shouldered by colleagues or so-called experts. Outsiders
may have creative and striking ideas that shed new light on a situation
you have been wrestling with for some time; but they have much less
knowledge of the web of idiosyncrasies and routines – each with their
history – that are such a strong influence on what happens in the classroom. In addition, outsiders don't have to live with the consequences of
their suggestions and this makes it easy to give advice too lightly.

M44 NOMINAL GROUP TECHNIQUE (NGT)[1]

Nominal Group Technique (NGT) is a highly structured procedure for
decision making in groups. It ensures that all members of the group
voice their ideas. It prevents discussion from getting stuck on just
a few aspects of an issue, helps to bring more ideas to light and
enables quicker decision making than many other procedures (e.g.
an unstructured group discussion).

A group undertaking NGT is a group only nominally; its inter-actions are strictly controlled by the group leader according to the NGT rules. It may help to think of it as a development from the idea of individual brainstorming (see M5): by comparison, NGT offers more participants the chance to contribute their ideas, and ensures that priorities for a choice between decision-making among suggested alternatives become visible. Clearly NGT is a technique that can be used if you are part of a research group. If you are not, you may be able to assemble a group of colleagues or critical friends who find it personally rewarding to work with you.

Procedure
The NGT process contains the following phases:

1 *Explanation of NGT and its stages (5–10 minutes)*
   The objectives of the method and its stages are explained. With most groups it is useful to visually display them.
2 *Clarification of the question (5–10 minutes)*
   The question to be considered by the group is announced. This needs to be decided in advance, either by the person whose problem it is, the group leader or a planning group of some kind. Group members are given a short time to clarify the issue. If appropriate, the question may be reformulated. Discussion at this stage should only deal with the wording of the question. Substantive comments come in the later stages and should be discouraged by the group leader at this point.
3 *Individual listing (7 minutes)*
   Working individually, participants list short statements and phrases that come to mind in answer to the question. Silence is important at this stage to ensure that group members write down as many ideas as possible without being influenced by one another.
4 *Collection of statements (15–35 minutes)*
   Each participant *in turn* is asked to read out *just one* of the state-ments he/she has listed. The group leader writes these on a flip-chart in an abbreviated version using the original words as much as possible. During this stage no evaluation, interpretation or dis-cussion of statements is allowed. The collection of ideas continues to rotate around the group until all ideas are recorded on the flipchart. Meanwhile, completed sheets are torn off and posted on the wall or a display board. (Participants who have run out of statements or whose answers have been anticipated by other group members "pass" in later rounds).
   The duration of this phase depends on the complexity of the question and the size and ingenuity of the group. The phase must

not be stopped prematurely, but should be extended until all ideas are collected. If time is scarce it is better to negotiate a limited number of "collection rounds" in advance (e.g. 3 rounds) rather than to break off the exercise at a point that is not expected by the participants (e.g. when the group leaders consider the ideas not to be "relevant" any more). This highly structured procedure gives an equal voice to all the participants, in a way that seldom or never happens in normal group discussions.

5 *Clarification of statements (approx. 15–45 minutes)*
Participants can ask for any necessary clarification. At this stage there is an opportunity to eliminate repetitions and reword statements, provided the original author is in agreement. If possible, very general statements should be avoided in favor of more specific, concrete ones. Comments and judgments should still be avoided at this stage. Evaluations (e.g. if idea X is relevant or is to be included in the list) should not be accepted by the group leader in this phase. Since this phase makes visible what wealth of ideas there are in a group, provided there is enough time, we suggest that the group leader stimulate more ideas by asking questions (Why is it important? What would be your first step in order to get this idea going?).

6 *Individual selection and ranking (7 minutes)*
The participants are asked to study the statements on the flip-chart paper. Working individually, they then select and write down on a piece of paper the five statements that seem to them most relevant with respect to the initial question. Then, they individually rank these five statements in order of importance, giving the most important statement "5", the second most important statement "4", and so on.

7 *Collection of rankings (10–15 minutes)*
The ranking points awarded by each individual are recorded in turn on the flip-chart paper beside each statement. After all the participants have given their rankings the group leader adds up the points and identifies the six or so statements that have the highest scores.

A suggestion for the layout of a poster on which the ideas are collected is shown in Figure 7.2. Briefly note ideas in the center column. In the left-hand column all ideas are numbered. (This can be easily done during the participants' individual work in phase 6). In the right-hand column 'ranking points' are written during "step 7".

8 *Discussion and interpretation of results (30+ minutes)*
In this final stage the participants discuss the results and their implications. The NGT process usually breaks a problem down

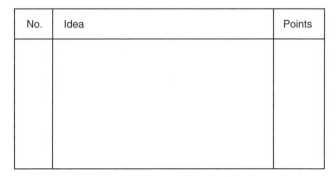

No.	Idea	Points

Figure 7.2 Layout of a poster for collection of NGT ideas

into its constituent parts, with the result that the context and relationships between the parts may be lost. Therefore, it is important at this stage to recreate an understanding of the problem as a whole.

The following questions can help to direct discussion:

- Which statements do participants generally agree about in their rankings, and which create the greatest divergence of view?
- What are the reasons for agreement? Are the statements so general that everybody finds it easy to agree? Do they represent generally shared prejudices?
- What are the reasons for differences of view? Do they relate to different working conditions, different styles of work or differences in attitudes or aims?
- Does the result suppress minority views (statements that are important to just a few people)? How does the group want to deal with that?
- Do the "winning statements" deserve the weight that has been attached to them by the NGT procedure?

Afterwards the group may move on to discuss what consequences should result from the exercise.

Group size
The optimal group size for the NGT procedure is 8 to 10 people; with more, the whole exercise becomes too cumbersome, and with fewer there is increasingly less need for such a procedure. If there are many more potential participants it is possible to run two (or more) parallel NGT processes. The results of the parallel groups can be shared in analogy to stages 6 to 8 for the whole group.

The role of the group leader

Leading a group in NGT can be quite challenging. The leader's task is to structure the information flow and promote the development of ideas by keeping the group to the NGT rules. However, they must not do this so strictly that group members lose their interest and enjoyment in participating. The following advice may be useful for NGT leaders:

- Don't reinterpret people's ideas.
- Use the participants' wordings as much as possible.
- Don't develop ideas of your own – you are not a participant.
- This is not a debate – don't allow people to challenge or attack each other.
- Give participants time to think.
- Don't offer interpretations or search for patterns.

Occasions for use

NGT may be helpful in the following situations:

- A group wants to decide on a starting point for group research, such as the study on patient discharge preparations by a group of nurses that we looked at in Chapter 3.
- A group wants to explore possibilities for clarification of the starting point for their collaborative research. For example, having identified lack of support for pupils with special needs as the focus for a collaborative project, a group NGT exercise may address the question: "What are the most important reasons for lack of support for pupils with special needs?"
- A group wants to think of a number of action strategies and select one or more for collaborative action. For example, they might address the question: "What actions and organizational changes would better prepare patients for their discharge from the hospital?"

Problems and drawbacks of NGT

- Some participants may react against the strict rules of NGT. You can guard against this to some extent by explaining the reason for the rules.
- The rules of NGT change the dynamics of a group. Sometimes power struggles, suppressed early on, surface later.
- As always with voting, there is a danger that minority views may be neglected. Steps should be taken to ensure that the result fairly represents the whole group, particularly if the group is intending to go on working together.

- The wording of the initial question is very important and can be difficult. If it is too narrow, the participants' thinking is unduly limited. If it is too broad, there may be the problem that different participants interpret it differently. When in doubt it is probably better to err towards breadth.
- The leader's role in NGT is quite demanding. It may be difficult to see that the rules are kept without spoiling participants' enjoyment by policing the procedure too tightly. Sometimes this can be a little daunting.

HOW CAN I PLAN CONCRETE STEPS TO MAKE SURE I FEEL COMFORTABLE WITH MY ACTION STRATEGY?

Earlier in this chapter (p. 200) we gave the example of a teacher deciding "to take a deep breath" as an action strategy to be used at certain points in her teaching. What concrete form might this strategy take in the classroom?

- Whenever the teacher feels that the students are having difficulties in understanding, and she is in danger of producing a rushed explanation, she could give herself a mental order to "stop". This pause "to take a breath" would give her a chance to decide whether any reaction were necessary and, if so, what kind of reaction would be appropriate. The disadvantage is that it may not be easy to keep cool and pause for reflection in the stress of the situation.
- Alternatively, the teacher could announce that she is going to pause to think, and justify this to her pupils. The disadvantage mentioned above might also apply in this case and there is the additional problem that some teaching time will be lost.
- Another possibility would be for the teacher to ask a question (or "bounce back" a pupil's question) to keep the pupils thinking while giving herself time to think. Here, the drawbacks are that the students are deceived about the teacher's real intentions while she still cannot concentrate her full attention on thinking.
- Yet again, the teacher could interrupt the flow of work and explain what she sees as a problem: "I don't think you have understood everything. Perhaps I'm not being clear. Is that true?" A disadvantage of this strategy may be that the pressure to react precipitately will rise if more students say they have not understood. Also, it is often difficult and time-consuming to decide on a solution in collaboration with a large group of pupils.

This example makes it obvious that it is necessary to plan concrete steps to put an action strategy into practice, taking into account the advantages and disadvantages of different alternatives.

In order to put an action strategy into practice it is necessary to feel comfortable with the idea and have confidence that you can carry it out. Does this action strategy suit my way of working? Can I do that? Are these actions part of my repertoire? If not, could I develop the necessary competences? Here are some possible ways of developing confidence in action strategies:

- Imagine the situation and play it through in your mind. Mental training, similar to that used by athletes to prepare themselves for specific movements, is useful preparation for simple, relatively isolated actions. It is more difficult to use this method for complex sequences of interactions, although it can alert you to possibilities and consequences that you have not thought of before.
- Try out the action strategy in advance by piloting it with one or two people or a different group. This is good advice for any new activity in practice, but especially makes sense when you use the action strategy to test your practical theories.
- If a colleague is already using this action strategy, try to arrange the opportunity to observe it in action and talk it over with him/her afterwards. In cases where you cannot directly observe your colleague in action, it still helps to discuss it. This will help you to develop a clearer awareness of the possibilities and limitations.
- Try to arrange an opportunity to become more familiar with certain action strategies within a training program, e.g. setting up a short course or working group.

As a rule it is not possible to feel completely comfortable with an action strategy until you have put it into practice. It is easier to try out something new if you normally have an experimental attitude to your practice. Putting an action strategy into practice is a "test" and we can't expect everything to work out well immediately. However, we can expect to learn something that will add to our professional development.

HOW CAN I CHECK THE RESULTS OF ACTION STRATEGIES AND RECORD THE EXPERIENCES I HAVE GAINED?

The most important and most interesting tests of an action strategy do not lie in cross-checking with yourself (as in M43) or in any procedures for group decision-making (as in M44) but in putting it into practice. In order to learn as much as possible from trying it out, it is important to consider in advance what data to collect and for what purpose. In general terms, all the methods of data collection and analysis that we have already described are suitable. A *time plan* may help you to think through and prepare the complex task of coordinating research activities with different action strategies.

M45 TIME PLAN

It is often a good idea to plan the steps of your research before you put the first action strategy into practice, so that you don't develop unrealistic expectations and find that you run out of time at the end of the school year. The following time plan was developed by a Physics teacher who was researching the issue: "My students learn Physics by memorizing facts. They do not seem to develop an understanding of the concepts and processes on which the facts are based" (see Kemmis and McTaggart 1982: 11 and 30).

Step	Date	Monitoring	Comments
Finalizing general plan	30 March–3 April		Availability of audio-recorder to be finalized. Ask Ms X to agree to swap rooms.
First action step	Two weeks beginning 3 April	Audio-record 20 mins of Year 10 Science in the two single periods each week. Write impressions in spare period that follows (research notebook). Interview students (three to begin with) for impressions	Allow two periods on Friday pm to transcribe part of the audio recording. (Just write out questions and answers.) Collage with impressions (mine and students).
Evaluation	After vacation week		Verbal report to Science Faculty first Friday after vacation.
Revise general plan	24 April–27 April		
Second action step (plan and implement)	Two weeks beginning 27 April	As previously	Place microphone so it better records class conversations.

Figure 7.3 Time plan

M46 THE "ORGANIC TO-DO LIST"

A simple way to incorporate action strategies into your practice is to develop an organic to-do list. A to-do list is a list of things that you want to remember to do or accomplish. Traditionally it would be in the form of a list written on paper, possibly made fresh every day. As an item was accomplished, it would be crossed off. Recently with the development of computer-based calendars and PDAs (personal digital assistants), it has become possible to construct what we call "organic to-do lists". An "organic to-do list" can be sorted into categories that correspond to the different varieties of activities that we do in our complex lives: tasks for our everyday lives, whether they are shopping, doctor appointments or family responsibilities; or tasks that relate to our professional practice that could include preparing lessons, grading papers, preparing reports, and so on. It is possible to subdivide these categories further and get to the point where one of the categories relates specifically to our action research and our action strategies. It is also possible to give these categories a priority so that different tasks or actions are ranked as 1st priority, 2nd, and so on. It is even possible to attach "alarms" to them so that you are reminded to do them. What makes a computer-based to-do list "organic" is that there is no need to rewrite the list every day. It is also possible to write memos that record what you did and what immediate effects you observed.

If an action strategy does not bring about the expected results there may be several reasons:

- *A problem in the way the action strategy was put into practice* – you may not have been sufficiently comfortable with the action strategy and may have carried it out in a diffident manner or in a different way from what had been planned.
- *A problem in the conceptualization of the action strategy* – for example, too little time may have been allowed for the action strategy to make an impact, or you may have misjudged how much preparation the pupils would need before the new approach was implemented.
- *A problem in the analysis of the situation* – your own prejudices may have seemed more convincing than the data so that you never engaged in a 'reflective conversation with the situation'; or you may have failed to take alternative interpretations into account, or jumped to premature conclusions.
- *A problem in the collection of data* – important sources of data may have been overlooked.
- *A problem in the problem definition* – perhaps the problem you investigated was not the "real" problem, or alternatively the problem, your aims or the context may have changed in the meantime.

To check the results of action strategies you need criteria of success. When can you say an action strategy was successful? Perhaps, if it:

1 has resulted in an the intended "improvement of the situation", in such a way
2 that it has not also caused unintended, negative side effects that detracted from the main, positive effects, and
3 if the "improvement" is not "short-term" (vanishing after only a short time).

In saying this we have, however, uncovered another layer of the problem. What practitioners, their pupils, patients and clients and other interested parties consider to be "improvements" varies, depending on their objectives and the values that guide their action. For example:

- Your aims and values, which are the basis for regarding something as an improvement or progress, may be more or less explicitly stated. The less explicitly they are stated, the less clear it is that there has been actual improvement. On the other hand, highly explicit aims and values can unduly restrict your research and your actions.
- Your aims and values may change in the course of the research. You may begin by stating an interest explicitly that recedes into the background in the course of the research, because values that you had neglected become more important.
- Some improvements are in terms of processes, while others are products. The outcome of your action research could be a new way of doing something or even a new way of thinking about your practice. This could result in changes in your practice situation without directly observed products. For example, an action research study could convince a nurse that he/she should provide patients with as much information as possible about their conditions and possible treatments. This could cause a significant change in the practice situation without necessarily improving anyone's health. On the other hand, if the goal of the action research is more end-product oriented, such as pupils performing better in exams, patients who better take care of their own health or clients who are less depressed, then one should expect to see some evidence of these products.
- Some improvements refer primarily to your emotional well-being or that of your pupils, patients or clients, some refer to performance and some to new or deeper insights.

Many of these improvements are subtle in character rather than spectacular. In our experience improvements in practice often appear rather inconspicuous on superficial examination: practitioners and/or their pupils, patients and clients feel a little better and/or perform a little better than previously. However, in the long term this "little" can make a difference.

What is considered to be an improvement depends also on *who* is making the judgment. What appears to be an improvement to a practitioner may not be regarded as such by a pupil, patient or client. What any one of the participants or stakeholders welcomes may not conform to the values of the others (e.g. different community interest groups) or to the values of the State as embodied in laws and regulations. We want to distinguish four voices to show clearly the multiplicity of criteria that action researchers should use to evaluate improvements.

1 The voice of the individual practitioner

All the examples just provided exemplify this voice. Practitioners try to improve a situation; in doing so their personal values are uppermost in defining what may be considered as improvement. In addition to the individual interests of action researchers in changing unsatisfactory situations there is also a collective, societal benefit in practitioners taking responsibility for the development of their own practice.

2 The voice of other people concerned

Action research assumes that effective development of social practice is only possible with the collaboration of all those concerned in this practice. There are both ethical and epistemological reasons for this. For ethical reasons action researchers need to collaborate with others in a negotiated evaluation of the situation. Epistemological considerations lead to including all the other people concerned because the knowledge developed through action frequently depends on their willingness to cooperate (see Chapter 5).

Who counts as a person concerned cannot be definitely and finally settled in advance, however. Certainly, all the participants in the situation that is being researched, and all those who will be affected in any way by the action strategies being implemented, must be included: in most cases this means the pupils, patients or clients. The participation of other people concerned, such as family members or colleagues is sometimes uncovered in the course of the research. For example, in an interview with a patient another caregiver is mentioned and he/she then becomes a 'person concerned'. Of course, the ethical code should apply to all those concerned in the situation in even an indirect way, but another important consideration is that, in the long term, successful action strategies will depend on tapping into their knowledge and expertise.

3 The professional voice

A characteristic of professionalism is that the practice of an individual member of the profession should be open to scrutiny by professional colleagues. Evaluating practice is not only a matter for the individual action researcher and those directly or indirectly concerned, but in some sense concerns all practitioners as a professional group. This professional evaluation begins when teachers, nurses, social workers or other professionals voice their knowledge, experience, and professional values in conversations about their practice situations. If such conversations go beyond the narrow circle of close colleagues, they contribute in the long term to a shared stock of knowledge and values that connects practitioners as members of a professional community and distinguishes them from other groups.

This dimension is evident in the particular responsibility the profession has to society. This professional responsibility requires both specific expertise and a professional ethic – a reflexive understanding of educational aims, willingness to undertake what society expects of the profession in an autonomous way and willingness to be accountable for the freedom necessary to carry out these responsibilities. (For more about responsibility in action research, see Feldman (2007a).) The development of such a professional community depends upon both external solidarity and continuous internal critique of professional action, knowledge and values. As a result, the tenets of the profession can be communicated to the public in good conscience.

4 The voice of the community

Practitioners' action research also has an effect on the community as a whole, which also affects the action researcher. Some of this is due to the fact that many practitioners are employed either directly by the community (as in the case of most teachers) or indirectly through the use of public funds (as is the case for many nurses and social workers). It is also due to the fact that practice situations do not exist separately from the rest of the social sphere – they are embedded in the world of the communities in which they are situated.

What counts as "improvement" is ultimately the result of a – sometimes implicit – process of negotiation among these four voices, each of which can claim some legitimacy. However, we think

- that the complexity of the professional practice necessitates freedom of action, which, in turn, requires a high degree of professional knowledge, self-critique and responsibility;
- that therefore there is a necessity for a high level of professional debate that takes into account both the interests of the pupils, patients and clients, and the interests of society more generally;
- that this dynamic process of self-reflection and continuous development must be embedded in a professional community and promoted by it.

Community interest groups and state institutions should both challenge and support this process, but they should not replace it with a multitude of restrictions or regulations. Such regulations can certainly solve some problems in the short term. In the long term, however, they will prevent schools and other institutions from becoming capable of coping with society's developing needs in a creative and constructive way.

Decisions about what counts as improvement, success or failure are judgments about complex situations that are shaped in a multi-faceted, social process. Not least for this reason, it is only seldom possible to speak of success or failure in a strict sense. Only a more cursory inspection will suggest successes without any negative side effects, or failures without any positive side effects. This should be a source of confidence to us all in continuing to research and develop our professional situation (even if progress seems small), accepting discrepancies and "problems" as natural characteristics of complex professional work; on the other hand, it should remind us to be cautious and skeptical about claims of large-scale improvements.

Action research is an "art of the possible," which does not aim for a predefined ideal state, but helps us to see the potential that is implicit in a situation, and to put into practice action strategies that correspond more nearly than previously to our present values. To this end its cyclical character is most important. The test of action strategies leads to everyday practical action, to new starting points for reflection and, thus, in some cases, to new research cycles. To explore a new starting point, resulting from the implementation of action strategies, the ideas in Chapter 4 are relevant. This new starting point will often include novel questions, which have only emerged because "improvements" resulting from prior research have raised the level of aspiration, making it possible to see further potential for innovation and, thus, leading to a further spiral of professional development.

Chapter 8

Making practitioners' knowledge public

For Lawrence Stenhouse (1981; 1983) research was systematic inquiry made public.[1] In this chapter we look at how action research is made public. We begin by explaining why, in our view, "going public" is an important part of action research. We will then discuss different ways of reporting your own research, and possible audiences, and end by giving some advice on the most common form of presentation, that is, the written report. In the next chapter we will present some examples of action research reports that have been published in journals since 2000, so that you can look at the decisions others have made and compare them with both our suggestions in this chapter and your own ideas.

Before we begin, we want to make clear that there are many ways to make your action research public. Traditionally we think of publishing articles and books but practitioners can also make their research public orally by reports in staff meetings, presentations at professional meetings and workshops for colleagues. While oral presentations do not provide a permanent record of your work, they are a way to make it public. The Internet is also an important means of disseminating your work. However, it is important to remember that anything "published" on the Web should meet the same ethical and copyright requirements as any other publication.

WHY IS IT IMPORTANT TO MAKE PRACTITIONERS' KNOWLEDGE PUBLIC?

While the knowledge that social scientists and scholars construct is an important source of information, the books and articles they write usually have little connection with the world of the practitioner. In some fields of professional practice there is a tradition of the reporting of clinical studies written by people working in the field. Often professional associations publish these clinical studies. In nursing, clinical studies are published in journals such as the *Journal of Research in Nursing*, the *International Journal of Nursing Studies* and *Nursing Times*. In the teaching profession professional bodies such as the Classroom Action Research Network (www.did.stu.mmu.ac.uk/carn/) and the journal *Educational Action Research*, regularly publish writing by teachers (and other professionals). In addition, the growth of school-based in-service education has done much to break down the unspoken rule that teachers should not tell colleagues about their achievements. We believe that because action research can produce the type of knowledge that leads to the enrichment and improvement of practice, it is imperative to make this knowledge public.

Public reporting prevents professional knowledge from being forgotten

> Between the classroom and the staffroom teachers destroy their most valuable property, the knowledge borne from their experience.
>
> (Adapted from Gürge 1979: 46)

This quotation from a teacher's autobiography is symptomatic of the low regard in which many teachers hold their own knowledge and experience. Action research aims to rectify this by giving practitioners practical methods to develop knowledge from their experience and make a contribution to the shared knowledge of the profession. Reporting is an important final step in realizing this aim. It saves knowledge and insights from being forgotten in two senses of the word: by reporting and communicating your own experience you root it more deeply within your own memory, and by making it available to other teachers, nurses and social workers and your professional community as a whole it becomes part of the collective memory of the professions.

The process of reporting practitioners' knowledge increases the quality of reflection on practice

Your preparation to report the experiences and outcomes of action research involves further reflection and analysis that sharpen your initial interpretations, and give rise to additional insights. In addition, in actually reporting research to colleagues you engage in further theorizing upon practice. It is as true here as in any other situation that one of the best ways of learning is by having to present and explain it to others.

Reporting the outcomes of your action research is also a prerequisite for getting feedback and critique. Through reporting you make it possible to receive comments and at the same time demonstrate your own willingness to think more deeply about your practice. It is also true to say that the publication of results is considered to be an essential part of the quality control procedures for more traditional forms of research. That is, an important method for ensuring validity is to make your research available for critique by your peers.

By reporting their research knowledge, practitioners meet the requirements of professional accountability

Your professional standing depends to a large extent upon other people: the cooperation of pupils, patients or clients and, to some extent, their families; and the support of administrators, policymakers or inspectors and so on. Practitioners cannot afford not to care about the impression they make on others. Most of what you do, particularly anything innovative, relies on the cooperation of those concerned. This, in turn, depends upon their understanding and knowledge of your aims. Communicating the outcomes of your research to those concerned has a twofold effect:

- It shows your commitment to those concerned (for example, clients and their families) as partners in a common endeavor, and places a responsibility on them that is likely to strengthen their cooperation.
- It disseminates knowledge about your practice and the conditions of your practice situation and, in this way, empowers those concerned to make a constructive contribution of their own.

By reporting their research knowledge, practitioners reinforce their professional self-confidence

After a number of years in the job many practitioners feel that their professional development has come to a standstill, and that their work has become routinized and they themselves isolated. For example, when we used the Nominal Group Technique (NGT) (see M44) to find out what teachers find most detrimental professionally, a sense of lack of co-operation from colleagues came out on top. Reporting on research can help to overcome this problem because it documents individual professional development and makes it visible. In the long term, research knowledge developed by individual practitioners can build up a collective knowledge base upon which individual members of the profession can draw, and that forms a bond between them (see Elliott 2007). We think that such a knowledge base, primarily produced by teachers, nurses, social workers and other practitioners, is an indispensable prerequisite to strengthening the collective self-confidence of practitioners and overcoming their damaging sense of isolation.

By making their research knowledge public, practitioners can play a more active role in professional education

Mentors, who are involved in the training and induction of new practitioners, and those leading professional programs need to have a range and depth of practical experience, and be able to explain professional practice and draw meaning from it when working with novices. They need to open their knowledge and their practice to critical questioning and be ready to change on the basis of experience. Last but not least, they need to be open to differences in novices' ideas and practice (which could imply criticism of their own practice) and use critical questioning as the basis for their own and the novices' reflection on their practice – becoming a sensitive partner and adviser in their education. In short, they need to be "reflective practitioners", able to communicate their practical theories and knowledge to their (future) professional colleagues (see Schön 1983)

By reporting on research, practitioners' professional autonomy increases

If practitioners contribute to the professional and public discussion and credibly show professional competence they pave the way to increasing their professional autonomy. If they demonstrate that they are willing to study and evaluate the quality of their own work and draw consequences from new understandings, trust can develop and it can be shown that a reduction of professional autonomy based on lack of confidence is unnecessary and even counterproductive.

By reporting their research knowledge, practitioners improve the reputation of the profession

Many practitioners in the caring professions (e.g. teachers, nurses and social workers) are aware of having a low status in society and find themselves subjected to adverse public opinion. They may feel powerless victims of the media. We believe that there is a relationship between low self-esteem and low profile in public debate on professional matters. As a result, practitioners receive very little feedback on their contribution to the formation of public consciousness. For example, teachers passively accept scandals in the media and the complaints of dissatisfied parents, because they have no voice in public, educational debate. We believe that by contributing to building up a professional knowledge base, and participating in public debate, teachers, and other practitioners can raise the self-esteem and status of their profession.

Through reporting research, practitioners clarify their own position and bring influence to bear on policy by means of databased rational argument

In analyzing data from your own experiences and reporting them, you make it clearer to others where you stand and why. We do not want to overestimate the importance of rational arguments in public debate but we believe that teachers and other practitioners could strengthen their ability to shape policy and improve conditions in their institutions and workplaces if their voices were more often heard presenting well-argued reports on professional matters. Practitioners need to show that they are not only passive recipients of demands from other institutions in society but that they are also willing and able to express and realize their views of the society they want to live in, and that they deserve and demand respect as partners in the solution of problems in society.

DISSEMINATING PRACTITIONERS' KNOWLEDGE: WHAT?, TO WHOM?, HOW?

If you believe that it is important to make your knowledge public, you still have to decide how this should be done. When choosing the method of reporting it is helpful to ask yourself three interrelated questions.

- *What* – what should you include (descriptions, research methods, analysis of findings, action strategies, etc.)?
- *To whom* – who are your audience?
- *How* – what method of reporting do you want to use?

Having already spent some time discussing the 'What' we now want to concentrate on the other two questions.

Possible audiences for action research

Often practitioners underestimate both the degree of likely interest in their research and the size of their potential audience. In courses with an action research focus we sometimes use the following exercise to clarify this point.

M47 POTENTIAL AUDIENCES FOR ACTION RESEARCH REPORTS

You have been studying your professional practice for some time, have collected some data, analyzed it and come up with some insights. Make a list of whom you believe might be interested in this work.

Please compare what you have written with the list below, which was drawn up by participants in an action research course. Which potential audiences did you leave out? Was this because of the content of your research, the plans you have already made for reporting your research or did some of these audiences simply slip your mind? Did you have a tendency to forget particular kinds of audiences – for example, people external to your practice situation or your pupils, patients or clients? Are these "forgotten audiences" really irrelevant or are you simply unused to addressing them? Are they particular to your practice field? Or were they left out because of the ever-changing nature of professional practice?

Possible audiences for action research reports
A list drawn up by participants in an action research course:

Myself, my colleagues in my own institution, professionals in other institutions or groups in my region, participants in professional development courses, my pupils, patients or clients, their families, administrators, policymakers, researchers, the media, the local community.

Methods of reporting

Sometimes the same research results would interest several different audiences, but different methods of reporting would be needed. For instance, you could report to the local community by writing a short article for your local newspaper or a letter to the editor. For a colleague this kind of article or letter would be too short and provide too little information. Let's look now at different methods of reporting that you could use.

Involving others in the research

If you ask other people to cooperate with you and participate in the research process, it is important to keep them informed of your research aims, methods and results so far, if you want them to make a useful contribution.

1 INVOLVING PUPILS, PATIENTS AND CLIENTS

Professionals have everything to gain by including clients and other stakeholders in their action research activities. For example, Baker *et al.* (1986) did research on group work with "able" and "less able" pupils. They used a video camera to collect data and then discussed the recording with both groups of pupils. Here are some results from the teachers' point of view:

- The self-confidence of the less able pupils increased.
- When some pupils saw on the video that they did not ask any questions, they changed their behavior.
- The teachers were made aware that as the self-confidence of the more able pupils increased and they contributed more in discussions they received even more attention than before, whereas less able pupils gradually received less attention because their participation did not improve to the same extent.

The first two results probably could not have come about if the pupils had not been involved in the research process.

Another aspect of action research is stressed by Jinny Hay, Prevention Strategy Manager for Essex County Council Social Services: she emphasizes the "collaborative nature of the approach to solving a practice dilemma when the question has been agreed by all participants who want to learn from and with each other and change the way that they work" (personal communication). Action research "offers a different approach to a 'live' problem by involving those people whose problem it is and who want to do something about it to improve the way they work" (personal communication). (See also Hay (2002).)

2 INVOLVING YOUR CRITICAL FRIEND

When you invite an outsider to support you in collecting data about your practice, good communication is important. The partnership might begin with a preliminary conversation so that you can explain the starting point for the research and some of the initial insights. The next step would be to talk over ideas for the first stages of the research. This not only helps your critical friend to get a clearer picture of your concerns, but also helps you to clarify ideas by talking them through. We have found that students and novices across the professions can make good critical friends if the partnership is properly established through this kind of discussion and takes place in a relaxed environment.

3 COLLABORATIVE RESEARCH

We use the term collaborative research when several practitioners collaborate in their research by sharing experiences and discussing outcomes, though not necessarily sharing the same focus. This is the typical situation in an action research group. As with working along with a critical friend, the more that members of your collaborative action research group know about your situation and your research, the more they can help you in clarifying ideas, developing research plans and identifying action strategies.

Sharing ideas and research experiences with visitors

It can also be helpful to share your ideas and research experiences with those who have not been involved with your research from the beginning. When you explain to a visitor what you are doing and why, it causes you to think about your research in new ways. If the visitor is also doing innovative work in his/her practice, and is familiar with action research, even though they have little knowledge of your situation, they can help you to think about your work from a new perspective.

Graphic forms of presentation

Sometimes research can be presented graphically in the form of diagrams, tables, caricatures, etc. If you can present a surprising or thought-provoking finding in this kind of concise form (perhaps on a staffroom noticeboard), there is a good chance that it will attract attention and give rise to discussion.

Oral reports, workshops and in-service education

Teachers and other practitioners who research their practice acquire experiences and material that is very often interesting for fellow practitioners. An oral report is the most familiar way of communicating experiences. However, this kind of reporting is not necessarily stimulating and effective. It is useful for action researchers to think of different ways of sharing their experiences with other practitioners, taking into account that reporting orally is a form of teaching and needs to be effective in those terms.

A potentially more worthwhile way of communicating these experiences and insights to colleagues is through workshops and professional development courses. In light of this, many action research-based programs and projects include opportunities for practitioners to develop their competencies for running workshops and holding in-service courses (see e.g. Feldman and Minstrell 2000, Somekh 2006).

Multimedia presentation

Multimedia presentations also typically use presentation software like PowerPoint but add sound and video clips. This allows you to include audio and video data in your presentations. Remember that you must have permission from your participants to show others the data. For reporting back to pupils, patients, clients, family members and colleagues it is not necessary to produce finished products that stand by themselves without a commentary. For example, you can present clips from video and talk about them, followed by discussion, rather than spending a lot of energy on the production of perfect videos.

Acting on results

One way of disseminating research experiences and outcomes is to turn them into practical action. This can mean planning and carrying out changes in your practice as a result of your research. Another possibility is that research findings can lead to strategic or political action. For example, if you find that organizational structures are blocking changes you want to make it might be useful to raise this in discussions of policy within your institution or region. For example, a group of mentor teachers in California used the results of their action research to successfully argue for the continued funding of their program (Ashton *et al.* 1990).

The Internet

The Internet has become an important way to disseminate research. It is relatively easy to establish a website for your research that you can add to as your work progresses. There are also tools on the Internet that allow you to share files for data analysis and collaborative writing. Even if you do not have access to the more sophisticated tools on the Internet, there is much that you can do with email. Although it is not as effective as face-to-face meetings, much of what happens in a research group or with a critical friend can occur through the Internet. With the rapid rate of innovation in this medium it is not possible for us at the time of writing to predict what you will have available when you are reading this. It does seem, however, that videoconferencing will be more readily available, which may greatly improve the efficacy of meeting on the Web.

Written reports

Written reports are only one method of disseminating action research. They may not be the most useful way of communicating your knowledge to other practitioners, but at the moment they are the most usual and often the most visible method. Written documents can take very different sizes and forms, including letters to the editor in local or regional papers, notes on the staffroom noticeboard, short articles in a magazine or journal of a professional association or longer papers in a journal, such as *Educational Action Research*, to give a more comprehensive report of the research and its findings. Information about submitting articles for publication in EAR are given on its website. Those who have not written for publication before can enlist the support of a more experienced critical friend to submit their article for them as a "Supported submission". The reviewers' comments are then sent to the "Supporter" for discussion with the author about any additional work that may be required. Because written reports currently have such importance, we will deal more fully with their writing and design in the next section.

WRITING REPORTS TO DISSEMINATE PRACTITIONERS' KNOWLEDGE

Case studies are the most usual format for writing about action research. We will also describe a format that might be called a *cross-case analysis*.

Case studies

Case studies – in our wide definition of the term – are written reports, in which practitioners present information about one case taken from their practice, including the context and starting point, research methods, the stages of the research, findings, proposed action strategies, and emerging issues that may be the subject of further work. There are many different ways of structuring a case study and no fixed rules, but here are some suggestions:

1 Following the chronological sequence of the research

The simplest and safest way to write a case study is to communicate your experiences and findings in the step-by-step sequence in which they occurred. It helps with writing and with reading if you also illustrate the chronological sequence in a diagram or list. The chronological form of presentation is not always the best, because the whole research process is included irrespective of what is more or less interesting. Sometimes it is difficult to make links if the sequence of events and interpretations is chronological. In addition, the chronological order of presentation can occasionally entice the researcher to concentrate too much on description at the cost of analysis and interpretation.

2 Developing a case study from an issue

Many action researchers do not report the whole of their research, but select one or more issues that appear to be of special interest and discuss them in more detail. Writing the case study then becomes a continuation

of the analytical process by which the central insights and their supporting data have emerged. The following is an example of a case study from
action research on nursing practice.

*I was conducting an action research study into the organization of care for older
people in the accident and emergency department (A&E) at a large, busy hospital.
Staff members from A&E and Services for Elderly People (SEP) were involved in
the study and early interviews, focus groups and observation work had led to a
variety of suggestions for improvement. However, as we worked to make these
improvements, a major barrier to change emerged. While many of the changes
were dependent on co-operation between A&E and SEP, their working relationship was in fact poor and when external pressures such as high admission
numbers or resource restrictions increased, the relationship deteriorated further.
As I gathered data on the processes and outcomes of change, I made use of this
finding in gathering and analyzing further data. For instance, I would always
invite comment from A&E and SEP staff on issues that emerged, and probed
them as to theirs and the other department's contributions to patient care and
collaborative working. When I analyzed the data, I compared responses from staff
between the two departments. This focus led to an understanding that some
patients whose quality of care relied on good co-operation between the two
departments were in fact losing out because neither department saw those
patients' care as their primary responsibility (Bridges and Meyer 2000, Meyer
and Bridges 1998).*

Reports based on issues are particularly appropriate when reporting
extensive and complex research projects. They are also well suited to
action researchers' interest in development, which is usually directed at
specific aspects of the situation. On the other hand, readers of this kind
of case study may find it difficult to identify how your understanding of
the situation developed over time. If you choose this format you should
explain why certain issues were selected for close analysis.

3 Portrayal

In a portrayal an event is described vividly and in great detail without
much analysis and interpretation. The idea is that the reader should be
able to gain an understanding of the situation and bring his/her own
judgment to bear without becoming dependent on the interpretations
and value judgments of the authors. Texts of this kind can be very good
at stimulating a discussion. However, they are, in fact, analytical although
the interpretation is not made explicit, and sometimes this can make it
difficult for the reader to get a critical purchase on the situation. It often
helps to have a brief addendum that describes the research methods that
you used.

4 Shedding light on a case from different perspectives

We have experimented with a form of reporting in which we present a particularly vivid scene, event or short extract from data and illuminate it from different perspectives. The scene is like a prism with its facets illuminated from different sides so as to provide different meanings. The idea is to stimulate the reader to review the significance of the scene with respect to his/her own practical experience.

In an article "Intermissions – a discovery in higher education" (Altrichter 1984), Herbert included just two short scenes from observation data in which teaching was interrupted by the teacher leaving the room, and confronted these with a variety of materials that were relevant to a consideration of "intermissions" or "pauses": definitions from educational encyclopedias; statements from learning theory; a written account from our own experiences in teacher education; and a short story by Bertolt Brecht called *The Art of Stopping Teaching* (Brecht 1977). Similarly, in an article that he wrote, Allan looked at the practice of two teachers from a variety of theoretical perspectives (Feldman 2002).

One potential disadvantage of this form of reporting is that the desire to stimulate ideas may become stronger than the writer's consciousness of the importance of giving an exact account of what happened. In any case, to be successful, this kind of reporting must be clear and vivid so that it brings the reader to reflect deeply on the scene for some time.

5 Reporting action research through the use of key statements

An alternative to voluminous and elaborate reports is to condense an account into brief, carefully worded statements. You can, for instance, summarize the outcomes of your research in a well-structured, written presentation of about one or two pages (see Platten 1986: 12). For example, the article on the use of metaphors in divorce mediation that we referred to in Chapter 6 (p. 173) was only a few pages long.

An extreme form of reduction is a list of hypotheses. Elliott (1976: 44) tried to reduce the most important outcomes of the Ford Teaching Project to their conceptual core and formulate them as hypotheses. For example, the following statement is the first of 43 hypotheses on "developing self-monitoring ability":

> *The less a teacher's personal identity becomes an inextricable part of his professional role in the classroom, the greater his ability to tolerate losses in self-esteem, which tend to accompany self-monitoring.*
>
> *(Elliott 1976)*

The brevity of this form of presentation has its strengths and weaknesses. It is not easy to condense a lengthy research process while still retaining the analytic detail. However, if it is possible to master this conceptual challenge and present the main insights gained in a brief, but clear and intelligible way, this is an important achievement. Condensed forms of reporting are generally short enough to be easily read, but they are often too thin to be illuminating to the reader. In addition, supporting evidence and the implications of the research are often left out, so that the reader does not know how the statements were arrived at, and what conclusions can be drawn from them. A way of overcoming this is to follow each hypothesis with some extracts from data that provide enough of the context to enable the reader to understand it. This could be done, for example, by following the suggestion in M38.

Cross-case analysis

Sometimes a group of practitioners forms a project team in which each member of the team writes a case study about some aspect of the practice. In this situation it can be useful to analyze the cases as a set to uncover similarities and differences that further illuminate the overall project goals. Another possibility is that a group of action researchers may find that they are interested in a similar issue and decide to come together to analyze their case studies. An example of this was a group of doctoral students enrolled in a graduate seminar on action research who were involved in the supervision of student teachers. At the end of the course they decided to work together to see what they could learn by combining their individual cases. They reported their findings in a traditional academic format at conferences and in an article (see Feldman *et al.* 1998) and in the form of a play that they presented as readers' theatre.

M48 PRODUCING A CROSS-CASE ANALYSIS AS A TEAM

The method we present here was developed as part of the Teacher-Pupil Interaction and the Quality of Learning Project (TIQL). In that project teachers produced about 30 case studies. They then faced the task of preparing an analytical summary reporting the main points of agreement and any differences in their outcomes. Although the method was developed for a teacher research project, the procedure we outline below would be useful to any group of practitioners. You will note that this method includes the role of 'project coordinator'. It would be possible also for one of the practitioners in the group to take on this role.

Procedure

1 Each member of the research team brainstorms a list of the most important issues that had arisen in his/her research.

2 The project coordinator reads all the case studies and from these, and the team members' lists, develops a list of issues. It is possible for all of the team members to share in this part of the procedure and then use NGT (M44) or another group process to identify the list of issues.

3 The team members and any outside facilitators and/or critical friends set aside a significant amount of time (2–3 days) for a cross-case analysis retreat.

4 The whole group discusses the issues to clarify them. Some will be eliminated; others may be combined. The group then splits up into smaller groups, with each small group focusing on one issue of their choice. If there is an issue that no one chooses to focus on, that is an indicator that either the issue is actually a non-issue, or that it is so problematic that no one wants to deal with it. In any case, it is worth exploring why an issue that was identified by the team is "orphaned".

5 Each of the groups reads the case studies that appear to be relevant to the issue.

6 Based on their notes from reading, each group produces brief analytical notes including the following:

- hypotheses, summarizing in one sentence the main points of agreement and any differences arising from the case studies;
- comments, explaining each hypothesis, and references to illustrative material in the case studies.

7 The brief analytical notes can be used as the basis for writing analytical summaries on each issue, as a means of reporting the knowledge developed from the case studies. The cross-case analyzes can then be collected and distributed, either through print, as was the case for TIQL (Ebbutt and Elliott 1985), or the Internet. By this means practitioners are able to contribute to the development of a common stock of knowledge about professional practice. This accumulation of case studies to provide insights and strategies to guide the practice of other professionals was envisaged by Stenhouse (1978) as a resource bank akin to the accumulation of case law in the legal profession. More recently, practitioners' case studies have been seen as part of a "knowledge base for teaching" (Shulman 1992; Reynolds 1989).

CRITERIA TO USE IN WRITING REPORTS

Let's assume that you are about to produce a written report. You have thought carefully about its contents and possible audience, and you now have to decide what criteria to use in writing your study. While there are some criteria that are commonly agreed upon, there is not enough agreement to make the decisions unproblematic. It is important to remember that while these criteria relate to the writing of action research reports, there are the more general criteria for the quality of action research that we discussed in Chapter 5.

The criteria listed below are the ones that we use ourselves. We can give good reasons for them but that does not necessarily make them any more valid than a different list that someone else might put forward. If you are not dependent on other people to assess your written reports, we recommend that you develop a personal style that suits you and is accessible to the reader. It may be helpful if you begin by defining the criteria that you yourself use in judging written texts, for example, by asking questions such as:

- What kind of texts do I enjoy reading?
- Thinking back to the last two texts I have read, what did I like and what didn't I like about them?

It is also useful to compare your ideas with other people, such as your research group or critical friend. Below are some of ours.

Is the writing supported by data so that a reader can easily visualize what happened?

Are the points made sufficiently clearly to be understood by readers who have no direct experience of the case described? Do you give supportive arguments for your claims and credible evidence from the data? Later in this chapter we give some practical suggestions for writing. When you are thinking about answers to these questions, see in particular: (6) the "backbone" of the writing, (7) the introduction, (8) the conclusion, (10) substantiating your points from the evidence and (13) structuring a report (see pp. 241–3).

Are conflicting evidence and alternative interpretations considered?

Do you present arguments and data only in support of your own opinions? Or are conflicting data and other possible interpretations made available to the reader? Do you discuss any potential sources of error? Are comparisons drawn with colleagues' experiences or with findings reported in the research literature? Is the study more generative (inviting the reader to reflect on his/her own practice) or more definitive (presenting results as final and unquestioned)?

When writing a research study, we all hope to be able to present clear-cut results and, in trying out action strategies, we hope to be able to report success. Practitioner and academic researchers both share these expectations. Practitioners often feel under pressure to take action and be successful – especially if they are involved in innovations. This may sometimes mean there is an even stronger tendency for them to want to come up with definite findings and demonstrate success than is the case with researchers who enter the situation from outside. We call this the "need to know". For example, Andria Erzberger did action research on innovations that she implemented in her physics classroom. She wanted to know whether what she was doing differently was more effective than what she had done in the past. That is, by embracing new forms of pedagogy and assessment, were her students learning at least as much physics content as before while coming to a better understanding of how physics relates to their everyday lives (Feldman 1994)?

There is a real danger of cheating oneself and others with definitive success stories. Reporting research knowledge *does* serve to increase a practitioner's personal profile and that of his/her profession; however this should not be its primary and dominant function. The main aim of writing reports of action research should be to enable more reflection on your work and situation and in so doing improve professional practice. For this purpose, discrepancies in the data, contradictions and inconclusive ideas have their value in reports. They provide much better starting points for both the writer's and the reader's further learning than clear-cut success stories (see Chapter 3).

Is the context of the research made clear?

Are the specific characteristics of the situation and the research context put forward? Are your judgments of the conditions and likely validity of your insights presented? Are your own preconceptions made clear?

Action research findings are not directly transferable to other situations. They can only have the status of hypotheses that may serve to stimulate thinking about other situations. (See Stenhouse's telling phrase: "Using research means doing research" (1985: 92) To be able to reflect on other people's experiences in his/her own context, the reader must have an understanding of both the general context and specific features of the case described.

Is the text written in a way that is understandable, vivid and interesting?

Do the linguistic and formal characteristics of the text make reading enjoyable or must the reader fight his/her way through the text? Does it arouse emotions? Are there striking and interesting passages? Are examples and metaphors used (see M37)? Are stimulating ideas put forward? Unfortunately, too many authors write their research reports in a boring and long-winded manner. When writing action research reports it is important to take the trouble to make them readable and linguistically attractive.

Is the report ethically defensible?

Did you negotiate with all those concerned as to what would be put into the report and tell them that you intended to make it public? Was their feedback incorporated into the report? Have you respected the confidential nature of some of the information? We have already addressed ethical issues in Chapter 5. They are part of the whole research process but are of special importance when it comes to producing written reports of the insights gained through the research.

Does the presentation include analyzes or is it primarily descriptive?

Is there interpretation and explanation of the events as well as description? Are links established between points? Does the report draw conclusions for subsequent action and provide open questions for further investigation?

There is a tendency, especially the first time you write a report, to offer very few analytical points and interpretations in order to reduce the risk of getting it wrong. We want to challenge this view. An aim of action research is to gain a better understanding of professional practice and this is not possible without developing specific explanations and *practical theories*. You should take the risk of giving interpretations and drawing conclusions, if they appear to be plausible and relevant for developing new strategies. Luckily, the risk of being wrong often goes with the opportunity to learn something new.

FURTHER IDEAS ABOUT WRITING

Two further constraints on teachers researching were, first, the difficulties of writing about one's own practice, and second, the reservations that teachers have about whether they have anything worthwhile to say. Many teachers have not written at length since college days and need reassurance about their ability. Teachers seem to be very skeptical of their colleagues' ability to say things of importance about the profession.

(Wakeman 1986b: 90)

Writing is difficult. It is often hard to put ideas down on paper, even if they seemed clear and logical when thinking or talking about them beforehand. There are gaps in your argument and you find that some concepts are too vague, as new connections and implications come to mind. These difficulties spring from the fact that writing is not just about communicating the definitive outcomes of analysis, but is in itself a form of analysis. It is a continuation of the process of analysis under narrower constraints, because our inner thoughts have to be given shape and form. Writing is, therefore, a crucially important part of the research process, in which the writer-researcher goes through a powerful, reflexive process, and analysis of the data is deepened and clarified (Somekh 2006). Although we may see writings as provisional they become our product in a material sense and can be examined by other people. These very difficulties are a symptom of the fact that writing offers a new kind of depth to our reflection and research.

For many action researchers there is a sense of alienation that they experience in relation to writing. Wakeman (1986b: 90) has suggested that this is an expression of the low esteem in which they hold their own practical knowledge, and a symptom of low individual and collective professional self-confidence. Whether or not this is the case for you, many of us believe that our everyday experiences and the knowledge acquired from practice cannot be useful to anybody except ourselves. Practitioners are often pleasantly surprised when their work arouses the interest of their colleagues in action research projects or at conferences. Action research places a premium upon the dissemination of professional knowledge – including written reports – because one of the aims of the movement is to strengthen professional self-confidence. The aim is to prevent professional education, and research into practice, from being completely surrendered to experts who are external to the field.

Practitioners' difficulties with writing are also, in part, a result of the fact that their jobs do not require them to write at any length in the course of their professional work, and therefore, they have no opportunity to write. In terms of their career it is irrelevant whether or not they investigate their practice and/or publish written reports about it. Furthermore, their work does not usually allow the space or time to reflect deeply on their experience and write about it. Stenhouse (1975) and Schön (1983) suggest that the ability to reflect upon and develop practice, and present this for public scrutiny, is what distinguishes a professional. If they are right, professional organizations should strive to ensure that these qualities are taken into account in training and promotion, and suitable working conditions provided to promote them (for example, by creating time for reflection, and opportunities for debate with colleagues, during the working day). Action research projects try to provide practitioners with a better context for reflection (for example, by establishing research groups to discuss experiences, providing the guidance and facilitation of critical friends and suggesting practical research methods).

Part of practitioners' aversion to writing may spring from their perception that it is the traditional form of academic communication, but not the most meaningful method of disseminating knowledge within the profession. We agree with this to some extent, but believe that action researchers should master this form of communication as one among many methods of making their research knowledge public. Finding words to present meaning in writing is always a creative process that adds significantly to the potential impact of the action research work. All of this suggests that it is important to develop better writing skills and find ways of simplifying the difficult job of writing.

M49 WHAT DOES WRITING MEAN TO YOU?

This activity is structured to be used by a group of action researchers. It can be done by the members of an action research group, a research team in a project or as part of a professional development workshop or course. It is, of course, possible to do this exercise by yourself or with a critical friend. If this is done as group work, it helps to have someone act as the facilitator.

1 *Individual work (15 minutes)* Each person writes a short piece covering the following questions:

- From all the written texts you have ever produced, which piece are you most proud of? Why?
- What was your last piece of writing? What kind of writing have you done most often during the past year?
- What causes you problems in writing? What is fun?
- On the basis of your answers so far, try to respond to the following question, if possible in a single sentence: What does writing mean to you?

2 *Pair work (20 minutes)* Partners exchange their writing, read each other's and discuss any differences, similarities or surprises.

3 *Plenary (20–30 minutes)* Anything interesting or controversial that emerged in the pair work is reported to the group. At this stage it usually becomes clear that in one way or another everybody has

to cope with writing difficulties. It can be helpful if the facilitator joins in by presenting his/her own experiences and difficulties with writing.

M50 LEARNING TO BE FLEXIBLE IN WRITING

Many writers experience the block of not being able to give up "dead ends". The following exercise (based on an idea of Gibbs (undated)) can produce the right mental state for flexibility by showing from experience that there is always more than one way to describe something. This activity is also structured for a group. As with M49, you can do this exercise by yourself or with a critical friend. And again, if you are doing this as a group, it helps to have someone act as the facilitator.

1 *Individual work (part 1)* Participants are asked to write a description of an event that is part of the shared experience of the group. (An alternative is to watch a short extract from a video together and then describe it individually.)
2 *Individual work (part 2)* After about 10 minutes the facilitator interrupts this work and asks the participants to write a second description of the same event but in a completely different style.
3 *Pair work* Partners exchange their writing, read each other's and discuss the differences in their approach.
4 *Plenary* Partners report back on this experience in a plenary session and the group as a whole discusses whether it is possible to identify typical strategies.

You might also like to look again at M3, which can be a useful exercise to help develop facility in writing through in-depth reflection.

ASSORTED TOOLBOX FOR PRODUCING WRITTEN REPORTS

If you are writing a report of your research and its outcomes the following may prove helpful.

1 Take it step by step

Try not to think of the writing task as a huge enterprise in the future, but as a continuous process to be built up step by step. You have already taken the first steps: the records in your research notebook, your data summaries, analytical memos, hypotheses and so on.

2 Don't aim for immediate perfection

Don't expect to produce a finished manuscript straight off. Give yourself the right to begin by producing a draft that you will be able to revise later. This attitude helps to reduce the stress when writing.

3 Try to get feedback

Whenever it is possible, give your draft writing to someone in your research group, your critical friend or perhaps a colleague and ask him/ her to read it and comment on it. This feedback may be more relevant if you suggest some questions to guide the comments. When you are given feedback it is best not to defend yourself or to correct "wrong interpretations" (after all, you may not have written what you intended to say!). Try instead to get as much as possible out of your reader. Then spend an hour or so quietly reflecting on it and deciding which points you can use to develop your document and generally improve your writing. Most people find it stressful at first to receive comments on their writing (probably because writing is such a personal process), but it is ultimately very reassuring to go through this stage before publishing a report more widely.

4 Getting the right conditions

A relaxed atmosphere and a place where you cannot easily be disturbed provide the best context for developing your ideas and expressing them on paper. Obviously using a computer can greatly facilitate your writing. However, some people like to write a draft out first on paper and then type it into the computer for editing. At the end of some action research projects a writing retreat is scheduled, to provide time and quiet in a pleasant atmosphere for writing and consulting with colleagues and external facilitators (see Pickover 1986: 32).

5 Resources and materials

Before you begin to write, all the resources and materials you may need should be laid out near where you intend to work, especially:

- all the data that you have collected, such as diary, observation notes, and analytic memos;
- something to write on, whether it is paper or a computer. For those who write on paper, scissors, and glue are essential for editing draft

writing. For those who write directly onto a computer screen, disks, thumb drives and printed hard copies are essential and backups should be kept separate from the computer so that they survive disasters such as fire and theft.

- books and other resources that you may need to refer to (for example, a dictionary, a relevant policy document or report, the case study a colleague has written on the same issue or a book that has been important in your thinking during the research).

6 The "backbone" of the writing

Before you actually begin to write it is important to think about the shape of your argument and how this shape can best be expressed in the structure of your written report. For this purpose it is useful to think about the "starting point" of your research and to reread your data analysis. It is often helpful to make a plan, outline, or diagram of your argument: Which are the main points and what will be the best order in which to present them? The "clusters" exercises outlined in M3 can help you to start.

Above all, the purpose of this preparatory work is to get a mental vision of the thread of the argument that will form the backbone of the writing, and that the reader will be able to follow. The form that the backbone of the writing takes will depend on the theme of your study, your chosen form of presentation and the nature of the results. It might be a chronology of events, a step-by-step exploration of an intriguing issue or a telling metaphor used to establish connections between different areas.

7 The introduction

The introduction to a written report should tune the reader into the text and prepare him/her for what is to follow. The following suggestions may be helpful:

- What question will be investigated in the report? (It may also be useful to limit the scope by saying which aspects of the question will not be dealt with.)
- What was the context of the study? What background information is needed to understand it? What research methods did you use?
- Why is this question important to you? What importance might it have for your colleagues?
- What will be the structure of the report?

When planning the report you should try to give yourself provisional answers to these questions. However, some of the answers will change or develop during the process of writing. Therefore it is probably best to:

- jot down a few catchwords for the introduction while working on the plan of the report and make a note of other ideas while writing the report;
- write the introduction after you finish the first draft of the report.

8 The conclusion

If you want to be nice to your reader, spend time on the final part of the report, because it summarizes the main arguments. The conclusion is an opportunity for you, as the author, to emphasize once again the points that you believe to be important. The following should help in deciding what to include in the summary:

- What were the main findings of the study?
- What ideas for practical action emerged? Which of them were tried out and with what success?
- Which questions remained unanswered or arose as a result of the study?
- In what larger context could the issue(s) discussed be subsumed?

9 Defining central concepts

Most written reports contain a limited number of central concepts, which appear prominently in hypotheses, working theories, and diagrams and recur throughout the report. In working on an action research project you will have pursued an issue for a long time and become very familiar with its central concepts. They are likely to have a very specific meaning, which will be clear to you but not necessarily to the reader. It is therefore well worth the effort to decide which of these central concepts need to be explicitly defined. Diagrams are sometimes useful to illustrate the relationship between different concepts.

10 Substantiating arguments with data

When you come to the end of the action research process you can look back to a large number of experiences and a quantity of data that assisted you in developing insights. When you write the report these experiences and data should be used again and again to provide evidence for your main arguments and to illustrate them – by literal quotation, paraphrasing them or referring to them.

Sometimes action researchers use quotations from their data in the written report without noting their source. This seems to be not so much the result of carelessness as a failure to recognize that *their* data are important. This is unhelpful modesty because it is important to reference quotations properly to the data. An easy way of cross-referencing your report to the data is to list the data in an appendix, or as a table in a section on research methods, and give each item an abbreviated code and number that can then be used in references (see Chapter 6).

11 Procedures for quotations and references

When writing a report you will refer to your own data, but also to other people's ideas taken from published books and papers. Quoting is an established tradition. Quotations must be formally referenced to allow readers to cross-check with data and follow up ideas in the literature. The reference can also be helpful for you, as author, if you need to go back to an original source to make corrections or wish to refer to it again in a subsequent report.

There are several different traditions for setting out quotations and referencing them to their source. Thus, it is better to stick to one of the established styles that is used in your favorite journal or book rather than invent a new one. What is important is:

- that the method used is consistent throughout the report;
- that the source can be quickly identified by the reader without having to use detective skills.

12 Unrecorded data

While writing the report sometimes ideas and experiences come to mind, which support or modify the argument, but are not available as recorded data. It is useful to "quote" these kinds of experiences, by describing the event that produced the idea, for example: "This assumption is borne out by my experience in a role play with class, when the following happened . . ."

13 Techniques for providing structure

The inner structure of the writer's ideas, the logic and thread of the argument, should be clear in the design and presentation of the text. Here are some ideas:

Using linguistic patterns that imply structure

- on the one hand . . . on the other hand . . .
- both . . . and . . .
- at first . . . then . . . finally . . .
- first . . . second . . . third . . .

Highlighting passages

- underline
- capitalize
- italicize
- use bold type
- use large type

Employing structuring devices

- divide into paragraphs
- indent to show new paragraphs or quotations
- use single and double line spacing (e.g. present quotations from data in single spacing and the rest of the text in double spacing)
- use sub-headings
- use stars, bullets, numbered points etc.

Including passages of text that indicate the structure of the argument

- introductions that introduce the reader to the flow of the argument and provide necessary background information;
- passages that summarize the most significant points so far (either at the end of a section or as a conclusion to the whole piece);
- explicit transitions from point to point (e.g. "Now I come to my third point");
- diagrams showing the structure of particular arguments or concepts.

14 Giving examples

Examples drawn from personal experience are particularly important in writing that is addressed to an audience of practitioners. In everyday conversation we use examples if we are not able to explain something on a more abstract level. When we sense that we are not being understood we take a step back, so to speak, and draw on a concrete example (see M16).

Doyle and Ponder (1976) put forward the notion of teachers as "pragmatic skeptics" who judge new ideas and proposals for change first on the basis of a "practicality ethic". While Doyle and Ponder were writing about teachers, the same is true for many practitioners in other fields – that while theory and "outsider" research may strongly support certain actions, the real test is what happens when the innovation is put into practice. Elliott, again speaking specifically about teachers but with implications for other practitioners, stresses that this should be taken into account when presenting teachers with educational innovations:

If change proposals are to stand a chance of getting implemented under normal conditions of decision-making in schools they should:

1. Specify concrete procedures for accomplishing change.
2. Provide examples of how these procedures might be implemented in typical classroom environments.
3. Specify ways in which procedures can be legitimately adapted and modified by teachers in the light of their own assessments of particular situations.
4. Provide examples of the sort of benefits teachers can expect in return for the effort they are expected to put into the implementation process.

(Elliott 1984b: 159)

This does not mean that practitioners have no interest in the ethical and theoretical justifications for their practice. It simply means that new ideas must show themselves to be practicable, before they are given detailed consideration. It follows that it is important to include examples in written reports, to illustrate the practicability of theories and their likely consequences.

M51 FROM INTERVIEW TO TEXTUAL COLLAGE

If you are finding it very difficult to start writing a case study, this idea may prove helpful (modified after Prideaux and Bannister (undated)):

1 Ask someone from your research group, your critical friend or a colleague to interview you about your research and audio-record the interview. It is often easier to talk about experiences than to write them down, especially if your partner shows interest and prompts you with requests for detailed descriptions and explanations.
2 Transcribe the interview or parts of it (see M27).
3 Mark those passages that contain important statements referring to your research question, the research situation and its context or your methodology. Cut these passages out, spread them on the floor and try to arrange them in a sensible sequence. You may also want to try doing this using software that allows you to look at relationships intuitively, such as *Inspiration*.
4 Construct the case study from these passages. In some places it will be necessary to write intermediate passages to link the quotations from the interview. Such intermediate texts are generally much easier to write than the main text.

Chapter 9

Examples of action research studies published in journals

In this chapter we want to present some action research studies whose authors have "gone public" by writing up their work for publication in a journal. In Chapter 8 we suggested that before you start writing you need to decide on the possible audiences you are writing for and the criteria you might use in planning your writing. The studies we want to share with you in this chapter are intended to help you make these decisions by providing examples that may suggest ideas to you. Since 1993 the international journal, *Educational Action Research* (EAR) has published articles by action researchers in education and across other professions, particularly in the fields of health, social work and community development (www.tandf.co.uk/journals/titles/09650792.asp). All of us who are authors of this book have been involved as Editors or Associate Editors of EAR for many years so it is perhaps understandable that of the eight articles we have chosen, five were published in EAR and three from other journals – the *Harvard Education Review*, the *British Educational Research Journal* and *Social Work Education*. They illustrate a wide range of approaches to action research used in projects in education, health and community development carried out in five different countries – the USA, Canada, England, New Zealand and Sri Lanka. We hope that by reading the summaries of these articles and our commentaries on them you will be inspired to write your own articles for publication either in EAR or other journals. We hope you might also download the articles from the journal websites and read them in full so that you can see whether or not you agree with our comments.

TWO STUDIES OF CLASSROOM PRACTICE CARRIED OUT BY TEACHER-RESEARCHERS

The first two examples are of action research carried out by teachers in their own classrooms in elementary schools, the first in the USA with a focus on mathematics and the second in England with a focus on thinking skills. If you are intending to carry out action research on your own, perhaps as part of the requirements for a post-graduate degree, and/or with a leadership role for a research group in your own school, these two articles could make useful starting points for your thinking.

Gaining knowledge about fourth graders

"Learning from self-study: gaining knowledge about how fourth graders move from relational description to algebraic generalization" (Grandau 2005) is an article about a self-study of teaching young children the first steps in algebra. The class was participating in a pilot study with innovative algebra materials developed in the US using the theories of V. V. Davydov. Laura Grandau wrote the article while a doctoral student at the University of Wisconsin-Madison in the USA, which has a strong tradition in working with teacher researchers. She was in her tenth year of teaching, but had not previously taught this age group or used these materials. The class was diverse in ethnicity, socio-economic background, and prior achievement in mathematics.

Laura tells the story of her research with great clarity including information about the school, her own role as a maths and science teacher and a description of her classroom with its "rug" area where the children sit for discussions about algebra. The inquiry took place over a five-week period. This is an independent school with a policy of small classes, so there are only ten students working with Laura for a 45-minute class every morning. She started with a very open focus on "examining my own practice with the goal of improvement", so although she calls it "self-study" it exactly fits the definition of action research that underpins the core thinking in this book. Laura wanted to become more knowledgeable about the mathematical concepts involved, the children's learning and her own teaching. The inquiry involved "a systematic look at instructional strategies, specifically questioning and discussion, as well as children's verbal and written responses". She made video or audio-recordings of all classes and notes of her own reactions to the tasks in the teacher's guide, kept a separate journal to record thoughts and conversations and made copies of students' written work. From the extensive video-recordings she selected and transcribed "key interactions" for detailed study.

Laura was also supported by a "critical friend", Sean, who lived at a distance but with whom she had regular, often extensive, telephone conversations about her ongoing research. The descriptions of the relationship between teacher-researcher and critical friend are one of the most illuminating aspects of this article. He asks probing questions, provides expert advice on mathematical concepts, gives interesting examples from his own experience of teaching children of a similar age and is always interested and affirming. In three sections of the article, extracts from transcripts are used to look in minute detail at the teaching of key algebraic concepts: relational description (comparing quantities and describing the relationships between them), "true or false statements" (building inferential connections between statements) and beginning to understand generalization by exploring the process of making conjectures. The relationship between Laura and the children is as far as possible one of co-learners and this is signalled by often referring to "we" in the narrative.

Laura's article is, at one level, easy to read because of its clear story line, but the detailed accounts of each of the three teaching episodes require careful attention to understand the depth of analysis of the process of learning and teaching. Analysis is on-going through a habit of reviewing recordings regularly every evening and the outcomes of Laura's thinking and conversations with Sean are used in planning the next day's lesson. Throughout the article she tracks her own learning, for example:

- She learnt that starting with children's existing ideas on number and "mathematical knowledge" helped her to know what kind of language they used and "how they could interpret and use the models [in the curriculum materials] to understand concepts".
- She learnt the importance of "the visual support of the models in that they provided a rich, easy-to-interpret backdrop" for investigations.
- She learnt that when she could not answer a child's question it was helpful to both the child's understanding and her own if she opened the question up for discussion with the group.
- She learnt how to accept feedback from a critical friend, and through working with Sean she "gained comfort with not knowing".

The article ends with Laura reflecting on her role as a practitioner-researcher, the impact the study has had on her own learning and that of the students and her own feelings at various stages of the work. She is cautious, but also clear and convincing, in making claims about the outcomes of her work:

I believe this work can make a contribution to the larger body of knowledge about early algebra. Perhaps teachers like myself who have not experienced the kind of questioning and discussion promoted by this curriculum, would find it useful to read about this study. (. . .) If my ideas are not new to the existing body of knowledge, perhaps they can at least provide yet another piece of evidence, or counter-evidence, to already existing theories.

She also gives a clear summary of how the process of inquiry has helped her to improve her teaching and summarizes this as follows:

I have experienced how successful inquiry for me seemed to grow not only from my own interests and commitments, but also from those of my students and my colleague Sean. In fact, it seemed to be the interplay of these three key resources – the text, the students' reactions and written work, and the conversations with a critical friend – that made the biggest positive difference in my instruction. I feel strongly that I owe much of what I learned to them.

We think you may find this article interesting for its careful attention to presenting evidence to support the analysis – indeed, starting from evidence and drawing the analysis out from it. This is also an article that presents a careful justification of the validity of the research methods and its claims for knowledge. You might like to think about what other criteria Laura had in mind when writing it. If you read the whole article we think you will find the extracts from transcripts of classroom discussion particularly interesting as insights into the children's thinking.

Thinking skills in a primary school

The second article of this pair, "Researching thinking skills strategies in a primary school: challenging technical-rationalist orthodoxies of learning?" is by Gail Edwards (2005) from the University of Newcastle-upon-Tyne. It is similar to the first in its focus on classroom interactions and questioning techniques and illustrates how the analysis has been developed from close scrutiny of transcripts of teacher-pupil dialog in classrooms. However, unlike Laura, Gail begins by presenting theories of learning and teaching that are important background to her research before describing the study itself. This is the kind of choice you may need to think about yourself – but notice that Laura's study presents theories about the teaching of mathematics through the advice from her critical friend, Sean, rather than through discussion of the way the new curriculum was explained and justified in the teacher's guide. So, the articles provide two very different models of how to engage in discussion of theoretical concepts when reporting action research.

Gail's article is about the introduction of a "thinking skills pedagogy" in a primary school and the impact this had on children's understanding of learning and beliefs about learning. This was a collaborative action research project, led and conducted by a group of teachers, with Gail (herself a teacher in the school at the time) acting as coordinator and facilitator of her colleagues' work. The impetus for the research came from the teachers' sense of a conflict between their own values and the way they were required to teach the English National Curriculum to prepare children for high stakes tests. They were worried about low pupil motivation resulting from internalizing the values of a competitive model of education based on transmitting knowledge from teacher to learner, as in Freire's "banking" model of education (see Chapter 6). The work was grounded in the recent literature on thinking skills so that all the teachers had a shared research agenda, within which they had individual choice about the specific focus of their work. The research involved using two thinking skills strategies – "mysteries" and "community of enquiry". The "mystery" is a generic tool that starts with a story about an event, such as the Great Fire of London of 1666, whose cause the children have to try to determine. The children are given slips of paper in an envelope, containing statements that provide pieces of evidence to help solve the mystery. Different groups have different "clues" and no group has all the evidence so dialog between them is necessary to solve the problem. The "community of enquiry" starts with a stimulus (e.g. a story or a picture) after which the children raise their own questions and engage in a structured group discussion governed by simple rules to ensure they speak one at a time and take account of each other's contributions. In the research, data were collected by the teachers in their own classrooms (audio and video-recordings during lessons and follow-up, semi-structured interviews with pupils) and they then drew on these to present "descriptions of empirical instances characterizing improvement" to the whole teacher group in "validation" events.

This brief summary does not do justice to the dialogic process whereby these instances "emerged, expanded, shifted and refined" over time. The collection and analysis of data were also systematic and there seems to have been a balance between freedom for individual teachers to plan and develop their own research, and a shared responsibility for transcribing data and "where appropriate to the research question" sorting it into "coded categories" during the validation meetings. The research findings are developed from the data and show that the children learnt to "substantiate beliefs with evidence and reasonable argument" that are indicators of "intellectual autonomy", but also that this may have been hindered by the pressure that both pupils and teachers felt to prepare for national tests within the linear model of learning embedded in the National Curriculum.

We think you may find this article interesting as an example of research carried out in a school as a response to a problem identified by the teachers themselves. The teachers worked collaboratively, facilitated by one of their peers rather than a manager, but their action research also engages critically with existing educational policy and may have the potential to influence national policy development. This kind of critical engagement with policy is seen by some writers as an important feature of action research, so this is another criterion you might want to use (Carr and Kemmis 1986). Another interesting feature of this article is how it draws on philosophical theories and models of learning to contextualize the initial problem; the article then goes on to suggest how the tensions observed in classrooms were the direct result of a conflict between, on the one hand, the prescriptive policy assumption that learning was a product "reproduced" by pupils and, on the other hand, the thinking skills pedagogy that encouraged teachers and pupils to see learning as a sociocultural process of dialog and meaning-making. If you decide to include extensive discussion of theories from philosophy or psychology in your own writing a good criterion to follow is to ensure that they directly inform your research questions and analysis of data.

TWO STUDIES OF ACTION RESEARCH LED BY UNIVERSITY TUTORS, WORKING COLLABORATIVELY WITH STUDENTS

These examples both look at action research carried out collaboratively by university tutors and their students. The first, which comes from Wales, focuses on an undergraduate program for nurses who are studying part time and carry out action research in their workplace as part of the course requirements. The second, which comes from Canada, focuses on an intensive summer course for masters and doctoral students, some of whom are studying full-time and some part-time. Both courses are highly experimental in their methods by comparison with other classes in the university, but whereas this creates some stress for the Welsh students and their tutors it does not feature as a major issue in the Canadian study.

Nursing practice in Wales

The article from Wales, "Our story about making a difference in nursing practice through action research" (Jenkins *et al.* 2005), is written collaboratively by two tutors who were teaching action research modules for the first time in an undergraduate degree program and five nurses working in local National Health Service (NHS) Trusts[1] (in many, but probably not all, cases hospitals) who were taking these modules as part of their degree. The writers present their work as having seemed to them to be risky initially – they reflect on how they themselves felt uneasy with the new methods as well as sometimes receiving negative responses from university administrators and NHS Trust officials. The first introductory module (10 credits) included teaching of theory about action research, identification and clarification of students' workplace problems, 'reflective discussion' and planning of possible action research projects. The second module (30 credits) involved students in leading a collaborative action research project in their workplace, working with nursing colleagues to bring about changes that would directly benefit patient care. These projects included, for example, "Reducing falls by elderly mentally ill people in a residential setting" and "Developing a tool to aid nurses' decision making in dressing selection, during wound care". Although these projects had a strong orientation towards practical problem-solving and were clearly product-orientated, the action research methods necessitated a much more open and exploratory research design than was normally assumed to be mandatory by both the NHS Trusts and the university. There were some formal teaching presentations, but most of the time was spent on "reflective discussion". Innovatory approaches were adopted using techniques such as "picture interpretation" – for example, how did a photograph of a mountain and trees reflected in a lake in the foreground "relate to action research"? The intention was to "encourage more divergent thinking, using imagery, metaphor and analogy".

The open-ended nature of the teaching was unusual and therefore somewhat unsettling for the students, and they were nervous of how the quality of their work would be judged by the wider university. The students had to gain approval for their projects from the Ethics Committees of the NHS Trusts[2] that employed them and came up against difficulties – for example, some ethics committees "sought on-going updating on progress because of the 'unusual' nature of the projects". The reflective sessions operated within a set of ground rules drawn up by the group, which included: "support and constructive challenge will characterize our working together" and "sessions should involve the element of fun and good humor". Both tutors and students "kept diaries that recorded details of sessions and [their] feelings and thoughts about them". A culture shift took place as the group came to understand that "the invest-ment of self in [their] work" could be a focus for both personal and collaborative learning. An important outcome was that "Students were making a difference in their practice areas and teachers were part of that, helping to enhance reflective appraisal and evaluation". This was both in terms of concrete outcomes to their projects, which focused on practical problems (see above), and also through transformed working practices. These included, for example, a greatly increased capacity to 'relate theory to practice' because of a new realization of the relevance of theory and a much more active engagement of colleagues in a student-led collaborative research process. After the successful completion of their research pro-jects, the authors came together for a writing project that involved meta-reflection on the experience of teaching and learning in the modules – and led to the production of the article.

This article illustrates how action research courses in universities can become the stimulus for multiple action research projects in workplace settings. The authors describe how this work completely changed the nurses' relationships with their colleagues. In this sense it shifted the power relations embedded in traditional hospital hierarchies, putting the nurses into positions of leading meetings and facilitating discussions between colleagues of mixed status, some much more senior than them-selves. The course itself is described as action research in its own right, with the teaching organized as open discussion sessions in which the students could openly express anxiety and "negativity" if they wished. But, over time, the tutors and students learnt to understand the tensions and uncertainty of their joint venture and came to an understanding that "we all wanted to foster more critical and participative approaches to learning".

We think you will find this paper interesting for the openness and honesty with which it engages with tensions and problems. It also provides evidence of how action research has made the reading of background theory much more meaningful. At one point in the paper a nurse-student comments on how the action research greatly increased her motivation to read existing research that could inform her project, because "it's important to know what backs up what we're doing . . . it's made me more interested. I want to know more". These might both be criteria you would want to consider for your own writing. A third criterion might be in seeking to show a link between your own small-scale action research project and larger, organizational culture, because what is really exciting about this paper is that the action research projects not only had small-scale impacts on things like how nurses made decisions about dressing wounds, but also began to develop a culture of inquiry throughout the hospitals:

> Also, it's not just the unit . . . it's the hospital . . . people we went to for information . . . research and development nurse[3] . . . has asked us to talk at meetings . . . there is an interest . . . not just on the unit but elsewhere in the hospital.

Authoring identities

The second article of this pair, "Living action research: authoring identities through YaYa projects" (Nicol et al. 2004), is collaboratively written by a teacher educator and four of her graduate students, who work at the University of British Columbia and the Vancouver School District in Canada. The joint authorship of the paper – and the consequent need to shift the authorial voice between "I" and "we" – is a common feature with the Welsh article, but this article is much less concerned with the policy context of the work. Its focus is entirely on what happens in the university classroom – the students' workplaces are only referred to as one of the "figured worlds" that they must come to terms with individually through action research. The article describes "the authors' experiences of living action research through an art therapy activity known as YaYa[4] that involved creating and sharing visual representations of themselves as beginning researchers". This collaborative action research examined the power of the YaYa activity as a lever to integrate the processes of "learning how to do action research" with "doing action research".[5]

This article starts with a description of the care and excited anticipation shown by the 17 graduate students as they got ready to present their YaYa boxes to each other at the end of the first week of an intensive three-week summer school involving daily classes of three hours. The action research was in two parts: first the experience of creating the YaYa, which involved reviewing life experiences, selecting artefacts to represent the emerging research self and preparing for and enacting the presentation of the YaYa to the group; and second a series of follow-up meetings over four months at which students who had volunteered to participate "discussed, explored and put together what and how we might share this strategy with others". The focus of the action, as it is described, is related to the development of the students' identity as researchers through their learning in the class and their subsequent research activities. In addition, YaYa is an art therapy activity that is used in the class as a tool for the personal/professional growth of the students. Through the YaYa and other course activities the students come to understand what it means to conceive of research as "a living practice". The presentation of the YaYa was the first course assignment; the second was a "critical review of an action research project" and the third was to produce a plan for their own action research project. Students were also "encouraged to 'chunk' the course readings by finding intriguing, enlightening or meaningful chunks (quotations in the readings) to critically analyze and share with others in the class".

The students' response to the YaYa activity is described in the article as "powerful and passionate" and transformative in its "potential to help uncover layers of meaning" and "author [their] identities". The YaYa is a mechanism for involving the whole of the self in the action research process or, as the course tutor puts it, "imagining action research as a living practice". The aim is to allow the students to understand the poten- tial of action research as a means of social, personal and professional change. The article presents action research as a form of "evocative autoethnography and systematic introspection", grounding its methods in the work of Carson and Sumara (1997) on action research and Eisner (2002) on the power of art for the development of mind and identity. This personal transformation took place through the demands of YaYa production and presentation, first to create themes or metaphors that represented the selves of these emergent researchers, and second through interactive sharing of self at a deep level:

> *Understanding others and ourselves is a complex interplay. Presenting and listening to the presentations moved us back and forth between self and other, where distinctions between these became blurred.*

The work is also described as a process of making meaning out of the "figured worlds" of high school teacher, academic and researcher:

the YaYa activity placed students in a position of examining these figured worlds as they attempted to imagine how they might author themselves in multiple worlds.

More than any of the other articles described in this chapter, this one presents action research as involving the whole of the self: "Learning to live action research involves the mind and the heart". This is action research, which is focused more on personal growth than on systematic inquiry, grounded in the collection of data and its analysis. These might be interesting criteria for you to use in planning your writing, as many argue that one of the indicators of quality in action research writing is reflexivity. In this article the authors go further than this, however. Their world view appears to assume that what is researched is shifting and co-constructed by multiple identities, whereas the action research described elsewhere assumes that it may be possible to identify causes and effects and engage with change in a more concrete way within a world that is not always and only ambiguous and uncertain.

TWO ARTICLES ON RESEARCH WITHIN LARGE-SCALE PROJECTS WITH THE POTENTIAL TO INFLUENCE CHANGE AT THE MACRO LEVEL OF NATIONAL POLICY

The next two articles describe action research within prestigious projects that have a direct impact on improving service delivery and are intended to feed into the refining of government policy. Both projects took place in England within the prescriptive contexts of public services – the first in the National Health Service and the second in education. In both cases the action research took place in specific local contexts but the knowledge generated from the work has obvious application to other similar settings. In one, the action researcher worked as both a researcher and facilitator leading a group of co-researchers that was not entirely stable over the life of the project. In the other, the teacher researchers' work is kept in the background of the article and has to be imagined in the context of the writing about the project as a whole – albeit the teacher's action research is acknowledged as centrally important to the integrated development of theory and practice.

Stroke units

The first of the articles, "Stroke units: the implementation of a complex intervention", is by Cherry Kilbride and the three university-based advisers for her PhD study (Kilbride *et al.* 2005). The action research took place in a large teaching hospital in inner city London in response to a recognized need by the hospital's managers and medical staff for the care of patients who had had strokes to be radically improved. Cherry was funded by the hospital's Special Trustees, to be part-seconded from her role as Head of Physiotherapy, to lead a group of co-researchers from the newly established stroke unit. A stroke unit provides specialist care in one geographical location from a multidisciplinary team that meets at least once a week and is headed up by a consultant physician. It also provides specialist education for staff, information for patients and carers and has links with patient and carer organizations. The aims of the study were: "illuminating the process of introducing a new stroke service; describing the outcomes achieved; and identifying the key factors that influenced the outcomes achieved". The research built directly on the existing research literature on the treatment of strokes and the action research design built on other studies carried out in health settings and in education. It took place over two years and was "strongly underpinned by the action research ethos of undertaking research with, for and by people, and operated within a structure of collaborative intent". Cherry's continuing (though part-time) clinical and managerial role in the hospital was important in giving the project "a high degree of clinical credibility" but the "role duality" was very hard work and had the potential to create conflict. Both quantitative and qualitative data were systematically collected "to monitor the process and outcomes of change over time". Data collection began with seven focus groups "to explore how staff wanted to implement and develop" the new service, together with analysis of documents such as policy statements and minutes of meetings. Cherry kept regular, reflective field notes throughout and led weekly meetings of the research team at which issues arising from the data were explored, outcomes were validated and actions planned. At the end of the study 24 semi-structured, exploratory interviews were carried out to enable "staff to reflect on what had been achieved and learnt". There was also a five-question survey administered at the end to gather views from a wider group of staff.

Over its life the project involved three interrelated action research cycles: the first "valuing and profiling stroke"; the second "building a team"; and the third "sharing skills and knowledge". The article is full of detailed evidence on the issues and outcomes from each of these cycles and these are cross-referenced to existing research literature. The learning of all participants in the research team was considerable, but its membership was not entirely stable due to staff movements over such a lengthy period of time. Cherry's study was very much research led by an action researcher who straddled the roles of "insider-clinician" and "outsider-researcher" and whose doctoral studies ensured that the work was strongly grounded in existing knowledge and well informed by change theories, including both action research methodology and complexity theory. The outcomes of the project are on two levels: first, the establishment of the Stroke Unit had a very substantial impact on improving the care of stroke patients (the death rate fell from 24 per cent to 15 per cent over two years), and, second, an in-depth knowledge of the processes that were put in place to make the Stroke Unit so successful. Complexity theory, which explains social practices in terms of group interactions rather than individual agency and assumes that all human activity is interrelated and mutually contingent, is used alongside action research to understand the nature of the change processes involved in establishing the Stroke Unit. This explains why the study was not able to identify any one factor that "made a difference" because to change any one would immediately bring about a shift in all other factors. However, four "non-linear interrelated main factors arose from the action research cycles and were perceived to have contributed to the local success: building a team, developing and sharing practice-based knowledge and skills in stroke; valuing the central role of the nurse in stroke care; and creating an organizational climate for supporting change."

You may find this article useful for its focus on the importance of groups rather than individuals in the change process. For example, one of the valuable insights it presents relates to nurses' sense of professional identity and pride in expertise in stroke nursing once the Stroke Unit has been established. This is presumably related to the status of the Stroke Unit in the hospital and the relationship between individuals' sense of identity and the structure of their workplace organization. Drawing out these kinds of micro-macro links might be a criterion in your writing. This article also places priority on explaining the unintended consequences of assumptions embedded in traditional practices – which in action research writing often leads to an "aha!" sense of revelation. For example, the article describes the tendency for nurses who work with stroke patients in non-specialist wards to expect physiotherapists to lead the treatment while they keep the patients comfortable; and how this was turned around when the action research identified that nurses in the Stroke Unit were ideally placed, through their 24-hours/7-day care, to lead the treatment process. Nurses and physiotherapists started to teach each other new skills to enable much more sharing of responsibility.

Formative assessment in the classroom

The second article in this pair, "Developing formative assessment in the classroom: using action research to explore and modify theory" (Torrance and Pryor 2001), illustrates a different kind of involvement in action research, one in which the teachers focused on their own research projects within the larger framework of a high-status research project. The article was written by the university-based researchers who collaborated with a team of seven teacher researchers. It presents interesting quotations from the teachers on their experiences of working in this way. For example, this one that refers to the power of using action research to test out and come to understand how to use theories of assessment in practice:

> *I found it really interesting. It taught me a lot about the children in the class and my teaching . . . Until you've analyzed your own data, you can't really take it in, even though you're reading about someone else doing something.*

The "Investigating and developing Formative Teacher assessment in Primary schools" Action Research Project, known for short by participants as "Primary response" built upon earlier basic research carried out by Torrance and Pryor and was designed to "investigate the issues from a more practical and applied perspective; in short to put the ideas generated by basic research to the test of practice". The article describes a research process in which teacher-researchers "remained immersed in their own projects" and cross-case analysis of "the common issues" that inform research knowledge about assessment was left to the university-based team. However, the latter are clear in stating that the learning between the two "kinds" of researchers was interactive and co-constructive:

> *Successful collaboration was an outcome of the fact that neither TRs [teacher researchers] nor university-based researchers would have been able to accomplish what they did without each other: they had different agendas and priorities both at the level of role and of output.*
>
> *(Torrance and Pryor 2001)*

The Primary Response Project built on the outcomes from the TASK Project (Teacher Assessment at Key Stage 1 – i.e. with 5–7-year-old children)[6]. The TASK Project developed a framework for formative assessment made up of two "ideal types": convergent assessment, which looks at how learners have mastered the planned learning specified in the curriculum, and divergent assessment, "which emphasizes the learner's agenda rather than the agenda of the assessor". Within the policy framework of the English education system teachers were strongly oriented towards the former type of assessment, with the result that they saw assessment as a separate step rather than an integral part of teaching and learning. This embedded assumption would have been much more difficult to confront and explore without the support of the university-based facilitators of their action research. A framework for analyzing assessment practices had been developed as an outcome of the basic research and was used by teachers in the first phase of the Primary Response Project and modified by them in phase two. In phase one practitioners were supported through discussions at team meetings and investigations of their own classroom practice in making their premises about learning and assessment explicit and developing "practical arguments" (practical theories as described

earlier in this book) about their practice. This enabled them to make connections between their own practice and the theoretical knowledge
developed through the previous basic research.

Seven teacher researchers completed these initial investigations of their
practice and wrote reports. In phase two, five went on "to explore specific
interventions and new approaches" and wrote further reports. In the
process they uncovered unintended consequences of their teaching
behaviors. They analyzed "how they framed and managed classroom
activities" in their teaching and found in many cases that they were
"closing down opportunities for exploring student understanding rather
than opening them up", and that their focus was on behavioral goals (e.g.
task completion) rather than learning goals. In phase two "conceptual
distinctions, such as that between 'task criteria' and 'quality criteria' came
to be regarded as analytical tools". The teachers moved from a point
where their practice was grounded in tacit assumptions to one where they
could provide data-rich analyzes of their practice. They were then able to
use the theoretical framework from the basic research, alongside the data
from their classrooms, to develop action steps to change their teaching
and assessment practices.

The article makes it clear that the teachers' action research – and specifically the data they gathered on their own classrooms through audio and
video-recording – was the key element in transforming classroom practice. We included this article as an example because we think it is a mis-
take to think that professionals do not gain from participating in a larger
project of this kind. In the Primary Response Project teachers' action
research generated knowledge that could not have been generated by
traditional research *on* classrooms. Mediated by the university
researchers' support and ability to give the work a high profile, these
teachers' action research had considerable potential to shape national
policy for assessment. It would be mistaken to see them as having been
used by the researchers in a way that was disrespectful of their professionalism. They were volunteers who were quite explicit in saying that
they gained enormously both personally and professionally from the
opportunity of working in partnership with the university-based
researchers.

TWO ARTICLES FOCUSED ON DEVELOPMENT WORK IN SOCIALLY DISADVANTAGED COMMUNITIES: ONE IN A DEVELOPING COUNTRY, THE OTHER WITH A MARGINALIZED GROUP IN A "FIRST-WORLD", INDUSTRIAL SOCIETY

These two articles, like the previous two, report on action research within
major, funded projects. One, based in Sri Lanka, had funding from an
overseas donor agency to improve education in remote rural areas. The

other, based in New Zealand, had funding from a prestigious research council to bring regeneration to the families and existing support structures in a rural community. The first used action research as a strategy within a school improvement framework based on models developed in "first-world" countries. The second used action research within the theoretical framework of community work practice.

School improvement in Sri Lanka

In the first of the two, "School improvement: an action-based case study conducted in a disadvantaged school in Sri Lanka" (Wijesundera 2002), Subhashinie Wijesundera writes about a school improvement project in a rural primary school in "a difficult mountainous area" in the Kegalle District in Sri Lanka "where a single bus travels four times a day between the school and the nearest town". An important focus of the article is on her role as a "trainer" and facilitator of change processes – a role in which she has responsibility for, not one, but 25 selected schools, working as part of a team with five other trainer-facilitators within a national project sponsored by the Swedish International Development Agency (SIDA). Her objectives for the intervention in the case study school were:

- To develop a self-renewing school, which identifies problems in its functioning and finds out solutions on its own.
- To improve the total teaching learning situation by developing teachers, methods of teaching, the physical environment of the classrooms/schools and school-community relationships.

The teachers were involved in a kind of action research in which activities were orchestrated initially by Subhashinie. "Whole group, small group, and individual activities and discussions" were the core of the school-based work and staff were involved extensively in "brainstorming, data gathering and group presentations". The starting point was the development-planning model adopted by the project (see Figure 9.1). She had received "training" in "group facilitation, interpersonal skills, communication, conflict resolution, project management and organizational development" at the start of the project. The article reveals insights into how Subhashinie carried out her role as facilitator so that its focus is on both the school's development and her own learning. Work began in line with the accepted principles of school improvement but she was quickly aware that the principles of school improvement (e.g. its "bottom-up" orientation) had been adopted only at a superficial level. The Principal assumed top-down responsibility and the staff adopted passive roles rather than exercising agency. They worked with her to identify problems and select strategies but initially nothing happened between her visits. Development work only began when she asked teachers two open questions about

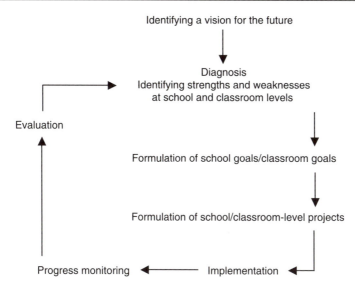

Figure 9.1 The development-planning model adopted in the processes of interventions

"the disorderly, cobweb-covered and dilapidated hall" while sitting with them over lunch: "Could you tell me what you see inside this hall? . . . Do you like to keep this place in this manner?" This led to immediate discussions during the afternoon and on her visit one month later the school hall was "whitewashed, cleaned and decorated". Her facilitation work is described by Subhashinie as "letting the participants themselves assess what is happening around them". From her second-order action research (Elliott 1988) she learns:

> *Although the facilitator has to have some objectives in her mind she doesn't have to impose them on the participants. She has to be a friendly guide who asks critical questions that help them to reflect upon their own actions. The facilitator always has to modify her planned strategies according to the responses of the participants.*

The school involved her in ten in-house sessions carried out on non-working days over a two-year period. The approach was informal and exploratory following a model of "learning by doing" rather than following any detailed guidelines.

Subhashinie's challenge was often to find a way of reconciling the school's preferred way of working with the framework of the project's objectives and strategies. Examples of outcomes in the school's work included very practical measures to improve school-community relations, such as "establishing parents' circles at the classroom level" and "organizing a mobile service to provide advice on tea plantation"; and others to improve the social well-being and sense of identity of pupils, such as establishing a student association, encouraging much greater participation in the class task of offering flowers to the Lord Buddha and taking pupils on field trips.

At the end of the article Subhashinie reflects on the barriers to change within the Sri Lankan education system and how these might be overcome. They include the reluctance of teachers to work in very rural areas with the result that there may be gaps in teacher supply in key areas such as mathematics. But the official response to this problem, which is to appoint teachers to "difficult schools" for only three years and then move them on, greatly undermines sustainable development. This problem is compounded by "punishment transfers", which place teachers in rural schools for disciplinary reasons. Subhashinie is careful to point out the limitations of her research in terms of the potential for its outcomes to be generalized to the whole system. However, she ends her article by reflecting on the need for research like hers to influence policy, and in particular to bring about increased involvement of educational officers and "master teachers" in the facilitation of school improvement. So, despite its focus on just one school, the article spells out messages for policy-makers in Sri Lanka and perhaps other developing countries.

You may find this article useful in developing criteria for your writing if you are in a position of being tasked to lead others in action research from the position of an "outsider". In many ways Subhashinie fills the same facilitation role as Sean in Laura Grandau's article described at the beginning of this chapter. The article is clearly written for several different audiences – one the international readership of the journal, another the sponsors from SIDA and a third the education officers running the service on behalf of the Sri Lankan Government. One of Subhashinie's criteria may be to provide leverage for the sponsors in influencing changes in national educational policy. Another appears to be to command attention in a "first-world" culture ("It will be necessary to include quantitative measurement of outcomes in the future endeavors of school improvement"). Yet, shining through her writing Subhashinie shows that a key criterion for her is to be respectful of her research partners in the school. She does a careful balancing act in meeting the needs of different audiences in her writing.

Community development in New Zealand

The final article, "Community development – action research in community settings" (Munford *et al.* 2003), is about a community development project in an area of New Zealand with a large Maori and Pacific Islands population. The authors were deliberately adopting participatory action research as a new approach to combining research with community development. They were committed to developing good ethical practice and giving participants "ownership of the research". The project was part of a larger research program funded by the New Zealand foundation for Research, Science and Technology. The focus of the action research was on "gaining further insight into what it is that leads to the achievement of well-being for families". It included investigating the way in which families themselves construct the meaning of "well-being", the reasons why some families do not have it and how external agencies could work with communities to generate it. They set out "to produce locally meaningful accounts ... that can be placed alongside official statistics to provide other interpretations of the meaning of well-being".

The funding for the project came before its location had been decided, so the first step was to find a community agency working with families/ *whanau* (the Maori word for family) and design a project that located this agency at its center. One of the schools responded and took the decision to come into the project and invite the researchers into their community, which the authors saw as "an important milestone in our work" because it set the right ethos for collaborative work. The school is described in the article as acting "in many ways like a social service agency" for its neighborhood. Many families were receiving state benefits, often as their only source of income. Poverty and other problems meant that they "daily met complex challenges as they raised their children". The school played a significant support role and worked closely with a local community center. Both the teachers and the community workers saw the project as an opportunity to access further help for their existing work with families.

The authors describe how they took immense trouble, over a considerable period of time, to develop the research methods. They "began to think critically about the research questions, the intention of the research and how the research project could be sustained over a long period". It was only after this that "a research team was formed and the community center and school became the sites for the research". An important factor in designing the research was to strike the right balance between involving the community fully in the research process and ensuring that their work was not unduly disrupted by additional demands on their time. Students at the university were useful in assisting with both research work and community activities to spread the workload.

The action research team included the principal of the school and workers at the community center and the action research focused on improving the quality of their work with families/whanau. Data collection and reflection were carried out at this level with the support of a full-time researcher and other workers from the university. Community participation was through being consulted and listened to, both formally in interviews and focus groups, and informally through participant observation, discussion of day-to-day issues and getting people to tell stories. These participatory research methods greatly increased consultation and shifted relationships so that the community workers focused increasingly closely on meeting the community's expressed needs. The research focused on "exploring the meaning of well-being, from the perspective of the families and young people", and learning from listening to individuals the kinds of factors and activities that had increased or undermined well-being for them in the past. The research fed back to the school and community center information they used to develop new strategies for more effective ways of working. In the course of the work a major focus emerged on developing improved ways of working with young people in the community.

The article also reports findings at the theoretical level that emerged in the course of developing new ways of working. Two that are likely to have relevance for other community work of this kind are:

• Recognizing that coming back into the mainstream (for example, by moving away from a life of crime) is difficult and painful for young people because it involves breaking up existing patterns of social relationships and joining groups who may not be welcoming.
• Recognizing that some families are living under such stress that the adults are "unavailable to parent", being unable to function effectively as parents even if they have good parenting skills without some alleviation of their living conditions.

The article ends by presenting a useful set of research principles and commentary that clarify that the action research work progressed very much along the lines of community work practice. These principles are described as "critical to understanding how best practice in research could be achieved". They provide a strong framework for others wanting to engage in community-wide participatory action research. Among the key principles are: collective decision-making about research processes; critique of research processes by participants and modification of methods as a result of feedback; including "indigenous and local models of practice" drawn from the participating community to ensure that "our understandings of well-being were informed by a range of cultural interpretations"; and "strengths-based approaches".

If your own research involves working with disadvantaged groups, in either a first-world or a third-world country, you are likely to be inspired by the criteria underpinning this article. It places a high priority on respect for participants, equality of esteem and privileging of local knowledge over knowledge imported from first-world cultures. That is in relation to the substantive focus on developing understanding of the well-being of families. However, the article is also interesting in importing a strong, theoretical framework from community work practice to shape the research design and methods, in much the same way that Kilbride imports complexity theory to inform the design of her action research into establishing a stroke unit and the analysis of data.

CODA

In music the coda is an occasional additional musical reflection that comes at the end in order to remind listeners of key themes raised in the main body of the work. Here we want to encourage you to reflect back on this chapter rather as you might at the end of a musical performance. We have not so much been presenting our own ideas in this chapter as giving performances of works composed by others. Different performers would be likely to give very different performances of the same works – and possibly give them much fairer and more interesting renderings. If you find the time to read the original articles you can judge that for your-selves. But, reflecting back on the articles as we have presented them, with all the inadequacies of our presentation, we hope you will sit for a moment and reflect back on the enormous range of kinds of action research and locations for action research revealed in just eight articles. All start from a vision of transforming social practices through grounding change and development in locally generated knowledge. The researchers are either participants in the social situation under investigation or work alongside the participants as co-researchers: the aim is for equality of esteem and mutual support among all those involved, whatever their role or responsibilities. They are concerned with developing practical theories that can be fed back and tested in practice and to varying extents they set out to understand and address issues of power, politics and ideology. Their orientation is towards deepening understanding of problems, developing vision of what is possible and taking action to improve the quality of professional practice. Action research is indeed a powerful approach to research capable of adapting to the needs of a very wide range of situations and projects. In the next chapter we present some key theories that inform our understanding of action research methodology, but this chapter is a reminder that action research should never be reduced to a narrow orthodoxy. What is important is that you approach the writing of other action researchers with an open mind to learn from their experience and the knowledge they have generated about learning and change. This is the first step in going on to writing with confidence about your own action research as a contribution to public knowledge about the complexities of practice.

Chapter 10

Behind the scenes
A theoretical foundation of action research

One of our goals in writing this book was to make it full of practical examples and methodological suggestions for action research. Now that we are at its end, we invite you to join us for a look behind the scenes of this research tradition. We will try to present a few ideas and arguments that we believe to be significant for practitioner research.

THE ROOTS OF ACTION RESEARCH

In Anglo-American literature[1] the development of the concept 'action research' is traced back to the work of John Collier, US Commissioner of Indian Affairs, Jacob L. Moreno, a physician, social philosopher and poet and Kurt Lewin, a social psychologist who received his degree from the University of Berlin and emigrated to the US in the 1930s (Noffke 1990; Kemmis and McTaggart 1988, Noffke 1997). Collier (1945), in his role as commissioner, worked from 1933 to 1945 to improve the conditions of life of the American Indian population by using an applied anthropology that was socially conscious and related to practice. Moreno was the inventor of theoretical concepts such as sociometry, psychodrama, and role-play. He also was probably the first person to use concepts such as "interaction or action research" and who insisted on principles such as participant observation, participation of lay persons in research, and social improvement as aim of research (Petzold 1980; Gunz 1996). However, Kurt Lewin is the person most often cited as founder of action research. For him, action research was "a comparative research on the conditions and effects of various forms of social action, and research leading to social action" (Lewin 1948: 202–3). From the middle of the 1940s he tried to implement this type of research in projects, e.g. to improve inter-group relations (Lewin 1948) or nutrition practices (cf. Lewin 1988). While Lewin worked with social workers in the 1930s and 1940s, action research had little influence on American schooling until the 1950s when it was taken up by Steven Corey of Teachers College, Columbia University (Corey 1953). Corey saw action research as a way for teachers to engage in legitimate educational research, and as a way to bring the then new scientific study of education into the classroom (Noffke 1990). Although under Corey's influence there was great interest in action research in the 1950s and into the 1960s, by the next decade it had nearly died out as a research methodology in the US (see Kemmis 1988; Sanford 1970; Neumann 2005). However, in the 1970s the critique of top-down curriculum reform in England and Australia generated an educational reform movement that operated under the name of action research or teacher research and spread to Europe and North America.

While we focus on the variety of action research developed in the UK and Australia, we believe that it is important to acknowledge a parallel, teacher research movement that developed in the US during the same time period (Feldman 1996). This movement arose from the work of the Writing Projects (Bay Area Writing Project 1979) and Pat Carini of the Prospect School (Carini 1978). The purpose of the Writing Projects, which are spread throughout the US but originated at the University of California at Berkeley, is to improve the teaching and learning of writing. Members of the Writing Projects engage in teacher research by paying close attention to their own work through journal keeping, and by paying close attention to children's work by collecting samples of their writing. Teachers in these collaborative groups then share and critique each other's work by making public their journal entries and exhibiting their students' writing. They expand upon their ideas by writing self-reflective documents that rely on their journals, the student writing samples, and the comments and questions of their peers. These documents are shared again with the collaborative group in a peer review process. This latter process may be repeated several times until there is an acceptable finished product. Collections of teachers' writings have been published by Writing Projects (e.g. Alaska Teacher Researchers 1991, Goodman 1988, Page 1992), and by university researchers (e.g. Cochran-Smith and Lytle 1993).

ACTION RESEARCH AS EDUCATIONAL INNOVATION

Much of teacher action research in the UK traces its roots to Lawrence Stenhouse. He was Professor of Education at the University of East Anglia in Norwich until his death in 1982. It was during the time that he was the initiator and driving force behind the Humanities Curriculum Project (HCP)[3] that he developed his ideas about the role of practitioners in the development and implementation of curriculum. Prior to the HCP the common strategy of instructional innovation was based on the classical Research-Development-Dissemination (RDD) model. On the basis of scientific knowledge ("research") researchers developed new instructional procedures and tested them ("development"). When the materials appeared to be technically mature they were handed over to practitioners ("dissemination") who were expected to apply them according to the intentions and specifications of the developers. In such projects it was observed again and again that the uses teachers made of the curricular materials were often far from the intentions of the researchers. Common explanations of these phenomena were that the teachers were not competent enough to implement the curricula properly or that they were "obstructionists" who "resisted" innovation.

Stenhouse (1975) developed another interpretation of this situation: What had appeared as distortion was the result of the pragmatic skepticism of practitioners (Doyle and Ponder 1976), and in fact was a kind of questioning, modifying, probing – in short an impulse towards research. Stenhouse concluded that if one wants to introduce an innovation one should not try to dodge or eliminate this pragmatic skepticism, but to incorporate it in a constructive manner. Quality in implementing an innovation is not achieved by asking practitioners to put its ideas – which may have been successful somewhere else – into action one to one. Rather, they should carefully observe the fit of the innovation with the specific conditions of their own practice. They should evaluate and modify the innovation as necessary. If innovations are developed, practitioners should not be regarded as technical operators applying prefabricated products. Rather, they should be seen as partners in a development process. With this, the idea of "teachers as researchers" was born (Stenhouse 1975; Elliott 1988). The Ford Teaching Project (Elliott 1991) and the TIQL Project mentioned in Chapter 1 of this book carried forward the tradition of Stenhouse, and Bridget, one of the authors of this book and a student of Elliott, was closely involved in its further development through a number of projects investigating the ways in which practitioner-researchers played a leading role in the process of innovation in different educational contexts (Somekh 2006).

PRACTITIONERS AS MEMBERS OF A PROFESSION

The idea of teachers, nurses, social workers, and other practitioners engaging in action research is not just a strategic idea to reduce frictions when implementing innovations. Instead, it implies a different self-concept of what it means to be members of a profession. The *Oxford English Dictionary* defines profession as

> A vocation in which a professed knowledge of some department of learning or science is used in its application to the affairs of others or in the practice of an art founded upon it.

> (OED 1989)

In everyday usage "profession" also refers to a typical combination of mostly monopolized work opportunities that are predominantly non-manual, that offer above average income, prestige and authority and that demand above average qualification (Hesse 1972: 69).

Stenhouse changed this conception of what it means to be a member of a profession so that it involves more than the acquisition of knowledge in a post-secondary institution – it must also comprise the ability to generate and further develop knowledge of one's practice situation.

> In short, the outstanding characteristics of the extended professional is a capacity for autonomous professional self-development through systematic self-study, through the study of the work of other teachers and through the testing of educational ideas by classroom research procedures.
>
> (Stenhouse 1975: 144)

PROFESSIONAL ACTION

Action research is primarily concerned with change, being grounded in the idea that development and innovation are essential parts of professional practice. At the heart of any practice lies the complexity of social interactions (usually involving large groups) in which there is always opportunity for improvement. In this context, the natural tendency of human beings to reduce complexity by establishing routine practices provides the advantage of freeing us to handle a large number of decisions and actions at the same time, but inhibits our ability to understand our own motivation and the consequences of our practice. Action research rejects the idea that changes and "improvements" are needed because there is some deficit or failure on the part of practitioners, and sees change instead as an inevitable and important part of being a professional. Moreover, as Stenhouse (1975) recognized in the practice of teachers, curriculum development has little chance of success unless it involves teachers in exploring the implications of the changes for their own educational values, and in finding out how to make any necessary alterations to the routines of their practice. We believe the same is true for the enactment of real, meaningful change in other professional practice situations. This approach to change presupposes a *reflective view* of professionalism, which is very different from the commonly held *technical rational view* (Schön 1983).

Donald Schön (1983) in his highly influential book, *The Reflective Practitioner*, distinguished between Technical Rationality and Reflective Rationality in the practice of professionals. To Schön, *Technical Rationality* is a way of conceptualizing political and administrative interventions in educational systems and other institutions that follow these three basic assumptions (Schön 1983):

- There are general solutions to practical problems.
- These solutions can be developed outside practical situations (in research or administrative centers).
- The solutions can be translated into practitioners' actions by means of publications, training, administrative orders, etc.

Technical Rationality is operationalized via the classical RDD model of innovation. Researchers produce the theoretical background for an educational innovation. In the development phase the theoretical framework is applied to solve a practical problem in general terms. The result is a product for a specific group of consumers (a curriculum, teaching and learning materials, clinical procedures, etc.). It is tested and directions for use are developed. The product is then disseminated to practitioners. Strategies are applied to reach, train, and stimulate or pressure them to accept the innovation and use it in a prescribed way (information booklets, training courses, administrative incentives, and pressures, etc.).

The result is a hierarchy of credibility. It implies that people are the more credible the higher they are in the institutional power structure, i.e. the closer they are to those who develop theories and make policy. The teacher is considered more credible than the pupils, the head of department more credible than the teacher, the principal more credible than the head of department, etc. In the same way the nurse is more credible than the patients, and the physician is more credible than the nurse. This hierarchy of credibility expresses a genuine mistrust of practitioners. Within the conceptual framework of technical rationality they work on a low level of theoretical knowledge and are merely applying what has been predefined in the academic and administrative power structure above them. Improvements of practice are in this view primarily a result of improved general and applied theories and norms transmitted to the teacher, nurse, social worker, or other practitioners (and of incentives and control mechanisms used to ensure their correct application).

Reflective Rationality, in contrast, follows these three very different assumptions:

- Complex practical problems require particular solutions.
- These solutions can only be developed inside the context in which the problem arises and in which the practitioner is a crucial and determining element.
- The solutions can only rarely be successfully applied to other contexts, but they can be made accessible to other practitioners as hypotheses to be tested in practice.

These assumptions imply the development of new types of communication among practitioners – dynamic networks of relationships to assist them in taking responsible action in the face of complexity and un-certainty. This kind of collaboration implies exchange processes among or between teachers, nurses, or social workers and other groups in which there is a symmetry, rather than a hierarchy, of power; it is often practitioner initiated and not bound to any pre-specified procedures.

Reflective Rationality depends upon the development of a dynamic learning culture, which is based on the understanding that local initiatives exist already, and that their growth process should be supported rather than ruptured and thwarted by imposed change. If specific innovations are forced upon people and institutions, this tends to reduce their coping power and problem-solving capacity and increase their dependence – because their existing potential for innovation is not encouraged but ignored and thus, in the long run, damaged.

To understand professional change in terms of Reflective Rationality, we need an adequate description of complex, professional action. Schön's (1983) account of "reflective practice" is based on an analysis of practice in a number of different professions. He formulated different relationships between professional knowledge and professional action, which we now discuss with respect to the principles of action research.

Action type I: Tacit knowing-in-action

When professional practice flows smoothly and appears simple to an onlooker, action is based on "tacit knowing-in-action". This type of pro-fessional action has these characteristics:

- Thinking and acting are not separate (skilful, practical activities take place without being planned and prepared intellectually in advance).
- The professional is frequently unaware of the sources of his/her practical knowledge or how it was learnt.
- The professional will usually not be able to give a straightforward, verbal description of this practical knowledge.

Nevertheless these actions could not have resulted without the know-ledge of the professional practitioners. Their skilfulness, their situational appropriateness and their flexibility indicate a knowledge base that is "tacit" for the time being. As Polanyi noted, "we know more than we can tell" (1966: 4).

The most important examples of tacit knowing-in-action are "routines". Routines are actions or "mind-sets" that have been built up through fre-quent repetition, are carried out comparatively quickly and are executed largely unconsciously. Routines have frequently been considered inferior to conscious, planned, and creative actions. It has been suggested that practitioners should increase the proportion of the latter and reduce our reliance on routine. This view is certainly too simple because routines also have positive effects. In teaching, for example, they contribute a certain stability that gives pupils the chance to anticipate what is coming and to gauge their actions accordingly. Routines are also essential in allowing us to do more than one thing at a time, which is one of the typical require- ments of practice. For example, a teacher can be explaining a concept, noting overall pupil involvement and keeping a special eye on a particu- larly "difficult" pupil, all at once.

The strongest argument for a re-evaluation of the relevance of routines comes from research on expert knowledge (see Bromme 1985: 185–9) in which it was found, for example, that less successful teachers take more information into account when they decide to deviate from the lesson plan than more successful ones. In other professional areas "experts" were found to need fewer words to define and solve a problem than less experienced or less successful colleagues. Bromme argues that these results may be explained by the prominent role of routines in "expert action". Routines do not indicate

> lack of knowledge but rather a specific quality of knowledge organiza- tion . . . a condensation of task related knowledge . . . which embraces concepts for problem perception, information on the conditions of problem solution and steps of problem solution.
>
> (Bromme 1985: 185)

Tacit knowing-in-action cannot sensibly be excluded from the concept of *professional action*. Routinized and flowing action that draws on implicit knowledge is the basis for competent, professional practitioner action in simple, or made-simple-by-experience, situations.

Action type II: Reflection-in-action

As important as knowing-in-action is to the professional in practice, there are those times when new and complex situations have to be dealt with, or disturbances and problems disrupt the smooth flow of routinized action. It is when we enter the "swampy lowland where situations are confusing 'messes' incapable of technical solutions" (Schön 1983: 39) that we need an alternative to Technical Rationality and knowing-in-action: reflection-in-action.

When someone reflects-in-action, he becomes a researcher in the practice context. He is not dependent on the categories of established theory and technique, but constructs a new theory of the unique case. His inquiry is not limited to a deliberation about means that depends on a prior agreement about ends. He does not keep means and ends separate, but defines them interactively as he frames a problematic situation. He does not separate thinking from doing, ratiocinating his way to a decision which he must later convert to action. Because his experimenting is a kind of action, implementation is built into his inquiry.

(Schön 1983: 65)

This "research in the practice context" need not be translated into words: it may take place in the course of action in an universalized form, in graphical form as sketches on notepads or partly verbalized in a process of demonstration, imitation, comment, and joint experimentation (Schön 1987) that is frequently used in the training of practical competencies. Reflection-in-action resembles, as Schön says, a "reflective conversation with the situation" (Schön 1987: 56)

The notion of reflection-in-action is compatible with the findings of some research on problem solving in complex situations. For example, Dörner (1983) summarizes his findings by sketching two main competencies that individuals need for autonomous orientation in complex environments:

- The competency for "self-reflexive transformation of one's own thinking": through reflection on one's own problem-solving actions, different strategies are compared and scrutinized for common elements; misleading stereotypes are eliminated.
- The competency to "import" knowledge' from one context to another, using analogs, to evaluate this knowledge, and to develop it on the basis of the evaluation.

Action type III: Reflection-on-action

As we have seen, "tacit knowing in action" draws on accumulated practical knowledge under simple or routine circumstances. "Reflection-in-action" begins whenever practitioners find themselves in more complex situations that cannot be coped with by routine: such reflection occurs within action, it is not at all rare and need not be verbalized to be useful in problem-solving (see Argyris and Schön 1992: 14). The third action type, *reflection-on-action*, is an important feature of professional action: it occurs when it is necessary to formulate knowledge explicitly and verbally, to distance ourselves from action for some time and to reflect *on* it:

- It improves our ability to analyze and reorganize knowledge: consciously reflecting on action slows it down and disturbs our smoothly running routines, but it also facilitates careful analysis and allows us to plan changes (see Cranach 1983: 71).
- It makes knowledge communicable: the knowledge underlying professional action can be made visible and communicated to others, such as colleagues, clients and interest groups.

In reflection-on-action, reflection distances itself from the flow of activities, interrupts it and focuses on data that represent the action in an *objectified* form. This ability is a constituent part of professional competency because it is the basis for fulfilling three requirements placed on today's professionals:

- We have to cope constructively with serious problems or complex new situations. By distancing ourselves from the flow of activities we have a better chance of dealing with the problems that entangle us, redefining them and reorganizing our response. For example, when we understand that there is some discrepancy between our expectations and what has actually happened, it is possible to become aware of the tacit knowledge embedded in our routine actions, to search consciously for mistaken assumptions and to reformulate our thinking. Many of the methods (Ms) included in this book aim at activating our tacit knowledge (see Chapter 4).
- We need to take responsibility for the education and induction of novices into the profession and for passing on professional experience to the next generation. To do this we need to express in a verbal and organized way the knowledge underlying our practice.
- We must be able to communicate our knowledge and our professional action to colleagues, pupils, patients, clients, and others, putting forward rational arguments for them and inviting critical discussion. This, too, requires the ability to put our professional knowledge into words.

To sum up: professionals need to be competent in all three action types. Our professional action builds on reflection-in-action. To be efficient in the run-of-the-mill situations of everyday practice, we have to rely on routines. To cope with difficult and complex problems, take control of our practice so that we can change it if we so wish and fulfill our responsibilities to society, we have to involve reflection-on-action.

THE VALUE ORIENTATION OF PRACTICE

So far we have used the terms reflection and action in our discussion of professional learning. For John Elliott, who was one of Stenhouse's collaborators during the Humanities Curriculum Project and later, like Stenhouse, professor at the University of East Anglia, practical actions are representations of professional values in a concrete form. Referring to the Aristotelian Ethic, he describes moral concepts as necessarily diffuse and open-ended, needing one of several possible concretions through action (Elliott 1998). For example, in an educational context, all actions (not only those that are intentionally value-oriented) are understood as explicit or implicit "interpretations of educational values". In other words, it is legitimate to ask what values are embedded in action. As the "translation" from general values to concrete actions is always uncertain, it follows that there is an obligation to reflect on the relationship between concrete action and professional values.

Professionality in teaching, nursing, social work, or other types of professional practice involves the acceptance of the value-laden character of practice and allows us to reflect on it. It provides a legitimation of action research as an element of professional practice: In action research not only is knowledge acquired but also the instrumental efficiency of action patterns for set aims is evaluated, as the fit between concrete actions and values.

> In reflecting about their teaching-learning strategies, in the light of a set of aims and principles, teacher-researchers will ask whether such strategies constitute a valid interpretation of them.
>
> (Elliott 1998: 157)

THE SOCIAL POSITIONING OF PROFESSIONAL ACTION

Until this point we could interpret professional action as reflected individual action. However, in Chapter 1 (p. 13) we claimed that *the long-term aspiration of action research is always a collaborative one.* In many action research projects groups of practitioners are involved in research and development. *Embedding individual research in a professional community* is supported by the following arguments:

- *Facilitation of research* – groups provide a social context for discussion on design, steps and results of research, and offer mutual support. They can also provide concrete assistance in specific phases of the research (e.g. in interviewing participants).
- *Dissemination of knowledge* – it is an important aim of action research to encourage practitioners to disseminate their experiences, concepts and results to contribute to a shared knowledge base of the profession (see Chapter 8). The cooperative exchange in a group of practitioners is a first step in disseminating knowledge in a professional community. Presenting experiences, case studies and ideas in a familiar group can be a good preparation for presentations in a larger professional community.
- *Development of a professional community* – the critical as well as friendly cooperation in a collegial group can initiate steps towards the building of a professional community. This is an indispensable condition for high-quality work in the profession.
- *A critical authority* – the community of practitioners can be seen as analogous to the *scientific community.* The final criterion for the scientific character and acceptability of research results is for Thomas

Kuhn (1970) a social-historical one: research results and the strategies behind them have to stand the test of critical discussion in a *professional community*. In collegial discussion action researchers have an opportunity to become conscious of possible misinterpretations, alternatives and strengths of their work (Capobianco and Feldman 2006).

The professional community is therefore an important location for reflection, further development, and learning of professional practitioners. Professional learning is not only an individual process nor an intellectual or practical further development alone; it is accompanied by the feeling of being at home and challenged at the same time in a social community. Lave and Wenger's theory of situated learning (1991) can make the importance of the social regard for professional action and learning still clearer (Altrichter 2005). This theory emphasizes the following *characteristics of learning processes*:

- *Learning is getting involved in the world* – learning is action, a form of being in the social world and not only a way of accumulating knowledge about it.
- *Learning is situated* – learning is involvement in specific social situations. It draws on them and is bound to them in a certain sense.
- *Learning occurs in and through communities of practice* – the primary locus of learning is not the individual mind but processes of co-participation in a community of practice. Primary actors are not individual persons but a community.
- *Learning occurs in socially structured situations* – being socially situated, learning necessarily involves controversial interests. The social structure of practice, its power relations and its conditions for legitimacy define the potentials for learning.
- *Learning is forming identity in communities of practice* – the acquisition of competence is associated with development of identity (in and through the membership in a community of practice). Both elements – learning of skills and development of identity – are part of one and the same process. Without participation there is no basis for identity – persons and communities constitute each other.
- *Learning occurs in communities of practice through "legitimate peripheral participation"* (Lave and Wenger 1991) – for this to happen,

  ○ learners must *participate* in a practice;
  ○ learners must be allowed to play at least a *peripheral* role – at least temporarily. In such a role the pressure to act is reduced in favor of a cognitive and emotional distance to the immediateness of practice (see Clases *et al.* 1996: 239).
  ○ learners' practice must be accepted as being a *legitimate* form of practice within the profession.

- *The value of action-oriented knowledge is dependent on a community of practice* – professional knowledge is situated and makes sense only in the specific contexts of the community of practice. Therefore, knowledge needs to be embedded in communities of practice.

> A community of practice is an intrinsic condition for the existence of knowledge, not least because it provides the interpretative support necessary for making sense of its heritage. Thus, participation in the cultural practice in which any knowledge exists is an epistemological principle of learning.
>
> (Lave and Wenger 1991: 98)

IS PRACTITIONER RESEARCH 'RESEARCH'?

According to action researchers in the UK, action research should contribute to the following aims:

1 *in-service training of practitioners*, who improve their "practical theories" and their action competence through reflection and action;
2 *improvements in the practical situation under research*, by developing the quality of teaching and learning through new and sustainable action strategies;
3 *collective development of the profession* by means of opening up individual practical knowledge to scrutiny and discussion and thus broadening the knowledge base of the profession;
4 *the advancement of educational research*.

This description of aims shows that for Elliott and his colleagues, action research is not only a model for the further development of professional practitioners but also a contribution to theory. Two concerns are fuelled by this claim:

- Based on his experiences, e.g. in the *Humanities Curriculum Project*, Elliott (1988) regarded the usual hierarchical relationships between academic researchers and practitioners as unjustified and disadvantageous. Action research calls for a *democratization of social science*. It places those who usually are only objects of research on an equal footing with academic researchers.
- To Elliott, an important precondition of the *practical relevance of educational research* is that practitioners are treated as reflecting subjects who contribute to research on equal terms. Innovative practice can only be achieved by working with the practitioners and not against them – this was already Stenhouse's argument. Educational theory will be meaningful for educational practice only if it is rooted in practitioners' self-concept and in their categories (which does not imply that practice is perpetuated uncritically). Dörner's (1983)

278 Teachers investigate their work

criticism of the relevance of psychology for everyday life is valid also here: empirical educational research has proceeded too swiftly to abstract categories, whose practical relevance cannot be understood by practitioners and very often does not even exist. Needless to say, we believe that Elliott's concerns are valid also for other professions such as nursing and social work.

Motives of this kind – even if many people share them – are not sufficient to substantiate the scientific character of action research. For this purpose solid theoretical and methodological arguments are necessary. The scientific character of action research, for example, is often questioned by the following statements:

- Practitioners are involved in action to such an extent that they are unable to attain the critical distance that is characteristic of research.
- The quality criteria of traditional research cannot be achieved if lay persons do the research.
- Action research leads to singular statements and not to statements of general validity common in traditional research.

We have examined these arguments elsewhere (Feldman 2007b; Altrichter 1986a; Altrichter 1990; Feldman 1994) with the following results:

- These arguments (lack of distance, quality criteria, generalization) are critical arguments that determine the usefulness and soundness of research results. Researchers who want to increase the quality of their research project are well advised to take them seriously.
- Research designs, which are able to eliminate these critical points from the outset, do not exist. Using the concept "validity", for example, we have shown that an examination of the quality of traditional research leads to relative and provisional results (Altrichter 1986a).
- Because the situation is basically the same for action research as it is for more traditional research designs, action research must also respond to these arguments. As we have shown in the section on "criteria for guiding the quality of action research" (Chapter 5, p. 148), this is achieved partly by comparable means.
- Neither the methods used in action research nor the fact that action researchers are "part-time" researchers allows others to devalue its quality conclusively. The results of action research as well as the products of other research approaches have to be examined by means of quality criteria and by critical public discussion in order to ascertain that they have been obtained with care and reflection and that they stimulate further research and further practical action.

THE ITERATIVITY OF ACTION RESEARCH

If the same quality criteria are valid for part-time researchers as for full-time researchers, the former seem to be in a worse position, because they are generally unable to invest as much time, energy, and deliberation in elaborate testing procedures. On the other hand, researching professionals also have an advantage over academic researchers. In this final section we want to point this out.

All kinds of quality evaluation of research can be traced back to two ideas (see Chapter 5; Bammé and Martens (1985)): to *criticism* (evaluation of the logical coherence of the design of the research, of the internal coherence of the statements and of the coherence of the statements with those of other researchers) and to *practice* (experimental evaluation of the results of the research). Traditional social research is split in temporary phases: a phase of contact to practice is followed by a retreat to the research institution, in which experiences are reflected and analyzed. This is its strength, because much effort can be put into this phase of distanced criticism. However, there lies also its weakness, because the test through practice is temporary and discontinuous (see Altrichter 2004). Action research does not strictly separate phases of action from phases of reflection. Reflection occurs in part *within* action: the more distanced mode of reflection on action is not limited to specific phases in research. Again and again reflection of action researchers assumes a definite form in their actions that have to prove their worth under the day-to-day conditions of the classroom. If new discrepancies turn up between expectations (based on their practical theory) and the realities of practical action then a new process of further development of theory and practice is indicated. In this sense practice is a test of the quality of prior research. Research is less oriented towards a definite aim; it has a long-term character and is more continuous than conventional research. Reflective practitioners need not start from a hypothesis that is slimmed down to a few variables and is to be corroborated or refuted. They examine the consequences of action, the intended consequences as well as the unintended ones.

Argyris and his colleagues (1985) have clarified this difference as follows: Practitioners do not pose the question, "Did we reach the aims we set?" But rather, the apparently sketchier question, "Do we like what we get?" Thereby, they open not only a window to the complex texture of effects of their actions including their side effects (practitioners are responsible also for them), but also how their value orientations flow into reflection and change processes.

In a certain sense, the research of practitioners is also more rigid than conventional research, because they have to live with the mistakes of their reflection. They experience them as "situations talk back" existentially, while traditional researchers can escape these consequences by changing the site or theme of research (Altrichter 1993). We use the somewhat eccentric term "iterativity" to name this characteristic of action research in which results of reflection again and again gain practical form and in which this form again and again can stimulate new reflection and development: By repeating the movement from action to reflection and back again etc. (see Figure 10.1) it is possible to detect weaknesses of the practical theory and to develop useful action strategies. Because of this characteristic of action research the actions of reflective practitioners gain in quality. And through this characteristic action research processes undergo frequent tests of their quality.

We too must live with the consequences of our theorizing. The practical methods in this book have been developed and tested in practice, and, through a reflexive process over a number of years, we have shaped and reshaped the ideas about action research that it contains. But the book itself needs to be developed and tested by the thinking and actions of its readers.

This is what the reader will be reading last, closing the book and leaning back in a chair. What impressions will linger in the mind? What ideas will come after the book is finished? These are our wistful thoughts as we sit in front of the last pages of our manuscript. There cannot be a definitive statement on action research because it must always be context-specific and responsive to the values and practices of the participants in the situation. This book is as far as we were able to go in presenting a method of research that, for us, has spilled over into being a way of life. The book is not finished. There is an important chapter still to be written by you, the reader – on extending and redefining your own practice and, through this means, further developing theory.

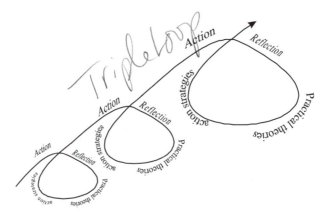

Figure 10.1 From action to reflection and back again

Notes

Chapter 1

1 See Chapters 3 and 4 of this book.
2 CARN is an international network linking all those interested in action research through regular conferences and publications. See the CARN website for up-to-date information www.did.stu.mmu.ac.uk/carn/
3 In everyday usage 'practical' can mean 'functional' and therefore may seem to have the same sense as 'technical'. Our use of the word 'practical' derives from Aristotelian ethics. Practical reasoning 'is concerned with human affairs and with matters about which deliberation is possible' (Aristotle 1962: 157).
4 LEA refers to 'Local Educational Authority'. This term is used in much of the English-speaking world and is the equivalent of the US 'school board'.

Chapter 2

1 Quotations from German sources have been translated by the authors.
2 In Chapter 5 we discuss other ethical issues in action research.

Chapter 3

1 See M25 'Quick methods for data collection' in Chapter 5.
2 The term 'rubric' is used in the US to refer to guidelines used for the assessment of pupil work.
3 For example, the Physics Teachers Action Research Project in California (Erzberger *et al.* 1996), the Formative Assessment Action Research Project in Massachusetts (Kropf *et al.* 2003), the evaluation of the ICT Test Bed Project (Somekh 2006) and environmental education teachers (Hart *et al.* 2006).
4 Modified from *Developing Teaching* (1984).

Chapter 4

1 At the time of writing, information about *Inspiration* can be found at www.inspiration.com
2 In teacher training courses we recommend to select no more than three indica-

tors; for the design of a self-evaluation project, of course, it is impossible to suggest a specific number. In most cases, however, it is advisable not to use too many instruments for data collection simultaneously.

Chapter 5

1 Another source is the Online Evaluation Resource Library (http://oerl.sri.com).
2 These include Formsite (http://formsite.com) and Survey Monkey (http://surveymonkey.com).

Chapter 6

1 Examples of this type of software include NVivo (www.qsrinternational.com), atlas-ti (www.atlasti.de), Ethnograph (www.qualisresearch.com) and Hyper-Research (www.researchware.com). There are books available to help you with the computer analysis of qualitative data but, because they quickly go out of date, we do not reference any here.

Chapter 7

1 For further discussion of this method see McCormick and James (1983: 160 ff., 240).

Chapter 8

1 In his inaugural lecture, entitled 'Research as a basis for teaching', at UEA (1979) Lawrence Stenhouse said, 'Research is systematic enquiry made public' (1983). In Stenhouse (1981: 103) it reads, 'Research is systematic, self-critical enquiry'.

Chapter 9

1 The British National Health Service (NHS) is organized in local Trusts that are centrally funded but locally self-governing.
2 NHS Trust Ethics Committees work with an awareness of patient sensitivities following a small number of scandals that received high-profile coverage in newspapers.
3 The article does not clarify the role of this person, but it appears to be a senior nurse with responsibility in the NHS Trust for leading research and development projects.
4 YaYa is not an acronym. No further information is given about it in the article. From a web search, it appears to have originated in 1988 in a community art organization in New Orleans that gives disadvantaged young people an opportunity to create art and gain entrepreneurial skills by exhibiting and selling art.

5 The authors of the article take issue with the contention of one of the authors of this book that these are necessarily different processes (Feldman, 1998: 28).
6 The English National Curriculum is divided into 'Key Stages' that correspond to specific age and grade ranges of pupils.

Chapter 10

1 By this we mean the work on action research in the English-speaking world.
2 Recent studies suggest that Collier's work may not have been in the interest of the native population. See, for example, Takaki (1993).
3 HCP was started in 1967 and intended to be an extensive curriculum in social education (Elliott 1998; Stenhouse 1968, 1971)

References

Adams, D. (1979) *The Hitchhiker's Guide to the Galaxy*, New York: Harmony Books.

Adlam, R. (1999) 'We need a night shift: notes on the failure of an educational design for police managers', *Educational Action Research*, 7: 51–62.

Alaska Teacher Researchers (1991) *The Far Vision, The Close Look: A Collection of Writings*, Juneau, Alaska: Juneau School District.

Altrichter, H. (1984) 'Pausen – Eine hochschuldidaktische "Entdeckung"', *Zeitschrift für Hochschuldidaktik*, 8: 527–38.

Altrichter, H. (1986a) 'Visiting two worlds: an excursion into the methodological jungle including an optional evening's entertainment at the Rigour Club', *Cambridge Journal of Education*, 16: 131–43.

Altrichter, H. (1986b) 'Professional development in higher education by means of action research into one's own teaching', *CARN Bulletin*, 7: 73–85.

Altrichter, H. (1988) 'Enquiry-based learning in initial teacher education', in J. Nias and S. Groundwater-Smith (eds) *The Enquiring Teacher: Supporting and Sustaining Teacher Research*, Lewes: Falmer Press.

Altrichter, H. (1990) *Ist das noch Wissenschaft? Darstellung und wissenschafts-theoretische Diskussion einer von Lehrern betriebenen Aktionsforschung*, Munich: Profil.

Altrichter, H. (1993) 'The concept of quality in action research', in M. Schratz (ed.) *Qualitative Voices in Educational Research*, London: Falmer Press.

Altrichter, H. (2004) 'Quality in action research for classroom development', in B. Ralle and I. Eilks (eds) *Quality in Practice-Oriented Research in Science Education: Proceedings of the 17th Symposium on Chemical Education*, Aachen: Shaker.

Altrichter, H. (2005) 'The role of the "professional community" in action research', *Educational Action Research*, 13(1): 11–25.

Altrichter, H., Messner, E. and Posch, P. (2006) *Schulen evaluieren sich selbst* (2nd edition), Seelze, Germany: Kallmeyer.

Altrichter, H. and Posch, P. (1998) 'Einige Orientierungspunkte für 'nachhaltige Lehrerfortbildung', in H.-J. Herber and F. Hofmann (eds) *Schulpädagogik und Lehrerbildung*, Innsbruck: StudienVerlag, pp. 245–59.

Angelo, T. A. and Cross, K. P. (1993) *Classroom Assessment Techniques: A Handbook for College Teachers*, San Francisco: Jossey-Bass.

Argyris, C. (1972) 'Unerwartete Folgen "strenger" Forschung', *Gruppendynamik*, 3: 5–22.

Argyris, C., Putnam, R. and McLain Smith, D. (1985) *Action Science: Concepts, Methods, and Skills for Research and Intervention*, San Francisco: Jossey-Bass.

Argyris, C. and Schön, D. A. (1992) *Theory in Practice: Increasing Professional Effectiveness*, San Francisco: Jossey-Bass.

Aristotle (1999) *Nicomachean Ethics* (M. Ostwald, trans.), Upper Saddle River, NJ: Prentice Hall.

Ashton, D., Dowling, L., Krumbein, S., Rausch, D., Rounds, A., Sullivan, V. and Traveler, L. (1990) *Where do we go from here in the California Mentor Teacher Program? Recommendations by seven mentors*, Stanford, CA: Stanford/Schools Collaborative.

Atkin, M., Coffey, J. E., Moorthy, S., Sato, M. and Thibeault, M. (2005) *Designing Everyday Assessment in the Science Classroom*, New York: Teachers College Press.

Attard, K. and Armour, K. M. (2005) 'Learning to become a learning professional: reflections on one year of teaching', *European Journal of Teacher Education*, 28: 195–207.

Baker, P., Cook, L. and Repper, J. (1986) 'From self-evaluation to staff development: beginnings', *CARN Bulletin*, 7: 252–65.

Bammé, A. and Martens, B. (1985) 'Methodenvielfalt und Forschungspragmatik: Zur wissenschaftstheoretischen Situation empirischer Sozialforschung', *Soziologie*, 1: 5–35.

Bathe, S. (2000) 'Case management', retrieved 6 August 2006, from http:// people.umass.edu/afeldman/ARpapersfall2000/Bathe/Bathe.html

Bay Area Writing Project (1979) *Bay Area Writing Project/California Writing Project/National Writing Project: An overview*. ED184123. Berkeley: University of California.

Belenkey, M. F., Clinchy, B. M., Goldberger, N. R. and Tarule, J. M. (1986) *Women's Ways of Knowing: The Development of Self, Voice, and Mind*, New York: Basic Books.

Bergk, M. (1987) 'Lernen aus Pausen für den Unterricht', in O. Ludwig, B. Priebe, and R. Winkel (eds) *Jahresheft V 'Unterrichtsstorungen'*. Seelze, Germany: Friedrich (quoted after the manuscript).

Bogdan, R. C. and Biklen, S. K. (2006) *Qualitative Research for Education: An Introduction to Theories and Methods, 5th edition*, Boston: Allyn and Bacon.

Bowen, M. (1978) *Family Therapy in Clinical Practice*, New York: J. Aronson.

Brecht, B. (1977) *Me-ti, Buch der Wendungen*, Frankfurt/M: Suhrkamp.

Bridges, J. and Meyer, J. (2000) 'Older people in accident and emergency: the use of action research to explore the interface between services in an acute hospital', *Educational Action Research*, 8: 277–89.

Bridges, J., Meyer, J. and Glynn, M. (2001) *An Action Research Study on the Co-ordination of Interprofessional Court: A Report for Basts and The London XIHS Trust*. London: City University.

Bridges, J., Smith, J., Meyer, J. and Carter, C. (2001) 'Meeting the needs of older people in rehabilitation care', *Nursing Times*, 97: 33–4.

Bromme, R. (1985) 'Was sind Routinen im Lehrerhandeln?', *Unterrichtswissenschaft*, 2: 182–92.

Calhoun, E. (1994) *How to Use Action Research in the Self-renewing School*, Alexandria, VA: Association for Supervision and Curriculum Development.

Canetti, E. (1981) 'Dialog mit dem grausamen Partner', *Das Gewissen der Worte*, Frankfurt: Fischer.

Capobianco, B. M. (2000) 'Making science accessible through collaborative science: teacher action research on feminist pedagogy', *Teacher Education and Curriculum Studies*, Amherst, MA: University of Massachusetts.

Capobianco, B. M. and Feldman, A. (2006) 'Promoting quality for action research: lessons learned from science teachers' action research', *Educational Action Research*, 14: 497–512.

Carini, P. F. (1978) 'Documentary processes', Annual meeting of the American Educational Research Association, Toronto, Canada.

Carr, W. and Kemmis, S. (1986) *Becoming Critical: Education, Knowledge and Action Research*, London: Falmer Press.

Carson, T. and Sumara, D. (1997) *Action Research as a Living Practice*, New York: Peter Lang.

Cazden, C. B. (1988) *Classroom Discourse: The Language of Teaching and Learning*, Portsmouth, NH: Heinemann Educational Books.

Churton, M. W., Cranston-Gingras, A. and Blair, T. R. (1998) *Teaching Children with Diverse Abilities*, Boston: Allyn and Bacon.

Clases, C., Endres, E. and Wehner, T. (1996) 'Situiertes Lernen zwischen Praxisgemeinschaften: Analyse und Gestaltung betrieblicher Hospitationen', in Geissler, H. (ed.) *Arbeit, Lernen und Organisation*, Weinheim: Deutscher Studienverlag.

Cochran-Smith, M. and Lytle, S. (1993) *Inside/Outside: Teacher Research and Knowledge*, New York: Teachers College Press.

Collier, J. (1945) 'United States Indian Administration as a laboratory of ethnic relations', *Social Research*, 12: 265–305.

Corey, S. (1953) *Action Research to Improve School Practices*, New York: Teachers College Press.

Cranach, M. V. (1983) 'Über die bewußte Repräsentation handlungsbezogener Kognitionen, in Montada, L. (ed.) *Kognition und Handeln*, Stuttgart: Klett-Cotta.

Cressey, P. G. (1932) *The Taxi-Dance Hall: A Sociological Study in Commercial Recreation and City Life*, Chicago: University of Chicago Press.

Cronbach, L. J. (1975) 'Beyond the two disciplines of scientific psychology', *American Psychologist*, 30: 116–27.

Dadds, M. (1985) 'What is action research?', Workshop Schulentwicklung an der Basis, Klagenfurt, Austria.

DeCharms, R. (1973) 'Ein schulisches Trainingsprogramm zum Erleben eigene Verursachung', in W. Edelstein and C. Hopf, (eds) *Bedingungen des Bildungsprozesses*, Stuttgart: Klett.

Developing Teaching (1984) 'Focus on teaching', INSET packet, Edingburgh: Moray House College of Education.

DeVore, I. (1970) *Selections from Field Notes, 1959 March-August*, Washington, DC: Curriculum Development Associates.

DeWitt, G. (2000) 'Gender and class participation'. Retrieved 6 August 2006 from www.unix.oit.umass.edu/~afeldman/ARpapersfall2000/DeWitt/DeWitt.html

Dörner, D. (1983) 'Empirische Psychologie und Alltagsrelevanz', in G. Jüttemann (ed.) *Psychologie in der Veränderung*, Weinheim, Germany: Beltz.

Doyle, W. (1992) 'Curriculum and pedagogy', in P. Jackson (ed.) *Handbook of Research on Curriculum*, New York: Macmillan Publishing Company.

Doyle, W. and Ponder, G. A. (1976) 'The practicality ethic in teacher decision making', mimeo, Denton, TX: North Texas State University.

Ebbutt, D. and Elliott, J. (eds) (1985) *Issues in Teaching for Understanding*, York: SCOC-Longman.

Edwards, G. (2005) 'Researching thinking skills stratregies in a primary school: challenging technical-rationalist orthodoxies of learning?', *Educational Action Research*, 13(2): 213–35.

Eisner, E. W. (1994) *Cognition and Curriculum Reconsidered, 2nd edition*, New York: Teachers College Press.

Eisner, E. W. (2002) *The Arts and the Creation of Mind*, New Haven: Yale University Press.

Elbaz-Luwisch, F. (2004) 'Immigrant teachers: stories of self and place', *International Journal of Qualitative Studies in Education (QSE)*, 17: 387–405.

Elbow, P. (1998) *Writing without Teachers, 2nd edition*, New York: Oxford University Press.

Elliott, J. (1976) *Developing Hypotheses about Classrooms from Teachers' Practical Constructs*, Grand Forks, ND: University of North Dakota.

Elliott, J. (1978) 'The self-assessment of teacher performance', *CARN Bulletin*, 2: 18–20.

Elliott, J. (1984a) 'Improving the quality of teaching through action research', *Forum*, 26: 74–7.

Elliott, J. (1984b) 'Some key concepts underlying teachers' evaluations of innovation', in P. Tamir (ed.) *The Role of Evaluators in Curriculum Development*, Beckenham: Croom Helm.

Elliott, J. (1988) 'Teachers as Researchers: Implications for Supervision and Teacher Education', Annual Meeting of the American Educational Research Association. New Orleans, LA.

Elliott, J. (1991) *Action research for Educational Change*, Philadelphia, PA: Open University Press.

Elliott, J. (1998) *The Curriculum Experiment. Meeting the Challenge of Social Change*, Buckingham: Open University Press.

Elliott, J. (2005a) 'Becoming critical: the failure to connect', *Educational Action Research*, 13: 359–73.

Elliott, J. (2005b) The teacher as a member of a networked learning community', *Learning for Democracy*, 1(3): 23–40.

Elliott, J. (2007) *Reflecting where the Action is: The Selected Works of John Elliott*, London and New York: Routledge.

Ellis, C. and Bochner, A. P. (2000) 'Autoethnography, personal narrative, reflexivity: researcher as subject', in N. K. Denzin and Y. S. Lincoln (eds) *Handbook of Qualitative Research*, Thousand Oaks, CA: Sage Publications.

Encarta (1999) *Encarta World English Dictionary*. London: Bloomsbury Publishing Plc.

Erzberger, A., Fottrell, S., Hiebart, L., Merrill, T., Rappleyea, A., Weinmann, L. and Woosnam, T. (1996) 'A framework for physics projects', *The Physics Teacher*, 34: 26–8.

Feldman, A. (1993) 'Teachers learning from teachers: knowledge and understanding in collaborative action research', unpublished dissertation, Stanford University, Stanford.

Feldman, A. (1994) 'Erzberger's dilemma: validity in action research and science teachers' need to know', *Science Education*, 78: 83–101.

Feldman, A. (1995) 'The institutionalization of action research: the California "100 Schools" ' in S. Noffke and R. Stevenson (eds) *Educational Action Research: Becoming Practically Critical*, New York: Teachers College Press.

Feldman, A. (1996) 'Enhancing the practice of physics teachers: mechanisms for the generation and sharing of knowledge and understanding in collaborative action research', *Journal of Research in Science Teaching*, 33: 513–40.

Feldman, A. (1998) 'Implementing and assessing the power of conversation in the teaching of action research', *Teacher Education Quarterly*, 25: 27–42.

Feldman, A. (2002) 'Multiple perspectives for the study of teaching: knowledge, reason, social context and being', *Journal of Research in Science Teaching*, 39: 1032–55.

Feldman, A. (2007a) 'Teachers, responsibility and action research', *Educational Action Research*, 15(2): 239–52.

Feldman, A. (2007b) 'Validity and auality in action research', *Educational Action Research*, 15(1): 21–32.

Feldman, A., Alibrandi, M., Capifali, E., Floyd, D., Gabriel, J., Henriques, B., Lucey, J. and Mera, M. (1998) 'Looking at ourselves look at ourselves: an action research self-study of doctoral students' roles in teacher education programs', *Teacher Education Quarterly*, 25: 5–28.

Feldman, A. and Capobianco, B. M. (2000) 'Action research in science education', *ERIC Digest*, Columbus, OH: ERIC Clearinghouse for Science, Mathematics, and Environmental Education.

Feldman, A. and Kropf, A. (1999) 'Teachers as curriculum decision-makers: the selection of topics for high school physics', *Journal of Curriculum and Supervision*, 14: 241–59.

Feldman, A., Kropf, A. and Alibrandi, M. (1998) 'Grading with points: the determination of report card grades by high school science teachers', *School Science and Mathematics*, 98: 40–8.

Feldman, A. and Minstrell, J. (2000) 'Action research as a research methodology for the study of the teaching and learning of science', in E. Kelly and R. Lesh, (eds) *Handbook of Research Design in Mathematics and Science Education*, Mahwah, NJ: Lawrence Erlbaum Associates.

Fetterman, D. M. (1989) *Ethnography Step by Step*, Newbury Park, CA: Sage Publications.

Freire, P. (1989) *Pedagogy of the Oppressed*, New York: Continuum.

Fuller, D. (1990) *Committed to Excellence: A Study of Child Learning using Desktop Publishing Programs*, Norwich: PALM Project Publications, CARE, University of East Anglia.

Geertz, C. (1973) *The Interpretation of Cultures*, New York: Basic Books.

Gibbs, G. (undated) *Learning to Study: A Guide to Running Group Sessions*, Milton Keynes: Open University Press.

Glover, M. K. (1992) *Two Years: A Teacher's Memoir*, Portsmouth, NH: Heinemann.

Goodman, M. (ed) (1988) *Visions and Revisions: Research for Writing Teachers*, Davis,

CA: University of California, Division of Education and The Campus Writing Center.

Grandau, L. (2005) 'Learning from self-study: gaining knowledge about how fourth graders move from relational description to algebraic generalization', *Harvard Education Review*, 75(2): 202–21.

Gredler, M. E. (1999) *Classroom Assessment and Learning*, New York: Longman.

Grell, J. and Grell, M. (1979) *Unterrichtsrezepte*, Munich: Urban and Schwarzenberg.

Griffin, E. (1990) *By Hook or by Crook: Putting IT into the Curriculum*. Norwich: Palm Publications, CARE, University of East Anglia.

Gunz, J. (1996) 'Jacob L. Moreno and the origins of action research', *Educational Action Research*, 4: 145–8.

Gürge, F. (1979) quoted in *Päd. Extra*, 7: 46.

Hammersley, M. (1992) *What's Wrong with Ethnography?*, London: Routledge.

Hammet, D. (1989) *The Maltese Falcon*, New York: Vintage.

Hart, P., Kyburz-Graber, R., Posch, P. and Robottom, I. (eds) (2006) *Reflective Practice in Teacher Education: Learning from Case Studies of Environmental Education*, Bern: Peter Lang Publishers.

Hay, J. (2002) 'The social model of disability and the assessment process: developing professional understanding through action research', MA dissertation, Anglia Ruskin University, Chelmsford.

Hesse, H. A. (1972) *Berufe im Wandel*, Stuttgart: Enke.

Hewson, P. W., Tabachnick, R. B., Zeichner, K. M., Blomerk, K. B., Meyer, H., Lemberger, J., Marion, R., Park, H. and Toolin, R. (1999) 'Educating prospective teachers of biology: introduction and research methods', *Science Education*, 83: 247–73.

Hiebler, S., Pliessnig, E., Teissl, R. (2001) 'Schuelerzentrierter Unterricht', in E. Messner (ed) *Chancen fuer Kinder – Chancen fuer Schulen*, Graz-West: Schulverbund, pp. 104–9.

Holly, M. L. (1989) 'Reflective writing and the spirit of inquiry', *Cambridge Journal of Education*, 19: 71–80.

Hook, C. (1995) *Studying Classrooms*, New York: Hyperion Books.

Hron, A. (1982) 'Interview', in G. Huber and H. Mandl (eds) *Verbale Daten*, Weinheim: Beltz.

Hull, C., Rudduck, J., Sigsworth, A. and Daymond, G. (eds) (1985) *A Room Full of Children Thinking*, York: SCDC/Longman.

Ireland, D. and Russell, T. (1978) 'Pattern analysis', *CARN Bulletin*, 2: 21–5.

Isaacs, J. (ed.) (1980) *Australian Dreaming: 40,000 Years of Aboriginal History*, Sydney: Landsdowne Press.

Jackson, P. W. (1968) *Life in Classrooms*, New York: Holt, Rinehart, and Winston.

Jackson, P. W. (1992) *Untaught Lessons*, New York: Teachers College Press.

Jago, C. (2003) 'The National Writing Project: a best idea from James Gray', *Voices from the Middle*, 10: 31–2.

Jenkins, E., Jones, J., Keen, D., Kinsella, F., Owen, T., Pritchard, D. *et al.* (2005) 'Our story about making a difference in nursing practice through action research', *Educational Action Research*, 13(8): 259–74.

Johnson, D. (1984) 'Planning small-scale research', in J. Bell, T. Bush, A. Fox, J.

Goodey and S. Golding (eds) *Conducting Small-scale Investigations in Educational Management*, London: Harper and Row.

Jones, C. (1986) 'Classroom research with seven to nine year-olds', in J. Elliott and D. Ebbutt (eds) *Case Studies in Teaching for Understanding*. Cambridge: Cambridge Institute of Education.

Josselson, R., Lieblich, A., Sharabany, R. and Wiseman, H. (1997) *Conversation as Method: Analyzing the Relational World of People who were Raised Communally*, Thousand Oaks, CA: Sage Press.

Kauffman, R. and Briski, Z. (2004) 'Born into brothels: Calcutta's red light kids', India, ThinkFilm Company.

Kemmis, S. (1988) 'Action research in retrospect and prospect', in S. Kemmis and R. McTaggart (eds) *The Action Research Reader*, Geelong, Victoria, Australia: Deakin University Press.

Kemmis, S. and McTaggart, R. (1982) *The Action Research Planner, 2nd edition*, Geelong, Victoria, Australia: Deakin University Press.

Kemmis, S. and McTaggart, R. (eds) (1988) *The Action Research Reader*, Geelong, Victoria, Australia: Deakin University Press.

Kilbride, C., Meyer, J., Flatley, M. and Perry, L. (2005) 'Stroke units: the implementation of a complex intervention', *Educational Action Research*, 13(4): 479–503.

Kropf, A., Emery, C. and Venemen, V. (2003) 'Formative assessment action research: using technology to increase student learning', Annual Meeting of the National Science Teachers Association, Philadelphia, PA.

Kuhn, T. (1970) *The Structure of Scientific Revolutions*, Chicago: University of Chicago Press.

Lave, J. and Wenger, E. (1991) *Situated Learning: Legitimate Peripheral Participation*, Cambridge: Cambridge University Press.

Lewin, K. (1948) 'Action research and minority problems', in G. W. Lewin (ed.) *Resolving Social Conflicts*, New York: Harper and Brothers.

Lewin, K. (1988) 'Group decision and social change', *The Action Research Reader*, Geelong, Victoria, Australia: Deakin University Press.

Lieberman, A. and Wood, D. R. (2002) 'The National Writing Project', *Educational Leadership*, 59: 40–3.

Likert, R. (1967) 'The method of constructing an attitude scale', in M. Fishbein (ed.) *Attitude Theory and Measurement*, New York: John Wiley and Sons.

Lincoln, Y. S. and Guba, E. (1985) *Naturalistic Inquiry*, Newbury Park, CA: Sage.

Lowenstein, S. (2006) 'Metaphors for divorce mediations and negotiations', retrieved 9 August 2006, from www.mediate.com/articles/lowensteinS1.cfm

Macdonald, B. and Sanger, J. (1982) ' "Just for the record?" Notes towards a theory of interviewing in evaluation', Annual Meeting of the American Educational Research Association, New York.

Malinowski, B. (1982) 'The diary of an anthropologist', in R. G. Burgess (ed.) *Field Research: A Sourcebook and Field Manual*, London: George Allen and Unwin.

Marshall, C. and Rossman, G. (2006) *Designing Qualitative Research*, Thousand Oaks, CA: Sage Publications.

McCormick, R. and James, M. (1983) *Curriculum Evaluation in Schools*, London: Croom Helm.

McKenzie, A. (2005) 'The high school principal: integrating vision and action', Amherst, MA.

Meyer, J. and Bridges, J. (1998) *An Action Research Study into the Organisation of Care for Older People in the Accident and Emergency Department*, London: City University.

Miles, M. and Huberman, M. (1994) *Qualitative Data Analysis*, Thousand Oaks: CA: Sage Publications.

Mohr, M. (ed.) (2003) *Teacher Research for Better Schools*, New York: Teachers College Press.

Moon, V. (1990) *Making the News*, Norwich: PALM Publications, CARE, University of East Anglia.

Munford, R., Sanders, J. and Andrew, A. (2003) 'Community development – action research in community settings', *Social Work Education*, 22(1): 93–104.

National Science Foundation (2004) *NSF Grant Proposal Guide*, Arlington, VA: National Science Foundation.

Neumann, J. E. (2005) 'Kurt Lewin at the Tavistock Institute', *Educational Action Research*, 13: 119–36.

Nicol, C., Moore, J., Zappa, S., Yusyp, M. and Sasges, M. (2004) 'Living action research: authoring identities through YaYa projects', *Educational Action Research*, 12(3): 311–27.

Noffke, S. E. (1990) *Action research: a multidimensional analysis*, Madison, WI: University of Wisconsin-Madison.

Noffke, S. E. (1997) 'Professional, personal, and political dimensions of action research', *Review of Research in Education*, 22: 305–43.

Nussbaum, M. (1986) *The Fragility of Goodness*, Cambridge: Cambridge University Press.

OED (1989) 'Oxford English Dictionary Online, 2nd edition', Oxford University Press.

Ourtilbour, B. (1991) *Concept keyboard with bilingual, year 1 and 2 children*, Norwich: PALM Project, CARE, University of East Anglia.

Page, E. (ed.) (1992) *Learning to Research, Researching to Learn: About Students at Risk*, Bakersfield, CA: Kern/Eastern Sierra Writing Project.

Peshkin, A. (1986) *God's Choice: The Total World of a Fundamentalist Christian School*, Chicago: University of Chicago Press.

Petzold, H. (1980) 'Moreno – nicht Lewin – der Begründer der Aktionsforschung', *Gruppendynamik*, 11: 142–66.

Pickover, D. (1986) 'Working with interested partners to meet individual needs in an infants school', in C. Biott and J. Storey (eds) *The Inside Story*. Cambridge: Cambridge Institute of Education.

Platten, D. (1986) 'Institutional self review and development', in C. Biott and J. Storey (eds) *The Inside Story*. Cambridge: Cambridge Institute of Education.

Polanyi, M. (1962) *Personal Knowledge: Towards a Post-critical Philosophy*, Chicago: University of Chicago Press.

Polanyi, M. (1966) *The Tacit Dimension*, Garden City, NY: Doubleday and Co.

Pols, R. (undated) 'The questionnaire', in B. Bowen *et al.* (eds) *Ways of Doing Research in One's Own Classroom*, Cambridge, UK: Ford Teaching Project, Cambridge Institute of Education.

Posch, P. (1985) *Beziehungen zwischen Lehrern und Schülern*, Klagenfurt: Interuniversitäres Forschungsinstitut für Fernstudien.

Prideaux, D. and Bannister, P. (undated) 'What to do with my data: reporting action-research', in J. Elliott and D. Ebbutt (eds) *Facilitating Action-Research in Schools*, Cambridge: Cambridge Institute of Education.

Putnam, H. (1995) *Pragmatism: An Open Question*, Cambridge, MA: Blackwell Publishers, Inc.

Radford, M. (1994) *Il Postino*. France/Italy, Miramax.

Reiners, L. (1961) *Stilkunst*, Munich: Beck'sche Verlagsbuchhandlung.

Reynolds, M. C. (ed.) (1989) *Knowledge Base for the Beginning Teacher*, Oxford: Pergamon Press.

Rico, G. L. (2004) *Garantiert schreiben lernen*, Reinbek, Germany: Rowohlt.

Robinson, M. (1984) 'A shadow study', paper presented at the annual meeting of the Collaborative Action Research Network, Cambridge.

Rowe, M. B. (1972) 'Wait-time and rewards as instructional variables: their influence on language, logic, and fate control', Annual meeting of the National Association for Research in Science Teaching, Chicago, IL.

Rumpf, H. (1986) *Mit fremden Blick – Stücke gegen die Verbiederung der Welt*, Weinheim, Germany: Beltz.

Sanders, D. and McCutcheon, G. (1986) 'The development of practical theories of teachers', *Learning Disability Quarterly*, 2: 50–67.

Sands, R. G. and Roer-Strier, D. (2006) 'Using data triangulation of mother and daughter interviews to enhance research about families', *Qualitative Social Work*, 5: 237–60.

Sanford, N. (1970) 'Whatever happened to action research?', *Journal of Social Issues*, 26: 3–23.

Schatzman, L. A. and Strauss, A. L. (1973) *Field Research*, Englewood Cliffs, NJ: Prentice Hall.

Schindler, G. (1993) 'The conflict', *Educational Action Research*, 1: 457–68.

Schön, D. A. (1980) 'Generative metaphor: a perspective on problem-setting in a social policy', in A. Ortony (ed.) *Metaphor and Thought*. Cambridge: Cambridge University Press.

Schön, D. A. (1983) *The Reflective Practitioner: How Professionals Think in Practice*, New York: Basic Books.

Schön, D. A. (1987) *Educating the Reflective Practitioner*, San Francisco: Jossey-Bass.

Seidman, I. (1998) *Interviewing as Qualitative Research: A Guide for Researchers in Education and the Social Sciences*, New York: Teachers College Press.

Selvini-Palazzoli, M., Boscolo, L., Cecchin, G. and Prata, G. (1978) *Paradox and Counterparadox: A New Model in the Therapy of the Family in Schizophrenic Transaction*, New York: Aronson.

Shulman, L. S. (1992) 'Toward a pedagogy of cases', in J. H. Shulman (ed.) *Case Methods in Teacher Education*, New York: Teachers College Press.

Somekh, B. (1985) 'An enquiry into the use of quinkeys for word processing in secondary English teaching', MA dissertation, University of East Anglia, Norwich.

Somekh, B. (2006) *Action Research: A Methodology for Change and Development*, Maidenhead and New York: Open University Press.

Somekh, B. and Davis, N. (eds) (1997) *Using IT Effectively in Teaching and Learning: Studies in Pre-service and In-service Teacher Education*, London and New York: Routledge.

Somekh, B. and Noffke, S. E. (eds) (forthcoming) *A Handbook of Educational Action Research*, Thousand Island, CA, and London: Sage.

Sorger, H. (1989) 'Fragen im Unterricht', in H. Altrichter, H. Wilhelmer, H. Sorger and I. Morocutti (eds) *Schule gestalten: Lehrer als Forscher, Fallstudien aus dem Projekt 'Forschendes Lernen in der Lehrerausbildung'*, Klagenfurt, Austria: Hermagoras.

St Cyr, K (2005) 'Do my supervisory skills promote teacher reflection?' Retrieved 14 July 2006 from http://people.umass.edu/afeldman/ARpapersSpring2005/KoreaFinalReport.pdf

Stenhouse, L. (1968) 'The Humanities Curriculum Project', *Journal of Curriculum Studies*, 1(1): 26–33.

Stenhouse, L. (1971) 'The Humanities Curriculum Project: the rationale', *Theory into Practice*, 10: 154–62.

Stenhouse, L. (1975) *An Introduction to Curriculum Research and Development*, London: Heinemann.

Stenhouse, L. (1978) 'Case study and case records: towards a contemporary history of education', *British Educational Research Journal*, 4: 21–39.

Stenhouse, L. (1981) 'What counts as research?', *British Journal of Educational Studies*, 29: 103–14.

Stenhouse, L. (1983) *Authority, Education and Emancipation*, London: Heinemann Books.

Stenhouse, L. (1985) 'How teachers can use research – an example', in J. Rudduck and D. Hopkins (eds) *Research as a Basis for Teaching*, London: Heinemann.

Strauss, A. and Corbin, J. (1990) *Basics of Qualitative Research: Grounded Theory Procedures and Techniques*, Newbury Park, CA: Sage Publications.

Strieb, L. (1985) *A Philadelphia Teacher's Journal*, Grand Forks, ND: North Dakota Study Group on Evaluation, Center for Teaching and Learning, University of North Dakota.

Suderman, E. M., Deatrich, J. V., Johnson, L. S. and Sawatzky-Dickson, A. D. M. (2000) 'Action research sets the stage to improve discharge preparation', *Pediatric Nursing*, 26: 571.

Takaki, R. T. (1993) *A Different Mirror: A History of Multicultural America*, Boston: Little, Brown & Co.

Tobin, K. and McRobbie, C. (1996) 'Cultural myths as constraints to the enacted science curriculum', *Science Education*, 80: 223–41.

Tomlinson, C. A. (2001) *How to Differentiate Instruction in Mixed-ability Classrooms, 2nd edition*, Alexandria, VA: Association for Supervision and Curriculum Development.

Torrance, H. and Pryor, J. (2001) 'Developing formative assessment in the classroom: using action research to explore and modify theory', *British Educational Research Journal*, 27(5): 615–31.

Tremmel, R. (1993) 'Zen and the art of reflective practice in teacher education', *Harvard Educational Review*, 63: 437–58.

Tripp, D. (1993) *Critical Incidents in Teaching: Developing Professional Judgement*, London: Routledge.

Turner, T. and DiMarco, W. (1998) *Learning to Teach Science in the Secondary School*, New York: Routledge.

Wakeman, B. (1986a) 'Action research for staff development', in C. Day and

R. Moore (eds) *Secondary School Management: Promoting Staff Development*, London: Croom Helm.

Wakeman, B. (1986b) 'Jottings from a coordinator's journal', in C. Biott and J. Storey (eds) *The Inside Story*, Cambridge: Cambridge Institute of Education.

Wakeman, B., Alexander, M., Bannister, P., Nolan, E. and Aspray, S. (1985) 'The TIQL Project at Rotherham High School', in J. Elliott and D. Ebbutt (eds) *Issues in Teaching for Understanding*. York: Longman/SCDC.

Walker, R. and Adelman, C. (1975) *A Guide to Classroom Observation*, London: Methuen.

Wang, C. C. (1999) 'Photovoice: a participatory action research strategy applied to women's health', *Journal of Women's Health*, 8: 185–92.

Watzlawick, P., Beavin, J. and Jackson, D. D. (1980) *Menschliche Kommunikation*, Bern: Huber.

Weiss, T. H. (2003) 'Scientists researching teaching: reforming science education and transforming practice', *School of Education*, Amherst, MA: University of Massachusetts.

Werder, L. V. (1986) ... *triffst Du nur das Zauberwort. Eine Einführung in die Schreibund Poesietherapie*, Munich/Weinheim: Psychologie Verlags Union/ Urban & Schwarzenberg.

Whyte, W. F. (1955) *Street Corner Society*, Chicago: University of Chicago Press.

Wijesundera, S. (2002) 'School improvement: an action-based case study conducted in a disadvantaged school in Sri Lanka', *Educational Action Research*, 10(2): 169–87.

Williams, B. (1990) *The Bury Project*, Norwich: PALM Project Publications, CARE, University of East Anglia.

Winter, R. (1982) ' "Dilemma analysis": a contribution to methodology for action research', *Cambridge Journal of Education*, 12: 161–74.

Wittwer, H., Salzgeber, G., Neuhauser, G. and Altrichter, H. (2004) 'Forschendes Lernen in einem Lehrgang zum kooperativen offenen Lernen', in S. Rahm and M. Schratz (eds) *LehrerInnenforschung*, Innsbruck: StudienVerlag.

Wong, E. D. (1995) 'Challenges confronting the researcher/teacher: conflicts of purpose and conduct', *Educational Researcher*, 24: 22–8.

Zeichner, K. M. and Noffke, S. E. (2001) 'Practitioner research', in V. Richardson (ed) *Handbook of Research on Teaching*, Washington, DC: American Educational Research Association.

Index

Page numbers in *italics* refer to figures.

Grandau, L. 247–9
graphical
    reconstructions/presentations 78–80,
    81, 227
Grell, J. and Grell, M. 112–13
Gürge, F. 221

Hammersley, M. 149
Haraty, J. 56–9
Hay, J. 103, 136
hierarchy of credibility 194, 270
holistic vs analytical perspectives
    72
Holly, M.L. 17, 60, 61
hypotheses 67, 198–9, 231–2; from
    categories to 83–6

in-depth reflections 31–4, 38
in-service education 227
index cards 80
individual brainstorming 205
inductive data coding 163–4
informed consent 22
institutional
    programmes/development as
    starting point 43, 44, 45–6
Internet 228
interpretive approaches 24, 113, 236
interviewer–interviewee relationship
    125–6, 132
interviewing: activating tacit
    knowledge 61; examples 134–6;
    learning 132–4; preparation 126–9;
    procedure 129–32;
    recording/transcribing 132; sources
    of misinformation 136–7; standard
    questions 134; and written survey
    137–43
Isaacs, J. 157
iterativity of action research 279–80

Jackson, P. 17
Jenkins, E. *et al.* 251–3
journals 220–1, 228–9; example studies
    246–65; *see also* research journals

Kenney, J. 166–7
Kilbride, C. *et al.* 255–7

knowledge: activating additional 60–3;
    see also dissemination of knowledge

ladder of inference 98–9
Lave, J. and Wenger, E. 276–7
learning process, characteristics of
    276–7
Lewin, K. 63, 266
Lincoln, S. 39–41
listening 130
Lowenstein, S. 173–4

McKenzie, A. 53–5
memos 23–4, 109
mentors 223
metaphors 172–8
methodological notes (MNs) 29–30
Meyer, J. and Bridges, J. 66, 230
Miles, M. and Huberman, M. 77, 176–7
mission statements as starting point 43
Moon, V. 146
multimedia presentations 227–8
Munford, R. *et al.* 262–5

negotiation, ethical principle of 154
NHS stroke units study 255–7
Nicol, C. *et al.* 253–5
Noffke, S. E. 12–13, 14, 266–7
nominal group technique (NGT)
    207–12, 222, 233
non-participants *see* others
nursing practice, Wales study 251–3

observation: by others 111–12; direct
    105–8; and documenting 104–24
observation profiles 121, *122*
open vs closed questions 140, 142–3
oral reports 227
"organic to-do list" 214–15
others: action strategies 203, 207;
    involvement 225–7; as observers
    111–12; views of 63; voice 217

participant control, ethical principle of
    155
participant observation 105
participation in institutional programs
    44